Burning
By Phil

Burning Religion:
Navigating the Impossible Space between the Religion and Secular Society

© 2015, Phil Wyman
All rights reserved. If'n you like my stuff, an' wanna use it, you oughta be a talkin' to me, an' asking fo' permishun. Prob'ly be jus' fine, but you best be remembrin' dis book 'ere be my intellechewal propurty.

Cover: Photo by Kevin (Kevissimo) Rolly, layout by Jeff Menasco
Cartoon: David Hayward (The Naked Pastor)
Biography Photo: Michelle Rogers Pritzl
Back Cover Photo: Shawn Fitzgerald

THE HEROES OF BURNING RELIGION

Dorothy Jones Jenkins (Mom!)
Josh & Ruth Jinno
Deb & Alan Hirsch
Timothy and Elizabeth Wright
Amber & Brian Barger
Michael Warrilow
Jeff Blackshear
Deanna Ogle
Jenn and Peter Gaffney
Jonathan & Rachel Meharry
Jimmy Melnarik
Rinus Oosthoek
Peter Lane
Jared & Erin Cyr-Robinson
Josh & Jane Turiel
Robert Watson-Hemphill
Alan Drake
Jide Alade
Mara & Glenn Coleman
Sandi Chai Brown
David Dashifen Kees
Ben Thorp
Paisley Rojagato
John Smulo
Trey & Amelia Black McCain

Robert Flaming
Renee Powell
Dee Cunniffe
Jodi & Greg Ainsworth
Joy & Paul Burwell
Paul Duffy
Donald & Amy Rylander
Stef & Mike Crockett
Dennis Huxley
Rob Petrini
Michael Toy
Anders Eskimyr
Ian Lynch
Pat Clarke
Andy Goldman
Papy Fisher
Lynne Krahn
Randall Shaw
Paul Bongiovanni
Ben Myers
Claire Bennett
Hope Deifell
Susan Parvis
Carl & Melissa Nystedt

THE FORWARDS

Like the forward positions in rugby, this forward is not just one. Using this rugby analogy, these multiple forwards are written by people who have played on the front lines of peacemaking in typically polarizing situations. They have been caught in the fray with everybody angry at them. These are people who know the pressure of being rebels with a cause. They are also people I have had direct contact with over the years, and it has been highly respected contact. They are my friends. But don't think for a minute that these friends of mine all think like I do about the world. Their foundations for reality and ethics may be radically different from my own little pastoral Christian world. These friends are the Hookers, Props and Locks in the scrum of life in this area where secularism meets religion. The Hooker, the Props and Locks are forward positions in rugby, and they are the positions of the players you find in the scrum. The scrum is that pile of muscly rugby humanity, which has large men bent over and locked head to head in a powerful crushing thrust against the competition – all for an oblong ball roughly the shape of a pig's bladder.

Mike Stygal is the current president of the UK Pagan Federation. He is a Neo-Shaman who has worked in interfaith dialogue for the last dozen years. Mike fits the title of "brother of another mother." I consider him one of my most cherished friends. Kile Jones used to be a Christian, who was one time a member of the little church I pastor in Salem, Massachusetts. Today, Kile is an atheist with two master's degrees in theology. Kile works creating open dialogue and understanding between atheists and people from other worldviews. He began a project called, "Invite an Atheist to Church Day," encouraging Christian churches to have a Sunday morning question and answer time with an atheist. Jim Henderson says he is not adventurous, but he is a Christian leader who once bought an atheist on eBay. That atheist (Hemant Mehta) offered to go church one hour for every $10 gained in the bidding. Jim paid a little over $500, and instead asked Hemant to go a small handful of churches, and blog about the experience so that Christians could learn what it was like to see church through the eyes of someone who is not a Christian. Jim is a serious provocateur. He challenges Christians to think outside the little boxes of our sometimes constraining faith systems. When I have had the chance to be involved in things Jim is involved in I always have walked away richer, and more open for the experience.

I realize that having people who represent such divergent worldviews is an unorthodox approach to creating a forward for a book, but it best represents what this book is about: navigating the impossible space between religion and secular society. More broadly, I believe the principles in this book are applicable to a myriad of polarizing issues in religion, in politics, and even in interpersonal relationships. So, here they are, some of my friends who represent the forward positions in navigating these impossible spaces today.

Phil Wyman, September 13, 2015

Words from an Edge-Walker: Mike Stygal

I've known Phil Wyman for over a decade – closer to 15 years. I first 'met' him on an email list he started called Circle and Cross Talk. It was a platform for Christians and Pagans to enter into dialogue with one another, a place where some of those thorny topics of potential conflict could be discussed and a mutual understanding might be explored. It was a place on the edges of two faith communities. I found Circle and Cross Talk, because my wife had just converted back to her Christian faith, away from our shared Pagan spirituality. I was scared. I had been thrust up against the edge and was fearful that I might be looking at the end of my marriage. I remember ranting at what I thought I knew of the cruel Christian faith: it's hatred of Pagans, and a fiercely held belief that we were all devil worshippers out to destroy lives, marriages, churches. Phil seemed to absorb all the fear and hate I was projecting, gently correcting my misinformed thoughts, holding the Christian hand up in acknowledgement to bad things that had been done in the name of his faith. He didn't respond to my hostility with defensive hostility of his own. I learned lots about his faith. I also learned to walk the edges – to be with people at those meeting points between different faiths, cultures and communities.

I formed my own compassion towards those of the Christian faith, whose unacknowledged fear of difference to their rigid, or possibly staid perspective of the church they belong to motivated them to hostility. I considered the possibility of that motivational fear and hostility was something that was actually evident in the accounts of those who demanded the crucifixion of their Christ. Then, I extended that reflection to recognize in others and in myself, how fear can blind people to their own behavior. I also began to notice similar motivational fear and hostility in some of my own Pagan community. I had, like Phil, become an edge-walker – a witness to the fears of those on both sides of the edges. I recognized that edge-walkers might have been among the fearful at some point in their lives, but had learned to face and overcome those fears with an open heart and mind.

Some of Phil's edge-walking experiences, and some of my own too, have suggested that those who might identify as spiritual, not religious (sometimes mislabeled as secular) could be exploring edge-walking for themselves, and in doing so, finding something deeper and personally more meaningful than adherence to 'tradition' for the sake of tradition. In choosing to explore friendly relations with people who are different, one learns much about one's own perspective, what underlies those things we hold dear and possibly sacred, whilst also gaining an insight into what is dear and sacred to others and why it is so. Some may fear that this will affect their faith. They're right, of course. It will. But it will affect their faith by deepening their understanding of the faith, and by shedding greater light on the sacred, and why it is sacred.

Phil has modeled edge-walking for me and for many others, being supportive of the fearful – not without personal cost. <u>Burning Religion</u> will provide the reader with a window into the world of the edge-walker. It will be of value to those of all faiths and of none, and could provide the reader with an invitation to join Phil, myself, and others in walking the edges.

Mike Stygal, President, Pagan Federation England and Wales
Walthamstow, London, England

The Man with Strange Connections: Kile Jones

I first met Phil Wyman many moons ago at the Church he was pastoring in Salem, Massachusetts. At the time I was a conservative and Evangelical Christian. I thought Phil was kind of strange for all his postmodern and subversive ministerial methods, but I was also rather intrigued. Shortly after meeting Phil we both decided to start a group called "The Dead Philosophers Society" where people from all different perspectives met and discussed various philosophical topics.

Shortly after, I finished my Masters degrees in Theology and came out of my studies as an agnostic. The more I studied the history and multifarious forms of religious beliefs, the more my world was turned upside down. Atheism was the terminus I found best fitting for my views. And even though I began my atheism with a less than gracious approach to religious persons, I soon discovered my desire to work with various religious traditions. It's one thing to spend your time propping up your tribe and another to create what I call "strange connections."

Some of the projects I created to harness these strange connections include "Interview an Atheist at Church Day," "Claremont Journal of Religion," and "Ahmadis and Atheists for Freedom of Conscience." These projects would fall under Bahktin's notion of Carnival "familiar and free interaction between people." They are "familiar" in the sense that these different groups (often unknowingly) share many of the same assumptions and life-worlds, and they are "free" because they are under no external compulsion to participate.

I can see why the notion of Carnivalesque inspires Phil. He's always been rather odd. First, he looks like Alan Moore, or at least some post-Marxist ex-hippie. He also seems drawn to the subalterns and marginalized peoples of the world. The way that other Christians "play the game" doesn't seem to catch his fascination. He's a theological carnie, and those types don't enjoy the typical bowling teams in Norman Rockwell's America.

I cannot underplay the radical gifts that emerge from the strange connections Phil and I try and create. Phil is well-known for finding these unique avenues--whether between Wiccans, Pagans, or even atheists, and Christians--and I am lucky to count myself as one of those influenced by his enthusiasm to step outside of dominant modes of discourse and create ruptures that well into beautiful lakes.

Kile Jones
Founder Interview an Atheist at Church, Claremont Journal of Religion
Fallbrook, CA

From the Man "not that adventurous" – Like Bilbo Baggins

I read a lot of books about explorers. People like Magellan, Columbus and Vespucci. I'm not sure why I do this. I'm not that adventurous. I think I'm trying to measure myself against their courage and craziness. I'm sobered by the role "luck" played in their accomplishments and think often about the many unnamed explorers who were no less accomplished but far less lucky.

Phil Wyman is an explorer. He has keen spiritual insights and an intellectual curiosity that easily surpasses many of his better-known contemporaries. He has devoted his life to doing field research among the people formerly known as lost, the people I like to say that, Jesus misses most.

John Fremont didn't discover California but he was the first to create a map of his discoveries so that people who were not explorers but did like to travel, had a way of heading west and still making it back alive.

This book introduces us to some of Phil's' explorations. It's a spiritual map for those of us who watch from a distance but dream about doing something like this ourselves. I think Phil's' desire is to show us a path that gets us a little closer to the people Jesus misses most who are in our life.

There are those who teach and those who do. Phil is a doer. Which are you?"

Jim Henderson
Executive Producer Jim Henderson Presents
Author Jim and Casper Go To Church

THE TABLE OF (DIS)CONTENTS

The Forward(s)	-5
The Table of (Dis)Contents	Ø
My Freestyled Intro.	1

The First Ring – Spinning Fire: the Self-immolation of Christianity

1. Burning the Temple	9
2. It must be a Cult	15
----*Birth of Gwyn Dee*----	page 17
3. Cultura animi philosophia est	21
4. Lessons from the Garden	23
5. The Self Immolation of Christianity	25
• YouTubers and a Growing Dissent	
----*The Long Barefoot Journey*----	page 33
6. What Are You Doing Here?	37

• Salem, MA • Druid Gathering, Southern England • Palenque, MX 2012

7. Paralyzed in Parallaxis: or, The Preacher's Naked Backside	43

• End Time Prophecies of Apocalypse • Worldwide Religious Revival Predicted • Moral Failure in the Churches • Theological Tension • Non-Religious Apocalyptic Warnings •

---- *Peddlers of the One Thing*----   page 50

• The Preacher's Naked Backside • The Excited Crowd • The Intimately Betrayed • The Confused Bystanders

---- *The Strange Mass*----   page 61

• Paralyzed in Parallaxis • Parallaxis as the Infinite and Impassable Distance • Parallaxis as Isolation • Myself as Subject - Enslaved by what I Observe • Bad News as Hope • Approaching the Elephant

8. Flat Faith   77

The Second Ring – Trapped Between the Ringmaster and the Clowns

----*The Paper War*----   page 81

9. An Apology — 87
10. Everyone has it Wrong — 89
- Denominations to Demon Nations? • Celebrating Easter with Blood (the Waldensian story) • Denominations Abusing the Most Innocent • Forced Child Labor in the Church • Keeping up with the Joneses • Witch Hunts in the 21st Century • The Non-Christian Religious Wrong • Buddhism and Violence • The Irreligious Wrong • What's so Great About the Great Society? • The Opium War on our Children • In the Name of Science • None Righteous, No, Not One

----*The Valley of Heeling*----   page 107

11. Everyone has it Right — 113
- When Right is Right • A Short Reprieve for the Waldensians • The Abused and Forgotten Hero • Pius or Impious? • The Pastor and the Imam • Heroes in Scarves • When Salvation Came from the Atheists • Generosity from Every Tribe • Where Nobodies are Somebody: Postman's Park • Saved by Scientists • Whistleblowers: Public Safety versus Private Safety

12. Where Adolf Hitler Met Mother Teresa — 129
13. Four Year Sentence – Cubism meets Frankenstein — 131

---*Red Faced in the Valley of Decision*---   page 137

14. Lex Rex or When Rules Rule — 141
- When Rules were Written in Stone • Is the Bible a Book of Rules? • Caritas Rex • Externalities to Internalities • Iesus Rex

----*Dancing in Salvatown*----   page 156

15. Between the Circus and the Carnival: from control to revolution — 159
- The Three-Ring Circus of Capitalism • Let Them Eat Cake • The Changing Face of 21st Century Gathering Patterns • Religion meets Bread and Circuses • The Carnival Flip: Philosophers, Artists, Revolutionaries, and Preachers • Carnival and the Gospel • Carnivalesque in Scripture – a Hermeneutic of Wonder • The Carnival Flip and the Individual • The Carnival and Freedom

----*The Feast at Little Finger*----   page 185

16. The Big Stink Bomb — 189
- The Fourth Square Meal: A Pythagorean Tale • Lower-Stratum vs. Upper-Stratum Illustrations (Rabelais and the Gospel contrasted) • Learning to Wipe Up After Cain's Spicy Bean Dip •

17. Validating Reductio ad Hitlerum — 201
- Slouching Toward Nuremburg • Power Corruption • Reductio ad Hitlerum • Reduced to the Worst Possibilities

18. **Imago Dei and Developing Culture**   209
   - Afraid of Witches?

   ----*The Great Wall of Jaw*----   page 212

   - Two Men, Two Stories, Two Critiques of Dominant Culture
   - The Distance of Othering • Killing Otherness • The Othering Other • Common Suppressive Roots of Relativism and Fundamentalism • Listening and Believing: an Antidote to Othering • Looking for God in All the Wrong Places

The Third Ring – The Carnival Canon

   ---*The Nameless Ones*---   page 236

19. **I am What's Wrong with the Church**   241
   - The Inherent Health of a Self-Critiquing Community • Self-Critique as a Healthy Deconstructionist Hermeneutic
20. **One Big Sorry Church**   247

   ----*The Cod Slappers of Peter Harbor*----   page 250

21. **Uncomfortable Sexual Positions**   255
   - Into the Deep, Dark Woods • The Deeper, Darker Woods? • Foucault as a Voice of Conservatism? • How to Get a Crowd • Where Cognitive Dissonance and Sexual Practices Meet

   ---*The Inquisition*---   page 267

22. **The Man in Middle: personal poetry from the struggle for a Carnivalesque authenticity**   269
23. **When God was Lost**   273
   - Finding Jesus at Burning Man • Of Pillars and Fire • God's Voice in the Wilderness
24. **The Clown in the Canon**   281
   - Our Corporate Attention Deficit • Fear, Loss of Control and the Clown • Emerging from the Space in Between • The Cost of Clowning

   ---*Bloody Full Circle*---   page 294

Bibliography   301
About the Author   307

A Freestyled Intro

My vision for this book is grandiose, but my words are small and in my own eyes insignificant. Years ago, I discovered a painful truth: the job of a preacher is a simple thing. We talk about one thing: God, and we don't even do a good job of that. The average laborer often learns more skills on a single jobsite than the tasks of a preacher teach him in a year – at least in respect to marketable, respected skills. All we preachers do is talk about God, or navigate our way to talking about God. The Apostle Paul, who was one of the first truly great preachers, called this the simplicity of the Gospel. He pretended to know nothing but the simple things about Jesus. Turns out he was fooling us all along, and he became one of the great philosophical minds of all the ages. Philosophers and theologians have been struggling with him ever since. He made us mad, and he wooed us back to God, and then he chased us away again. Somehow God became illusive (and yes, my editing friends "elusive" too) in his words, and simultaneously accessible. God became great, and somehow God was behaving in weakness. God became mysteriously wise, and somehow uncommonly foolish under the pen of Paul. The story of God, and the interactions of God with humans were wild. Well, that is if I have been reading Paul and Jesus properly for the last number of years; but I started reading them differently a while back.

My new reading glasses were given to me when I started befriending outsiders – the ones Christians thought were the strange and the scary people. Then I experienced betrayal at the hands of the "church," and some of those closest to me. Suddenly, Paul and Jesus looked different, and they surprised me with their intellectual muscle.

I, on the other hand, felt like a novice in a vocation with one goal. I was a preacher talking foolishly about God, hoping that people wanted to listen to me. Some people listened, but those people were kind of old fashioned. I, and my friends were fuddy-duddies. We were holdouts from those days that mom said were the good old days, but the world around us was saying that they were the oppressive, biased, unreasonable, unscientific past.

So on the heels of tragedy (or I suppose the better way to describe it is, "on my heels because of tragedy," or better yet, "on my ass") I found Paul being unreasonably brutal towards me. He called me out of the comfortable places. I suppose that was okay, because the comfortable places had all disappeared anyway, and I was positioned like the people of my distant heritage – the Welsh.

"Welsh" is not a particularly comforting name for the people of Wales. Its etymology is sourced in Anglo-Saxon. Someone else called the people of the land "Welsh," or "strangers." In their own tongue, they are called Cymry – compatriots, or friends. I feel like a man out of place in his own land. Called a stranger by invaders who have stolen what belongs to me, and only when I speak "iaith y nefoedd" (the language of heaven, which the Welsh call their own language) do I sense the friendliness of heaven enfolding me. But, the language of heaven is a strange tongue, and I am not an easy language learner.

Put it on paper, I can learn it, parse it, and translate even a dead language. Place it on the tongue and in the ear, and I stammer, and struggle to understand. But life is not about what is on the paper, it is about what is on the tongue and in the ear. Jesus was even tougher on me than Paul. He wouldn't let me put it on paper – at least not until now, because theories are best written in mud and blood, and scratched into the flesh like scars from a war.

It has not been put on paper in a holistic manner until now, because it was not holistic until it fought with a world and a church and a God, who all turned out to be wilder than I could have imagined. The experiences of life were wilder than I expected. The people I befriended – those who loved me, and those who betrayed me – were wilder than I had anticipated. God too, was wilder than the best of dreams, and the worst of nightmares. And I was wilder than I expected, and perhaps even now am fooling myself to think I have a holistic worldview. Even this short book tends against believing such a holism exists in a broken world.

And so, in the tragicomic story that is my life, I come to these pages. Of course, my vision is grandiose. I want to accomplish great things, and lay down deep wisdom, but at the end of the day, I expect that the "people who matter" will pay no attention to me, and at the end of the day, I will be fine with that. The "people who matter" are not my concern. The people who don't matter are the people who matter to me. The lost, the outcast, the broken, the lonely, the doubting, the disenfranchised, the broken-hearted, the hopeless, the homeless, and those who feel homeless even though a roof is over their head – you are my people. Those who have labored long for little, those who have given all without thanks, those who laugh as a replacement for tears, those who cry for joy for the little things, and those who continue to do what they believe is right, right to the end – you are my heroes and heroines.

And for you I pretentiously write, attempting to make the blank page more noble than the pure white of its unprinted beginning, but I fear that my words are chicken scratches on the page – ignoble cowardly attempts to describe a wild world, its wild people, and the wild God who seems to silently hover over the face of this wild-erness, and who on occasion violently, surprisingly, and passionately breaks onto the blank page of our lives. This is the beginning of what I hope shall become a series of my thoughts on a "Wild Theology" – a term perhaps best reserved for heretics, but which I am unreasonably comfortable to use in describing myself.

Somewhere back in the days of being a young pastor I felt uncomfortable with the descriptions of my Pentecostal/Evangelical theology, because it wasn't mine. It was too tame. The descriptions of the world were too tame. The descriptions of humanity were too tame. The descriptions of God were tragically too tame, and consequently, the practical outworking of the mission of God was too tame.

Through struggle, and through the adventures I signed up for, I discovered some interesting lessons. I saw the Christian church through the eyes of those on the outside. I saw why they didn't like it. I saw the rebellious disenfranchised outsiders, and they became my people. I also saw my new friends through the eyes of a traditional Christian worldview, and looked across what appeared to be an un-crossable gap. That gap is the concern of this first foray into my Wild Theology. Burning Religion is a look at the church world from the perspective of my non-Christian friends, and back again from the church to their worlds. It is an attempt to navigate the impossible space between the two without pretending that the space is not an impossible space. Yes, I am sure the phrase, "without pretending that the space is not an impossible space" must be some kind of literary illegality, an uncomfortable triple negative. At least I hope it is, because Burning Religion might best be described as a theological triple negative. It is an attempt to cross the impossible gap between religion and today's non-religious culture by not trying to cross it at all, because there seems to be a disappearing middle with no place to put a bridge. Perhaps we only understand the God of the impossible in a triple negative experience. To try, to fail, to give up, and perhaps to discover that not trying is maybe the same thing as not failing.

If you have been burned by religion, I identify as a poster child for the burned, and these words of triple negation are for you. If you think religion is tragically out of touch with a needy world, I do too – sometimes – and these pages are for you. If you see religion harming people, and justifying its actions under the banner of God's Will, I empathize, and these pages are for you. But don't come to these pages for comfort, or at least not for comfort alone, because these pages are like a grade school butt kicking contest.

I lived in the California high desert in the 5th and 6th grade. On the playground, we would try to kick our own butts, by snapping our feet up behind us, and trying to get the loudest butt kicking sound we could possibly make when our feet slapped against our butt cheeks. This book encourages seeing the best in others, and seeing the worst in ourselves. This is the grade school butt-kicking contest and we will be kicking our own butts.

A few apologies must begin this book:

First, I recognize that the terms "religion" and "secular" are ill defined in our culture. I struggled with the idea of using the words "church" and "state", which are equally ill defined, and saying so carries a far more controversial intonation. In the end, using the word "state" was far too limiting, but you can read the word "state" into "secular society" as a small subset of its meaning. Actually, these words have so much meaning that they have almost no meaning at all. Buddhism is called a religion, and yet it has no deity structure. Academics argue about the secular and/or religious framework of nationalism, even in respect to the atheist governments under Mao and Stalin. The argument is typically framed to benefit biases, and that argument often blows wildly around the subject of violence. Nonetheless, I use the words "religion" and its cognates, and "secular" and its cognates, because they are part of the ethos of our culture, and I do not attempt to define these words, because they are so ill defined in our daily references. Instead I will allow the reader to experience a re-framing of the space between these words on her/his own terms in hopes of helping us look at that space differently.

Second, this is a quirky book. It is a combination of philosophy, theology, psychology, sociology, history, autobiography, poetry, and tall tales. I suppose the book goes well beyond the typical overused multi-disciplinary model. My reason for this crazy combination of material is to attempt to take your emotions in the same direction as your intellect, and to model one of the basic theses of this book: that the power of Carnival (in the Bakhtinian sense of the word) is a radical transformative power, and it traverses impassable spaces. Treat the inserted tall tales called, 'Tales from the Land of Jaw: The Adventures of Gwyn Dee' as fun commercial breaks. They hold a hidden purpose, which is to take you on a subtle emotional ride.

Third, the major voices speaking into this project are dead. They passed away between the 1st Century AD and 2003. I never met them face-to-face. I have seen videos, read books, and spent countless hours pouring over material from them and about them, but I have discovered that there are two conflicting popular concepts that make me feel quite uncomfortable with my observations: 1) hindsight is 20/20, and 2) history is written by the victor. Obviously, these platitudes contradict one another, and neither can be a universal statement, and that leaves us in tension. Hopefully, we understand our own past decently enough to place our lives properly into the mythos of our culture, and hopefully we understand our culture fully enough to live within it redemptively.

Let me introduce you to these dead voices, whose words still live inside me. They are each exiles, and this is why they speak so loudly to me. Paul – that is the only name we have for him, and yet, the man from Tarsus remains one of the most formidable voices in human history. We still argue with him today, and a good body of the New Testament Christian scriptures was penned by this heavily persecuted former Jewish religious leader. He stood precariously between the Jewish religious elite, and the Roman Empire. Mikhail Bakhtin – a one-legged Russian literary theorist and philosopher. He was a survivor from the brutality of Stalin. He spent 20 years in exile, and his work was buried until the mid 60s. Bakhtin, through his concepts of Carnival and the dialogical, is perhaps the greatest influence upon this ghostly tome. Emmanuel Levinas was a Lithuanian Jew, who moved to France, and was captured in WWII by the Germans. His thoughts on the Other as an exile inform the latter part of this book. Edward Said – a Palestinian academic, who brought about the demise of an academic field of study formerly known as Orientalism. Single-handedly he gave the academic field a negative and patronizing connotation, and helped establish post-colonialism as we know it today. Said was 12 years old when Israel became a nation in 1948, and his family left for Egypt.

I don't pretend any scholarship concerning these voices from the past, but then theoretically I have been approaching life with the assumption that we are all correct and have something valuable to offer, and simultaneously we are all a hot mess and get it wrong a good deal of the time. Consequently, I view truth as I view my typing skills – it is a hunt and peck experience with a lot of need for correction. Although, I have to admit my primary bias from the beginning: concerning the Christian Scriptures, I approach them differently, and give the Genesis through Revelation words heavier weight than all other voices in my life.

Some thanks are necessary here. To friends who have walked with me through good portions of this text, or some of my thoughts contained herein: Aled Llion Jones, Megan DeFranza, Kelly Williams, Heather Leigh Mitch, Matt (the Pirate) Bender, Chris Reiss, David

Gerard, Stephen Martin, Joshua Jinno, Dennis Huxley, Peter Gaffney, Paul Drake, Rebecca Ver Straten-Mcsparren, Deb and Alan Hirsch, Hilary Davis – thank you for discussing the issues herein, or for reading, encouraging, and challenging my thoughts here. Those of you who were the most critical, were the most helpful. Mike Crockett, your skilled librarian services made this a less expensive process when I needed all that scholarship on Mikhail Bakhtin – thank you. Kevin (Kevissimo) Rolly – whose friendship is honored greatly and whose artistic skills grace the cover – thanks bro. David Hayward – the Naked Pastor, it was good to work with you. Michelle Rogers Pritzl and Shawn Fitzgerald – your photographic skills make me look pretty good – thanks. To the Tuesday night Pub Theology group – you helped hash out quite a few thoughts in this book. Most of all to a group of friends who have walked through some of these stories with me – the whole of The Gathering, former and current members of our little church in Salem, MA. Jeff and Diane Menasco, Stef and Mike Crockett, Jeff and Kellie Gentry, Rennie Treantos, and Joanne Joyce especially need mention here. Hope Deifell, thank you for being a fabulous Burning Man guide, a great support, and for offering a beautiful location in the mountains of North Carolina to write parts of this book - has anyone told you how awesome you are today? And to the distant people who were there when I needed a hero: Steve Pate, Shah Afshar, Dale Downs, Jim Henderson – thanks. To all the Neo-Pagans and atheists in Salem and even abroad, you too are a part of this story – thank you. Cern, Christian, Laura, Leanne, and a nod to Shawn Poirier (we miss you) - thanks. Jonas and Mary-Alice, you have been a part of this story in so many ways – love is the reason we are gathered here today. A massive thanks has to go to the nation of Wales, and my friends there – I might not be alive today without you.

Diolch yn fawr iawn. Dw i'n eich caru chi.
Phil Wyman
July 30th, 2015 on a hot muggy day in Witchcity, USA

THE FIRST RING
SPINNING FIRE – THE SELF-IMMOLATION OF CHRISTIANITY

BURNING THE TEMPLE

The Temple burned. Twenty thousand people stood in silence around the holy place as the flames leaped into the star dotted heavens. The fire climbed the walls, engulfing the pagoda-like roof, and licked the night sky. Tears were streaming down the faces of the quiet crowd. An occasional gasp broke the silence.

No one fought the fire. The temple's complete destruction was a foregone conclusion. As the fire grew, the flames reached hundreds of feet like grasping hands into the dark night. This had been the only temple the city had ever known, and its burning marked the end of their existence as a cohesive community. It held their dreams, and their fears. Years of loss and struggle were etched in the walls now consumed by flames. Lost loved ones had been dedicated to eternity here. Addictions had been surrendered here. Hopes clung stubbornly to the burning walls. Long held dreams rehearsed themselves in the smoldering thoughts of the silent crowd, and the people watched those stubborn hopes billow upward choking heaven with its thick smoke.

The temple had been one of the first structures erected. During the life of the city, it was the tallest building, and helped to serve as a navigational guide in the network of communities - perhaps as a premonition of the central place it would hold in the lives of the people. Already the once strong city of over 50,000 had begun to scatter. Fire and destruction had engulfed much of the city in the previous days. These 20,000 souls were the last holdouts - perhaps they were those who had the greatest emotional and physical investment in the community. Perhaps they were merely those who were afraid to leave. The silence was dark, dense and awesome. Vocal expression beyond the occasional gasp and sob was an invasion to this moment of dark holy crisis.

The blaze eventually consumed the walls. Roofs collapsed in leaping pillars of smoke, and when the main tower fell, the flames jumped high into the dark sky. The scattering embers joined the stars on the black canvas of the night, and dying fell back to earth.

I was there when the temple fell. Emotion swept over the city folk with the waves of pulsing heat.

The crowd broke the silence with a cheer. And I cheered with them.

This was Burning Man 2011. The week long festival on the barren

Black Rock Playa of the northern Nevada desert is a city-sized carnival of art, fire, lights, explosions, music, hedonism, spiritual pursuit, protest, and just about anything almost anyone might be looking for in an environment only the wildest dare to enter. During the week of its existence, it is Nevada's fourth largest city.

Burning Man is where Mad Max meets the Metropolitan Museum of Art meets the Fourth of July. Apocalyptic images and anarchy crash together with art and fire.

2011 marked the first time the temple was taller than the primary art structure of the event - the Man.

Burning Man began as beach party in San Francisco, California. That first year, in 1986, an 8' tall human-shaped structure was burned on the beach among friends, and it began this wild twenty-five year ride of experimental community and artistic expression. Each year, a newly erected Man, now five-stories tall burns among blaring sound systems, performance artists, and dance parties. But since 1999, a temple has been erected, and now the week concludes with the burning of the temple. The sound systems are quieted, and the last of the previously partying crowds stay to express something emotional, transformative, and somehow quietly celebratory as the temple burns in the final act of this absurd theater that is Burning Man.

The temporary temple serves as a catharsis for the participants of Burning Man – a type of postmodern non-religious evangelical altar. Pictures of loved ones who have died are hung on the walls. Permanent markers stain the temple with holy graffiti: words of release, words of pain, words of victory over addiction, words of surrender, words of grief, words of joy, words of dreams to come, words of pop wisdom, words of praise to the divine, words of blasphemy, words of confession, words of anger, and words of love. The burning of the temple becomes the release point for many of the hopes and frustrations of those who have decorated and violated its walls. The tears, which streamed during the burning flowed from both the sense of life's impermanence created by this temporary temple, and the release of the dreams and sorrows captured in the rising smoke.

Could it be that each year this temporary community of wild artists, hedonists, and subculture prophets are creating prescient moments speaking to the cultures and the religions in these days in which we live? Could the burning of the temple speak both to the potential power and the simultaneous impotence of spirituality in the 21st Century?

I came to Burning Man as a cultural missionary and a participating artist in 2011. The burning of the temple spoke like a mad prophet, and gave me a glimpse into my own religion from the perspective of those who usually look uncomfortably at it from the outside.

I wear a rough homemade copper Burning Man necklace around my neck sometimes. I do not wear jewelry of any kind typically, but this piece was "gifted" to me during the first year I attended Burning Man. It is a reminder to me of things all the crazy places like Burning Man have taught me.

I've lived most all my Christian life as a missional adventurer. I don't recommend this life to everyone. The price is high. Angels take out insurance policies for themselves while following adventurers. But, the lessons are deep for those who will brave the environments, which are so unlike the staid church world many people live within.

It is in these places we find the greatest critiques of Christianity: critiques both accurate and intelligent, as well as those birthed out the angry responses of pop-culture, and the politics of power. We would be remiss to dismiss these critiques, even when they are in many ways misdirected.

The little burning man around my neck reminds me of the impotent religion our society simultaneously cheers and mourns every time they see it fall. It reminds me of priests and preachers who have harmed honestly seeking people with the abuse of power and the sticky fingers of lust and greed. Yet, it also reminds me of a religion whose potential power in this temporary world reaches towards the eternal heights of heaven, and of a fire that still burns in the hearts of those who seek to express God in simple, honest and consequently – radical ways.

Religion burns.

This is both an indictment and a hopeful expectation. Marxist philosopher and atheist Slavoj Žižek recently wrote about the Spanish anarchist Buenaventura Durutti who was quoted as saying that *"The only church that illuminates is a burning church."* "He was right," said Žižek, *"though not in the anti-clerical sense his remark was intended to have. Religion only arrives at its truth through its self-cancellation."*[1]

Self-cancellation was the act of God at the crucifixion of Christ. It is the continuing act of the church, while it learns to walk in "the fellowship of His sufferings."[2] Unlike Žižek anticipates, I see this self-cancellation of the church as more than a Hegelian synthesis into

---

[1] Slavoj Žižek, Religion & Ethics: Content from Across the ABC (Australian Broadcasting Company) The only church that illuminates is a burning church - Slavoj Žižek ABC Religion and Ethics 8 Aug 2011, Also: Slavoj Žižek; John Milbank. The Monstrosity of Christ: Paradox or Dialectic? (Kindle Locations 4756-4757). Kindle Edition.
[2] Philippians 3:10

some(socialist)thing better.[3] Rather, I see radical renewal into the miraculous in every generation of a church re-birthed as the Phoenix from the ashes.

Perhaps both Durutti and Žižek are correct. The burning of the church is positive. It is a sign of our capacity to disconnect from this broken world. It is the fiery crucifixion[4] Žižek envisions. It may also be the loss of the oppressive human authority within religion, which Durutti celebrated.

The tensions of a burning religion are both a terrible loss and a hopeful expectation. That is what these stories, and musings are all about.

The little copper man around my neck reminds me of the fallen temple at Burning Man. It reminds me that people are simultaneously mourning and celebrating the falling of the temple of my faith. This copper man also calls me to apologize for, to respond to, to encourage, and to create a burning religion.

---

[3] Slavoj Žižek re-imagines the death of Christ on the cross as the loss of "the Big Other" – as the death of God. To Žižek, the crucifixion event marks the moment when we are completely alone in the universe, but consequently fully free. The liberating result is that we are called to become the community of the Holy Ghost, which he interprets as the ultimate egalitarian expression – people filled with love and serving one another. Žižek sees Christianity as a paradigm describing a philosophically materialist Gospel of human potential enacting justice and equality, "An egalitarian community outside of social hierarchy is possible. That is the good news." (God in Pain: inversions on apocalypse, with Boris Gunevic) Quote from LA Library dialogue with Slavoj Žižek. (https://youtu.be/sQ3g2zS6Tuk)

[4] Just in case this connection between death by burning and the crucifixion is misunderstood, let me be clear. This illustration has no connection to the Scottish rite of burning a cross on a hill to call people to war, nor to the obscene adoption by the KKK of the burning cross. If anything, this is a sacred inversion of such militaristic perspectives of the cross. It represents an intellectual and existential death through our own struggles, and the resultant loss of trust in corporate Christianity. The only warlike features to this "fiery crucifixion" are the internal war against the violent elements we hold within ourselves.

Engage: The Temple and You

The burning of the temple at the Burning Man festival illustrates the simultaneous rejoicing and grieving we see in our culture when religion fails. Is it possible that this tension over the demise of religion also resides within our own hearts? Do we feel a satisfaction at the loss of religion when we see it, even while secretly sorrowing for the loss of something ancient and innocent?

Interact with the Burning Religion community on the website at www.burningreligion.com.

IT MUST BE A CULT

People stroll the brick and cobblestone pedestrian mall on Essex Street in Salem, Massachusetts. It's a beautiful and weird, strangely romantic and quirky street with two fountains, overhanging trees, a world class museum, quaint tourist haunts, a glorious old dusty bookstore with not-quite vertical stacks of leaning books glaring out the windows,[5] a handful of witchcraft shops, and the former location of our church. I'm a people-watcher. I sometimes stood inside the church and looked out the windows facing the street. Often, the people stopped outside our doors.

"A Christian Church which is short on rules and long on relationships," the sign read.

Some people stopped and stood blinking, thinking - perhaps wondering what it meant. Others called to their friends or family. They smiled and made remarks about it. Maybe once a day in the high tourist season, someone would take pictures of the sign. Rarely, but on occasion someone would stop and look skeptically at it.

Some days I stood outside the front doors as I people-watched. I talked with interested passersby. More than half a million people would pass by our doors each year. Salem is a tourist town, and Essex Street is the pretty little pedestrian mall every tourist will walk, but it is not just tourists I watched. Locals stop and talk. I waved to the mayor and called her by her first name. I greeted the shop owners, the homeless, the people commuting by foot to and from work, the kids hanging out downtown after school, neighbors walking their dogs, and the growing number of people who simply thought of our church as a place to hang out.

A young man with close-cropped hair walked by one day. I was standing outside next to the sign. He was with a friend. He stopped. He stood still. He looked at the sign. He read it out loud.

The young man with the military haircut remarked to his friend, "How can you have a Christian Church with no rules?"

I interrupted the embryonic conversation gently, "It doesn't say, 'no

---

[5] During the writing of this book, the glorious old Derby Square books was sold, and for its fans, it was a sad day when the stacks of books disappeared from the windows, and the place that looked like something out of Harry Potter vanished.

rules.' It says, 'short on rules.'"

"How can you be a Christian without rules?" He repeated his critique with the slight variation, and directed the statement to his friend. With seeming intentionality, he ignored me, while talking about the church.

I repeated myself in the same gentle tone of voice, "It doesn't say, 'no rules.'"

He fired off questions loud and impersonally. He clearly wanted me to hear his questions, but he did not look at me, and he did not acknowledge my existence. Without waiting for a reply he asked questions like, "Well, what kind of Christian Church is this with no rules? I wonder if they even use the Bible?" Then he segued his monologue and began answering his own questions as he turned to walk away, "You can't be a Christian with no rules. This must be some sort of cult."

This brief one-sided encounter is a glimpse into another story: a story played out in our culture every day. It is a tale encircling religion, politics, our struggle to define and redefine freedom, and perhaps even the underlying presuppositions in many of our social interactions.

Tales from the Land of Jaw: The Adventures of Gwyn Dee
The Birth of Gwyn Dee

Brain vices, and blinders, and facial sin tattoos, and ear-corks, and olfactory filters, and tongue clamps, and taste bud benumbers, and veils, and face masks, and swallow restrictors, and voice suppressors, and mouth cages, and appetite suppressors, and spiked chokers, and neck stretching dzilla, and iron yokes, and stone yokes, and full burqas, sackcloth, and ponderous long sleeved shirts, and hair shirts, and hair shorts, and breast flatteners, and modesty dresses, and painful pinching gloves, and finger restrictors, and chastity belts, and leathern girdles, and locking cod pieces, and barbed cod pieces, holy underwear and bum whippings, and emasculations, and iron pants, and knee knockers, and anklet warning bells, and foot slappings, and foot bindings, and toe pinchers: these and many more were the devices of passion restraint in the Land of Jaw. Monitoring the behavior of people is always more difficult than a small bit of socially mandated prescriptive restraint, punishment and concealment. But, perhaps no people had so well adapted the arts of modesty and virtue as the people of Cominkingville with their stone shoes.

It had been a short 58 years since the founding of Cominkingville. Jane Foole the Jester of Jaw had come and gone, leaving a trail of new villages in her wake, and Cominkingville was one of a rumored thousand villages. Only a handful of the fading elders remembered meeting Jane Foole. The Clown Caste did their best to remember the ways of the great Jester of Jaw, and choose the wisest and most astute children for training in the traditions of the religious Caste. But now a mere generation and a half later, they translated rare writings, debated over doctrinal points, dictated edicts on community behavior, and forgot the arts of fire-spinning, costuming, tumbling, joke delivery, music, and painting. The only remaining art still practiced from the days of Jane Foole was storytelling, and all the people of Cominkingville were required to learn the art of storytelling. Secretly, a few rebels remained, who studied the other clowning arts, but they did so with itinerate jugglers in the illicit taverns of Cominkingville.

Gwyn Dee arrived in the 58th year of the founding of the village, born on the day of the Carnival of Clowns during a full eclipse of the sun. The village stared at the sky, and when the eclipse ended Gwyn Dee was lifted high in air before the cheering village, and to the declaration, "a child is born!" Gwyn Dee's birth was viewed as a premonition of great things to come – by some, but others thought this was an omen of trouble. Of course, history has taught us that great things and trouble are not exclusive of one another.

As soon as the children of Cominkingville could walk, they were fitted with stone shoes. Gwyn Dee was a happy, energetic, and precocious child, and the stone shoes were not easily kept on Gwyn Dee's feet. It is not difficult to imagine the frustration of a parent in stone shoes trying to catch their giggling two-year old running in circles, and laughing hilariously at them. Yet, Gwyn Dee was not a troublemaker at heart, so by the fourth year of life the stone shoes remained intact, but little Gwyn Dee did not stop running, and the people of Cominkingville watched in wonder and amazement.

As Gwyn Dee grew, the borders of the village grew more and more inviting. Tales of Jane Foole, of her exploits in the founding of many villages, and strange adventures beyond the borders of the Land of Jaw haunted the curious child's imagination, and when no one was looking, Gwyn Dee ran through the woods and strayed just beyond the border, or snuck up to the wide, wide road at the entrance to Cominkingville.

And Gwyn Dee heard of the adventures of the past and thought it strange that the people of Cominkingville sat comfortably and as adventureless as tired old dogs.

The elders were not ignorant of Gwyn Dee's excursions to the edges of the village. They watched to see whether these things were a good sign or an evil omen. So, Gwyn Dee was called to the Clown Caste, and trained personally by the elders of the High Clown Caste at an age younger than any in the short history of Cominkingville. But Gwyn Dee wondered why the Clown Caste seemed so serious, *and worked so studiously on dogma, and did not learn the arts of clowning, which were now relegated to dark nights in the illicit taverns.*

"CULTURA ANIMI PHILOSOPHIA EST"

Tully was a Roman philosopher and statesman. Some historians believe that he came from a family of landowner/farmers – probably growers of chickpeas. It was perhaps from this that the family name originated. Plutarch thought that the name came from an ancestor with a large cleft on the end of his nose that looked like a chickpea. He was urged to drop the name when he entered politics, because the name derived from "cicer" (garbanzo bean, or chickpea) appeared silly, even demeaning, and not a name for a prominent leader of an empire. He refused to change his common name. Instead, he said that he would make the name Cicero (the equivalent of "Garbanzo Beaner") glorious, and he did.

It was Marcus Tullius (Tully) Cicero, the powerful Roman politician philosopher from the garbanzo bean growing family who penned the phrase "Cultura animi philosophia est." Culture is the philosophy of the soul. Since Cicero, the agricultural term "cultura" has been applied to education, art and the developments of humanity.

So began the long descendancy of a family of words, which has given us such widely differing terms as "cultivate", "culture", and "cult."

The definition of "culture" has changed since Cicero's declaration, "cultura animi philosophia est". Yet, what has not changed is the understanding that society's ideas, actions, and long-term development have cultivated different attitudes in different people across the world. Different cultures are growing in the different climates of human interaction. Education, religion, language, art, politics, and economics have even cultivated different attitudes and world-views among next-door neighbors.

These differing opinions have often grown so disparate and so severe, that like the young man standing in front of our church sign: one group's culture has become another group's cult.

Engage: Cultural Dissonance and You

"...one group's culture has become another group's cult." To what degree have you discovered this to be true? Have you been mocked for your faith, or lack thereof? or perhaps for your political position? Have you found family gatherings difficult to attend, because family members' opinions are impossible to stomach? What is your experience with the issues of faith and politics in situations with differing worldviews and presuppositions?

Interact with the Burning Religion community on the website at www.burningreligion.com.

LESSONS FROM THE GARDEN

For about a dozen years I lived in a park. At least it felt like a park. Not far off the beaten path of downtown Salem, the boundaries of that little piece of turf and our 1830's farmhouse were surrounded by a five-and-half-foot fence. In that small quarter acre I cultivated hundreds of daffodils, whose early spring appearance smiled like golden sunshine. More than a dozen varieties of rare daylilies splashed across the yard in a rainbow of color during the midsummer. Over the course of a couple months the daylilies individually bloomed for a day, and by the next sunrise shriveled into the wilted corpses of rotting petals. Each year the bulbs and tubers of thousands of flowers exploded into life for a short season and disappeared again, needing to be cut back to nothing in preparation for a healthy return the next year.

The growth from late Spring through Fall is dramatic and explosive. With a little work, a gardener can cultivate a carnival of flowers blooming through each of the short growing seasons before the harvest season comes to a close and the enemy winter encroaches - for as long as five months.

When the snow melted in our little yard, the first white and purple pansies peeked their fairy faces through the snow, having been hidden by the catacombs of ice. As the cool sun of Spring gently warmed the earth, crocuses, and shortly after, the bright yellow daffodils broke ground, and raced upward to lift their heads, taking their trumpeting heraldic post in the sun. Forsythia hedges exploded in buzzing yellow fountains, and as they faded, the white to imperial purple lilac clusters whose small flowers belied their powerful fragrance slowly relaxed their tight buds, and stood by the gate like Byzantine guards. Tulips of every color (those whose bulbs survived the squirrels - squirrels who would overcome my yearly dusting of the bulbs with cayenne pepper) would sway in a smiling festival parade of crowded happy bunches, and the bleeding hearts hung their little pink and white heads like friends of the bride weeping tears of joy.

As Summer began to approach massive deep purple, and lemon yellow irises crowned our front door in amethyst and gold. The white and mauve echinacea stood as formal as newly titled nobility, proud yet hapless against the thieving groundhog shiftily scuttering away with their petals in his belly. The wild, local rosa rugosa haphazardly stumbled against the stone walls like pink disheveled drunken clowns from early summer through fall, and the heather and heath poked their tiny heads up to watch as the daylillies juggled their flaming red and yellow explosions, danced the hot white and magenta fandango, or tumbled across the path in absinthe greens and flowing chiffon yellows. As Summer fell into Fall, the pauperish ruddy pink asters and buff mums argued for space in the fading garden like clumsy barkers in the town square, and the drunken, clowning rosa rugosa kept tumbling and laughing as the garden was being cut back and protected against the coming Winter. And even as the first snows fell, one last vagrant bluish-green heather with small, soft dusty pink buds tenaciously hugged the ground and remained in bloom through the freezing rains and ice, and even under deep snows.

Christianity is as adaptable, varied, crazy and hearty as the garden. Through different seasons of history, and radically different climates, through war and peace, through economic hardship and prosperity, through famine and plenty, through racial tension and unity, through heresies and internal strife, and even through its own tragic errors and oppressive violence it has adapted and survived. And the carnival of cultures created during these dramatic changes, have often been a glorious explosion of the beauty of humanity, despite the weedy gardens of the old churchyards.

Like the bulbs and tubers of the flowering plants of Spring, honest followers of the Nazarene have often overcome and returned - culture intact - from the cold death throes of calamity and struggle.

Often, but not always.

THE SELF-IMMOLATION
OF CHRISTIANITY

In the Fall of the year, after the blooming had ended, and it was time to cut back the year's growth, I would evaluate the enormous deep purple and bright yellow irises guarding our front door. On most years I would need to separate the tubers. Dividing them into groups around the door by their color - yellows in their bunches and the deep purple irises in their groups. Within a few years, there was a small jungle of tall explosive irises around the front door, and we were giving tubers away, or planting them in other sections of the yard.

Christianity should grow and flourish with this same gracious process. Jesus speaks of the gardening work of his Father. It is a work of pruning, digging, and burning in the leaf pile that which is no longer fruitful.[6] The evidence from the history of Christianity suggests that the Church has not always followed that pattern. Too often Christianity has burned itself, starting fires inside the walls of the Cathedral, accusing itself – dividing itself into factions and seeking to do away with variations of itself, sometimes based on things which seem as trivial as color. The times in which we live are filled with evidence that one Christian's culture has become another Christian's cult, and some of us are trying to burn down expressions unlike our own.

YouTubers and a Growing Dissent

During recent Sunday services our small church played two YouTube video clips illustrating the tensions over religion in our American Christian cultures. Our simple interdenominational Christian church is commonly visited and attended by people from all varieties of faith and/or lack thereof. On this day, we had our own faith-family comprised of people from evangelical, high-church, agnostic, and Pentecostal backgrounds. Also visiting were Catholics, former Catholics, agnostic/atheists, and a Raelian (who believes that life on earth was created by extraterrestrials, who scientifically engineered humanity.)

The first video was by YouTube sensation poet Jeff Bethke. He had to defend his spoken word video "Why I Hate Religion, But Love Jesus,"[7] after it received almost 20 million hits, including more than

---
[6] John 15:1-8

300,000 likes, and over 50,000 dislikes. Bethke's video touched the painful nerve of frustration with what has been called "religiosity." In its opening lines Bethke's poetry positioned him against two widely different groups: politically conservative Christians and mainline Christian denominations.

Bethke asserts that Jesus came to abolish religion, and says that voting Republican wasn't part of Jesus' mission. Then transitions to attack large church edifices while saying they fail to feed the poor.

"Why I Hate Religion, But Love Jesus" expresses what many people feel as they search for authenticity within spirituality. "Why I Hate Religion, But Love Jesus" was filled with the common sayings from the coffeehouse and twitter theology of our times:
- It's not about religion. It's about relationship.
- If Jesus came to your church, would they let Him in?
- Religion has been a major cause of the world's wars.
- Christian Churches are filled with hypocrites who will monitor your sex life, but won't feed the poor, or help the oppressed.

These ideas have become rallying cries for a generation of new Christians. They are calls to action against formality and tradition, which are perceived as the stagnant remains of what might have once been a living faith, and they are cries for an active, socially aware and theologically radical faith. "Religion" by this definition is seen as dead formality: formality housed in expensive trappings, devoid of Jesus' heart to serve the downtrodden, and oppressed. It is the dregs of a promised "new wine."

Strangely, many of these same arguments are also the rallying cry for a generation of new atheists. The validity of religion is being attacked from within and without.

Jeff Bethke put the nail in the coffin of religion by equating Jesus' death on the cross with the abolishing of religion, *"So for religion, No, I hate it. I literally resent it, because when Jesus said 'It is finished,' I believe he meant it."*

And in that moment, Bethke equated religion with Jesus" words, "It is finished," and declared that the anger and the judgment of God is against religion.

Showing "Why I Hate Religion, but Love Jesus" was followed by a discussion at our church services.

A Sociology professor and former Catholic turned Episcopalian turned Emergent/Evangelical identified with the video and loved it. Our Raelian visitor thought it was fantastic. One of the founding members of our church, mother of three grown children, daughter to a

---

[7] see Jefferson Bethke's video at https://youtu.be/1IAhDGYlpqY

Lutheran pastor, and mother-in-law to an Episcopal priest identified strongly with the video as well. My friend Chris, quintessential and certified geek with code in Google Chrome who had only recently started visiting church after 25 years without darkening the doors apart from funerals or weddings loved the video and raved about it when he first saw it. For the most part, our small church loved the spoken-word attack on "religion."

Then we played video number two: "Why I Love Religion, And Love Jesus"[8] by Spirit Juice Studios and hip-hop artist/Catholic priest Fr. Pontifex.

> *"What if I told you that Jesus loves religion, and that by coming as man brought His religion to fruition? You see this had to be addressed; your use of illogical terms and definitions. You clearly have a heart for Jesus, but it's fueling atheistic opinions. You see, what makes His religion great is not errors of wars or inquisitions, it's that broken men and women get to participate in His mission. Clearly Jesus says 'I have not come to abolish. I came to fulfill the law, and I came to fulfill the prophets, and lines about building big churches and tending to the poor sound a bit like Judas when the perfume is being poured."*

The video defends religion as the largest worldwide contributor of help to the needy. Fr. Pontifex quips that blaming religion for hypocrisy is *"like staring at death and blaming the hearse."*

"So as for religion," He says, *"I love it. I have one because He rose from the dead and won. I believe that when Jesus said 'it [was] finished,' His religion had just begun."*

Our Raelian visitor hated the second video, and could only see the Catholic priest defending religion as an attempt to protect economic and power structures. One might expect this suspicion from Raelians, who traditionally identify with controversial antiestablishmentarian positions.

The Lutheran pastor's daughter saw the camera angles, and setting inside the church on the Catholic response video as indicative of prideful religious practices, and struggled with the delivery of the message.

The sociology professor and confessing Episcopal, one of our church leaders simply identified with the first video more, but saw value in both videos.

My geek friend, Chris, who grew up in an atheist home, thought Fr. Pontifex had a more reasoned video and saw the response as a poetic

---

[8] see Fr. Pontifex video at https://youtu.be/Ru_tC4fv6FE

slam dunk on the first video.

And so the strange dynamics of our small community's response to the spoken word poetry about God and religion highlights a tension within Christianity. Christians who have been involved in large and small churches, people both marginally and actively involved, and those who are participants in denominations and independent churches are not immune to feeling distrustful and angry toward "organized religion." Much of the culture of Christianity is captured by terms of deadly passion. Hate and resentment are attached to our feelings about religion. This is true not only from the pews, but from many of the pulpits – from those who are the cultivators of the 21st century American spiritual landscape.

Many Christians believe God does not honor religion. He is in the business of ending it. Other Christians find great hope in religion. For them it is the flesh and blood expression of God's love to humanity – lived out in the activity of people organized to serve His mission together.

To one person, the attack on religion identifies hurts, legitimates frustrations, accounts for inconsistencies, and allows for God to interact with us in a place outside corrupted human expressions of the faith.

To another person, this attack on religion is perceived as an attack on God's work itself. It is viewed as war against those who have found solace and meaning in organized communities of faith.

Within these two videos semantic play is going on. The two artists do not have the same definition for the word "religion." For Jeff Bethke, religion is defined by the worst behaviors of Christianity in history, and manipulative efforts to control human spiritual pursuit. For Fr. Pontifex religion is the framework for Christ's mission on earth. Bethke defined it by Jesus' scathing critiques of the Pharisees. Fr. Pontifex defines it by James' definition, *"Pure religion and undefiled before God and the Father is this, to visit the fatherless and widows in their affliction, and to keep himself unspotted from the world."*[9]

Is Jefferson Bethke telling people to stop attending church? No. In fact, some people have returned to church after seeing his video. He identified their frustrations, and this was Bethke's goal as he outlines his thoughts about the video:

> *"Like I say, 'I love the church' in the video…why don't they quote that one. Do I think I'm pushing people away from the church, while promoting Jesus? I hope not, and I pray not…so, no you can't live without the church. So,*

---

[9] James 1:27

maybe if you took it that way, I'm sorry."

Yet, as Bethke continues to describe his opinion of religion he illustrates his view by using flying as an example.

"If we tried to fly, how many of us could get on top of this building and just jump off and flutter about? No one is flying. Let's be honest. We are all going, just one by one, to pile down on the ground, and there's going to be a big stack of dead bodies. And that's pretty much what religion is."[10]

It is clear Jeff Bethke's definition for "religion" does not include "church." "Religion" has a narrow definition. It is a corrupt human invention, which stifles true spirituality. It creates a barrier between the experience of God, and the individual. "Church" on the other hand, carries a mystical definition defined by the activities of God. A special connection is discovered through Christ's sacrifice, and it is a connection by faith alone. "Church" is the people with this connection who follow Jesus, and by extension "church" is the regular gathering of those same people. As a result, God hates religion, but loves the church.

This is a simplified iconoclastic definition of the word "religion," and it is the most prevalent definition among evangelical Christians. Christian America slowly adopted this definition as its own over the course of the 20th century, and it is now imbedded deep in our corporate psyche. Many people feel as though they have found a way to define their faith in a non-religious manner to what appears to be an increasingly anti-Christian culture.

Interestingly, Jefferson Bethke attended a now defunct megachurch in Seattle. His former pastor is famous (or notorious depending on one's opinion) for being controversially aggressive toward other Christian leaders and churches with whom he disagrees.

Fr. Pontifex was traveling between Evansville, Indiana, where his parish is, and Illinois when I reached him by phone. We talked about his experience following the release of his response video "Why I Love Religion, and Love Jesus."

Within a couple days of the release of Jeff Bethke's video, it had gone viral. Catholics were calling their priests with complaints, and questions about the video. Fr. Pontifex, whose name is Claude Burns, was asked by Spirit Juice Studios if he would be interested in giving a

---

[10] Transcribed comments from Jeff Bethke's teaching on YouTube video "My Heart Behind 'Why I Hate Religion, but Love Jesus'" http://www.youtube.com/watch?v=dN1iyJQGrcU

response to the Bethke's video. A week after the release of "Why I Hate Religion, But Love Jesus" Spirit Juice Studios had Fr. Pontifex' response online.

Concerning Bethke's video, Fr. Burns says that Jeff Bethke, "made good points about hypocrisy, but he should have stuck with the issue of hypocrisy."

Fr. Burns agrees that there are "gaping wounds from the priest abuse scandals, and historical abuse in the church." He sees that these are things many people have intelligently identified and their critiques are warranted, but warns against throwing the baby out with the bathwater.

> "When you see the abuse, and you see the hypocrisy and say I don't need [religion], it's like divorcing yourself from the situation, and saying I only need my relationship with Jesus. By saying 'its about relationship, not religion,' we run the risk of over-spiritualizing Christianity. Over-spiritualizing says there is no need for a concrete, tactile reality. People point at their chest, and say the church is in here, but the growth of the church came from the concrete structure – with Paul and the first church."

Claude Burns is a man who has stood on both sides of this issue. When he was younger, he had what he describes as a radical encounter with Jesus. He was brought up Catholic, but did not live for God until his encounter. Initially, he turned to evangelical Christianity, but when deciding to enter the ministry he returned to faith of his youth.

"I had very strong ties to non-denominational churches, and I still do. Those friends had a hard time understanding why I became a priest," says Fr. Burns.

The difficulty Claude Burns' friends had in understanding his desire to return to Catholicism is birthed partially from the semantics of this argument, and perhaps more critically from the inherent deep mistrust of organized religion. Not only do Christians from different traditions not have the same definitions for common words we use, we also do not see the world of our faith from the same perspective.

At some point Fr. Pontifex stopped checking the remarks on the YouTube video, which continued to grow and turned toward debate. "I had to get away from checking the comments, and check my blood pressure," he joked.

At one level Fr. Pontifex believes, "Both videos are saying the same thing – live with integrity, they are a statement against hypocrisy." And Fr. Burns was quick to identify hypocrisy in his own church, "Within the Catholic Church – there are the culturally Catholic, and there are converts. As we often say converts often make the best Catholics. But, there is a connectedness between Protestant and Catholic, because the church is more than Catholic, it is catholic."

Fr. Pontifex contacted Jeff Bethke. The two have been in positive dialogue about the videos, and the issue of religion vs. relationship. They are agreeing to disagree. Is a video with the two evangelists sharing the spoken word together on the same screen on the horizon? One can only hope so.

In our culture the debate is much more intense than a rap battle. On one side, we have a radically violent position. Believing that someone or something is hated and does not deserve to exist, is effectively a Lockean declaration of war. To speak for God – to proclaim that He hates religion – is to declare a holy war against religion.

On the other side, people less gracious and experienced than Fr. Pontifex stand in a stalwart defense of religion, carrying a nationalistic emotion found in the protection of countries, or empires – but empires control the world. Sometimes that control is a blessing, and sometimes it is a curse.

Christianity is pulled between these tensions. We appear to be either revolting against religion in a paradoxical defense of our faith, or blindly defending religion as the sole public expression and the carrier of our faith. Riffing off Hegel, Žižek reminds of us of the obscene hermeneutic, which may occur in choosing one side against the other, "...*in accusations about 'fundamentalism,' the Evil often resides in the gaze that perceives the fundamentalist Evil.*"[11] Fortunately, not everyone is comfortable choosing between these options. Not every revolutionary change is good, and not every defense of the establishment is proper.

As we look across the landscape of 21st Century Christianity, it seems that we have declared Jihad against ourselves. We are all spinning stories like politicians spin a campaign, but we have not recognized that we are spinning fire, and creating destruction around us. The temples are burning. We are cheering their burning, even while we are standing inside the temple warming our faith to the deadly fires we have lit.

And this is not a new thing.

---

[11] Žižek, The Parallax View, pg. 376

Engage: Between the Flowers and the Fire. Where do you stand?

In the two chapters "Lessons from the Garden" and "The Self-Immolation of Christianity" the tension between the beauty of Christianity, and its tendency to argue, split and fight is highlighted. The points of tension are often small things, but they have carried deadly ramifications historically. How have these tensions affected you and the people in your life?

How do you evaluate and compare the hip-hop battle of thoughts between Bethke and Pontifex?

Interact with the Burning Religion community on the website at www.burningreligion.com.

Tales from the Land of Jaw: The Adventures of Gwyn Dee
The Long Barefoot Journey

*T*he flag dropped. The Stone Shoe Race began. All the boys and girls in Cominkingville ran for all their might. The Stone Shoe Race had been a tradition in Cominkingville for as long as anyone could remember. In fact, wearing stone shoes had been a tradition in Cominkingville for as long as anyone could remember.

Stone shoes were a spiritual discipline preparing the wearer for the apocalypse. Someday the people would be called to remove their stone shoes and leap high into the air to be caught by the Lord of Jaw's Juggler, and be whisked away to divine protection. So, everyone in Cominkingville wore the stone shoes to strengthen their legs, except the religious elders — for some reason no one could remember.

Gwyn Dee had run the Stone Shoe Race with the children for seven full years, and now in the 12th year of life, this was to be the last Stone Shoe Race for Gwyn Dee. Even at a young age, little Gwyn Dee surprisingly kept pace with the older boys, and in the sixth year of running, Gwyn Dee won the race, beating out an overly mature 12 year-old boy by inches, but even then the win almost appeared as though Gywn Dee was just playing around until the finish line.

A few strong young men who seemed to have grown a foot in their 12th year were serious challengers to the Stone Shoe Crown this year, but midway through the mile long race little Gwyn Dee was easily running the hard pace with the taller boys.

At the halfway mark the race entered a narrow forest trail overgrown with tree roots. Gwyn Dee paced easily behind the three leaders, and in the dark of the forest trail, unseen by the eyes of the elders tripped and somersaulted like a tumbleweed in the wind and landed splayed out on the forest trail. The stone shoes flew into the air, and when Gwyn Dee regained composure, they were nowhere to be found.

The leaders disappeared around the turn in the narrow forest trail, and Gwyn Dee panicked. Jumping up and running with as much might as could be mustered, Gwyn Dee worked to catch up, and in few paces realized a lightness of foot not experienced since being a young precocious toddler. All thoughts of winning were suddenly lost in the joy of running barefoot and free, unencumbered by the stone shoes.

Swiftly and effortlessly Gwyn Dee passed the leaders, and flew like the wind. The surrounding world disappeared in the ecstasy of running barefoot, and in the seemingly timeless experience Gwyn Dee crossed the finish line to the shouts of the city.

But joy turned swiftly to fear. The people of Cominkingville booed and jeered the young Gwyn Dee. The elders turned their backs upon the little 12 year-old. Sticks and stones flew. Young children and older teens rushed in to spit and mock. The parents of Gwyn Dee stood near the dais where the elders were gathered, and Gwyn Dee looked up. Father dropped his head in shame, and they too turned their backs. And as tears formed in Gwyn Dee's eyes, a stone shoe flew from the crowd striking the 12 year-old on the side of the head. Three days later Gwyn Dee would wake up, and no one would ever mention the event again.

Now, in the 21st year of life, Gwyn Dee stood at the wide, wide road that led to the borders of the Land of Jaw, wondering if it was the right or the left hand path that led to strange places of lore and wonder and warning. The years of training by the High Clown Caste had not removed the memory of the experience at the Stone Shoe Race. It repeated itself over and over for 9 years in mental pictures, ghost pains, and most of all the memory of father's rejection. Gwyn Dee looked back at the fading "Welcome to Cominkingville" sign and sighed a heavy sigh with a touch of fear, and not just a touch of relief. Looking to the right, it felt "right" to go that direction, but after years of stone shoe living Gwyn Dee had learned that what felt right, and what was right were not always the same thing.

The left hand path led in a gentle downhill slope toward the northwest, and following it a short distance Gwyn Dee found a vaguely familiar and weary looking couple standing in the wide,

wide road arguing.

"I cannot follow your wild dream any longer. We have traveled for too long, with nothing to show for it."

"But, we must be nearly there."

"You have said that for years. I am turning back home to Cominkingville before I die, whether you come with me or not."

"Perhaps you are right."

Gywn Dee interrupted, "I am from Cominkingville, and am seeking the borderlands, have you seen them?"

The couple laughed mockingly, and turning away from Cominkingville said, "It is hopeless. The borderlands are nowhere to be found. You had better join us on the long road home back to Cominkingville, before you waste your life in empty searching."

Gwyn Dee blinked, "But...Cominkingville is just a short distance behind me."

The mad couple laughed and mocked and continued walking away from the village.

Gywn Dee decided that madness and confusion lay to the left hand path, and turned to find the borderlands to the right. Dropping the stone shoes off at the weary sign to Cominkingville Gwyn Dee began the long barefoot journey.

WHAT ARE YOU DOING HERE?

Salem, MA

I was new to Salem, Massachusetts – a pastor moving into one of the most famous, or to some, one of the most notorious small cities in the world. Witch City USA was nervous about conservative Christian churches and their pastors in 1999. I was hoping to relieve the pressure valve of that nervous tension.

Just a few years prior to my arrival a well-known evangelist had blown into town on the wings of revival, and "driving out the devil." He brought cameras. He brought a supposed former Witch newly turned evangelist. They held a community revival meeting in the Salem High School auditorium, and offended all but the few militaristic Evangelicals. They visited witchcraft shops, and brought their cameras with them. They taped a confrontation inside a Witchcraft shop, which later played on a well-known Christian TV show, and were ushered out by the police. In the end, they were asked to never return to Salem again. To some of the Christian audience, this was evidence of a satanic conspiracy, and a dark underbelly of evil in the City of Salem. To the Witches, this was an intrusion into their sacred world. It was filled with absurd accusations birthed from the urban myths of baby eating, and satanic ritual abuse. To the city leaders in Salem, this was evidence that Evangelical Christians and Witches all caused too much trouble for the little city.

Arriving shortly after this season of tension between Witches, Evangelical Christians and the city presented challenges to accomplishing simple tasks. Schools did not want to rent facilities to an upstart church. Event coordinators were afraid to allow Christians to participate in community events.

This tension was longer and deeper than the one-time televangelist intrusion. Pentecostal churches had spent years praying against the symbol of the Witch on the police cars, and prayed cursing prayers against the dozen or more witchcraft shops in town. Traveling evangelists came to town each Halloween season with signs and bullhorns declaring Hell and Judgment upon the celebrants. Local pastors held prayer meetings on Halloween night praying against the "evil" activities of almost 100,000 tourists visiting Salem every October 31st.

Salem is among America's first cities. Like a typical New England village it is dotted with steeples of old Congregational, Catholic, Episcopal, Methodist, and Baptist churches. During a meeting with one of Salem's School District officials I was asked why I would come to the city of Salem to start another church. The reputation of previous newer churches and visiting evangelists made any new church coming into Salem look like a cult, and certainly there appeared to be enough churches in town. Answers to that question were hollow whispers under the thundering echoes of the tumultuous past.

Druid Gathering in Southern England

Our little church navigated its way into the events of the city, and strangely, into the hearts of some of Salem's Witches who trusted us to treat them like regular people. A few years later six of us traveled to the UK. We found ourselves with a booth in a Druid Festival in Southwest England near the Welsh border. We shared our beliefs with Neo-Pagans, sang songs around the campfire at night, and made friends. On more than one occasion we were asked what we were doing at a Pagan festival. We were Christians in a Pagan world, and didn't belong there.

During one of these mini-reverse-inquisitions I asked in response, "Do you think Jesus would come to an event like this?"

"Of course, Jesus would be here, but Christians aren't supposed to come to places like this," she said as she looked around the rustic Pagan camp.

I smiled. I paused just long enough for the humor of her statement to sink in. We laughed together. My Pagan friends are the people who buy the bumper stickers that say, 'Jesus, save me from your followers.'

"I want to be the kind of Jesus follower who acts more like Jesus, and less like some of His followers." I winked.

We laughed some more. By the end of the festival, people were thanking us for being there, and for showing them that there might be hope for those who still appreciated Jesus, but have fled the strict confines of the Christianity they once knew.

Palenque, MX – December 2012

After the great flood of 12/21/2012, we packed up our gear. I call it the "great flood," because so many people had camped close to the river, and we had spent the dark early morning hours harboring wet fugitives under our large tarp, and helping pull their tents and other recoverable belongings out of the swollen river. During the exact hours the world was supposed to end, 4 inches of torrential rain fell in as many hours. We ran to the rescue of screaming campers in the middle of the night.

This was in the jungle of Palenque, Chiapas, Mexico near the impressive Mayan ruins. We had come to participate in the End of the World Rainbow Gathering, during the days of predictions from the Mayan calendar. Joshua, Jeff, and Chris had already left for home. Shlomy, Cate, and myself were the remaining people from the "Jesus Camp" along with our newfound friend, Benjamin.

I said a few goodbyes on the last day. There was an evening ceremony the day after the end of the Mayan calendar. I was asked to join the ceremony by presenting an invocation of Jesus, and I was honored to do so. Such ceremonies often avoid any obvious Christian presence, and so the invitation was a statement of acceptance by leaders of the Rainbow community.

Shlomy and I prepared some simple ideas. We would start with myself giving an introduction, Benjamin would pray and invite the presence of Jesus into the circle.

The gathering of the ceremony circle included a spiral dance. Leaders laid hands upon a 12-foot tall dead tree trunk decorated with symbols from many religious traditions, and chanted over it. There was a long "Om," and a moment of silence by the crowd of about 800. Then a Spanish speaking man offered a feel-good New Age devotional, and a time to hug ourselves and tell ourselves that we love ourselves. I did not participate in much self-hugging. Love of self has always seemed to me to be more of a human problem than a solution.

He finished, nodded to me. Shlomy, Benjamin and I stood on the perimeter berm of the fire circle.

With a translator converting my words to Spanish, I shouted loudly to the large crowd of celebrants, "We are wounded healers! We are impoverished philanthropists! We are philosopher clowns!" People identified personally and laughed. So, I continued, "We have nothing and everything to give. We are broken and yet we offer wholeness."

Despite the fact that many in the Rainbow family feel that there is no such thing as good and evil – no imperfection, this was still received well. And seeing this I pressed just a little further.

"I come from a broken tradition." There was the small titter from the leadership of this predominantly hippie crowd. "Everyone knows my tradition is broken. The whole world sees it. I am a Christian pastor!" And now everyone laughed loudly with me.

"But, even in our brokenness we have something to offer, and so we want to invite the spirit of Christ – not just the spirit, but the person of Jesus to join our circle. If you would like to join us in this invocation, we invite you to lift your hands."

And so, some sheepishly, some boldly, many people lifted their hands. Among the Spanish speaking Rainbow family a far larger number of people lifted their hands.

I nodded to Benjamin, and he prayed.

At first slowly, then increasing in a gentle rising meter he prayed. I had told Benjamin to use his spoken word, hip-hop poetry in the prayer if he felt so inclined, and a few sentences into the prayer he did feel inclined. He was poppin' rhymes about our brokenness and Christ's crucifixion, God's forgiveness and our sins, and God's power and Christ's uniqueness. The tall, thin, bearded, shirtless young man had his arms extended wide like the crucified Christ. His passionate poetic prayer sounded like an anthem of glory to God. His smile was wide and genuine, and I laughed with joy watching him.

A few hecklers made comments from the crowd, but it remained respectful for the most part, and was well received by others. Then our friend Jorge, a Mayan Christian from Palenque began to translate. As he did, the Spanish-speaking Christians began to join his prayer loudly, and others began to counter the rising prayers by trying to shout the prayers down, and then a crazy pandemonium broke out. The English-speaking crowd became confused, thinking that the prayers were angry responses. Suddenly, we were in the middle of 800+ New Agers, Radical Faeries, noisy Spanish-speaking Christians, angry Latin American travelers, and confused hippies. Some were shouting that there is no god but ourselves, and some were shouting that there is only one God and He is Jesus. Others were shouting that there should be no division – that, we are all one, and still others were ringing bells, or trying to create the all-popular Om.

I laughed openly at the silliness of it all, even though I realized it could get out of control in a quick moment. 'A lot of people get stoned at Rainbow Gatherings,' I quipped to myself, 'but this isn't what I expected.' The pandemonium continued for maybe five minutes. Eventually it subsided when the ever-present Rainbow "Om" spread to enough people.

The ceremony eventually continued under far less control than the leaders hoped for, with occasional rants from young hippies over trivial issues, but it ended peacefully. We hugged Jorge our translator and Ingrid (his girlfriend who led the ceremony). I blessed them and their life together.

As we left the Rainbow Gathering, Benjamin said, "I would not have felt complete without standing up for Christ like that. It could only have been better if someone had thrown a rock at me."

I like how Benjamin thinks. I understand. That was our last night in Palenque at the Rainbow Gathering, and it felt just a bit Pauline.

The negative opinions towards 'Organized Christianity' are birthed in part out of a familiarity with the dark history of the Church. Inquisitions, forced conversions, crusades, wars, and indulgences can be pointed to in the history books of Western Civilization.

The three stories above are contemporary responses from three different nations, and different language and culture groups. They are merely anecdotal evidence representing a cultural dissonance between Christianity and the surrounding cultures, but such anecdotes have followed me through 30 years of pastoring. They have been growing in intensity over time, and they are not unique to me. The trending polls of religion and culture have pointed to what has been called the rise of the "nones" and "dones." Those who identify none as their religious preference, and those who say they are done with church. Each of the stories above shows the uncomfortable relationship between Christianity and culture. That relationship vacillates between thankful acceptance and angry rejection.

We appear trapped in cognitive dissonance. The contradictory opinions, which vacillate between the Organized Christianity we hate and the Jesus we respect is doing something to our emotional stability, to our faith, to our relationships with one another, and to Christianity's reputation in the world. Our struggle with this cognitive dissonance is the focus of the next chapter.

Engage: Why are we so divided on religion and faith issues?

In the chapter "What Are You Doing Here?" the Christianity faces off in the public square in secular settings and with other religious and non-religious gatherings. The tension in the public square is viewed in three countries, and three different situations. Why do you think our world is so divided on issues of faith and belief?

Interact with the Burning Religion community on the website at www.burningreligion.com.

PARALYZED BY PARALLAXIS, OR THE PREACHER'S NAKED BACKSIDE

Cognitive Dissonance Theory rushed onto the field of psychology in 1956 with the publication of the book <u>When Prophecy Fails</u>. Cognitive Dissonance Theory suggested that people have a need to relieve the tension of contradictions in their life. According to this theory, contradictory, inconsistent, or competing information is resolved by seeking dissonance reduction. Our minds search for balance, as we attempt to make our expectations equate with reality, and we may go to extreme measures to accomplish dissonance reduction.

<u>When Prophecy Fails</u>, by Leon Festinger and his team was a study based upon a tiny religious UFO group during a time of apocalyptic pronouncements, and the subsequent season when their predictions of imminent apocalypse failed to come true.

In late September 1954, the headlines of the local paper read, "PROPHECY FROM PLANET. CLARION CALL TO CITY: FLEE THAT FLOOD. IT'LL SWAMP US ON DEC. 21, OUTER SPACE TELLS SUBURBANITE." Marian Keech (whose real name, Dorothy Martin, was hidden in the publication of the book) had been receiving messages from a planet named "Clarion" through automatic writing, and was warning people of an impending doom coming upon the world.

The world did not end in flood. The members of Martin's group were not snatched away by aliens as she had predicted. When it was clearly apparent that the prophecy had failed, the group broke down emotionally. Yet, quickly an even smaller number of the original small group adjusted, and with renewed vigor became evangelistic in their efforts to share their communications from the aliens. Those who were less committed and less connected slowly faded into the distance, and eventually rejected the teachings of the group.

Five conditions were listed in the book as necessary for a person to become a more fervent believer, even after the failure or disconfirmation of their beliefs. Festinger's sociology students were planted in the group, and acted as believers. As the day of apocalyptic warning drew near the students tracked the activity of the believers to these conditions:

- *A belief must be held with deep conviction and it must have some relevance to action, that is, to what the believer does or how he behaves.*
- *The person holding the belief must have committed himself to it; that is, for the sake of his belief, he must have taken some important action that is difficult to undo. In general, the more important such actions are, and the more difficult they are to undo, the greater is the individual's commitment to the belief.*
- *The belief must be sufficiently specific and sufficiently concerned with the real world so that events may unequivocally refute the belief.*
- *Such undeniable disconfirmatory evidence must occur and must be recognized by the individual holding the belief.*
- *The individual believer must have social support. It is unlikely that one isolated believer could withstand the kind of disconfirming evidence that has been specified. If, however, the believer is a member of a group of convinced persons who can support one another, the belief may be maintained and the believers may attempt to proselytize or persuade nonmembers that the belief is correct.*[12]

Festinger, Schachter, and Riecken had predicted that the renewed vigor of faith would occur among those who had the most significant personal investment in the beliefs, and kept in close contact with one another during the moments of the failed predictions. On the basis of their cognitive dissonance theory, they foresaw that these most devoted followers would need to intellectually and emotionally compensate for the great disappointment of the failed prophecies, and would do so not by confessing their failure, but by redefining the failure as a type of fulfillment.

When Chicago, and the central US were not flooded on December 21, 1954, Dorothy Martin received another prophecy stating that the flying saucers would pick their little group up in front of her house on Christmas Eve. The small band gathered on the lawn that night and sang carols, as they waited to be picked up by the "spacemen." 200 people gathered around the apocalyptic carnival, with newspapers present.

A small band of believers huddled on that frozen Chicago suburban lawn on Christmas Eve in 1954, sang their hearts out, and stood waiting for their salvation from their spacemen. The crowd watched and mocked, and eventually went home after spacemen failed to appear and the news reporters were finished.

Somehow, this second, and even more public disconfirmation of

---

[12] Festinger, Leon; Schachter, Stanley; Riecken, Henry W. When Prophecy Fails, Pinter & Martin, pg. 4

prophecy did not deter the few faithful. The lack of fulfillment would be re-interpreted as a sign that mercy was being extended to the world, and that the faithful needed to share the forthcoming messages from the aliens with the world. Instead of interpreting the moment as a failure, they interpreted it as a new calling to share their revelations more vigorously.

The experience of Dorothy Martin's little flying saucer cult is not a unique response to failure in the world of religion. In 1914, the Watchtower Organization (Jehovah's Witnesses) declared the coming of Armageddon. When Armageddon did not occur, believers pressed forward under a renewed evangelistic fervor declaring that the end time prophecy was fulfilled, because Jesus had invisibly come to earth and established His Kingdom in Brooklyn, New York – home to the Watchtower headquarters. Even those who love Brooklyn most might have a hard time equating the city with an eschatological fulfillment of the Kingdom of God. The original president of the church, Charles Taze Russell died on October 31st, 1916. Joseph F. Rutherford took over the presidency and was there until 1942. Between the date of their remarkably public failed prophecies in 1914, and the death of the second president in January 1942 the church grew from approximately 50,000 people to 134,624.

Could it be that we are living in season of cognitive dissonance similar to that of the UFO believers and followers of Dorothy Martin? Similar to the season following the 1914 prophecies of the Jehovah's Witnesses? Just as they experienced the failing of prophecies in 1914 and 1954, when the world did not end in Armageddon or flood, Christianity has been experiencing the ongoing failure of its prophecies, its institutions, and its personalities. Are we repeating the cognitive dissonance of 1914, and 1954 all over again?

End time declarations boldly announced

- 1981 – The book <u>The Late Great Planet Earth</u> predicts the rapture of the church, and the beginning of the Great tribulation. I am sitting in the congregation of a large, theologically conservative, culturally influential, 15,000 member Evangelical church in Costa Mesa, CA and the pastor says, "I believe this year could be the year Christ comes to take us away!" His statement of potentiality does not hide his sense of urgency and certainty, and the congregation of thousands responds enthusiastically.
- 1988 – A church in South Korea predicts the coming of the rapture, and the subsequent tribulation. I meet people standing

outside grocery stores in Southern California, passing out flyers, and saying that Jesus would suddenly take His people away to be with Him on October 28th of that year. This is based upon Edgar Whisenant's book 88 Reasons the Rapture will Happen in 1988. When it does not come true, the book is reprinted in 1989 under the title 89 Reasons the Rapture will Happen in 1989.

- 2011 – May 21st is declared to be the day of the beginning of the end of the world.[13] Believers will be caught up in the rapture, and God's judgment will begin to fall on the earth. Billboard signs are purchased around the world. People sell their homes, and begin itinerant ministry declaring that the end is coming. On that day, I stand outside my church with a group of friends, and we invite people to a "Left Behind Party" the following day. The rapture of the Church does not happen, and our little church in Salem has a party on the May 22nd. In a mock anti-apocalyptic parody, we predict the end will not come. Fortunately for us, the Left Behind Party goes on as planned, and the newspaper is there to document the festivity.

Worldwide religious revival predicted

- From 1983 to 1985 – I hear repeated predictions of a coming great revival of religion, which will sweep San Diego County, and then spread throughout the world; and this will be the last great revival of religion, before the end of the world. These predictions are supposed to come true in those years, but life goes on as usual for the churches, and the world around us. These were not predictions from the fringes of Christian culture. They were beliefs held by tens of thousands of people.
- 2000 through 2003 – I hear the same type of prophecies coming from the North Shore of Boston. God will begin His great worldwide Christian revival starting in the two cities of Cambridge and Salem, Massachusetts. This will spark a worldwide movement preceding the Second Coming of Christ. When one year stubbornly refuses to cooperate, the next year is boldly declared to be the appointed time. Until those prophesying finally give up. Strangely, no one admits they might have been wrong.

---

[13] My song about the false prophesy about being left behind on May 21st, 2011. https://youtu.be/t3j5-0ZxM58

Moral failure rocks the Church

- In the early 1980's, and again in 2000's famous TV evangelists fall to sexual sins, and financial mismanagement.
- In the early 2000's, The Boston Globe breaks the story of the priest sexual abuse scandal, which continues to be unraveled in different parishes across the US, and different countries around the world.

Theological tension on the increase

A neo-Calvinist movement has gained momentum with young adults across the US. A strong patriarchal system with its rejection of a woman's place in ministry is being accepted by an increasing number of millennial Christians in spite of the liberating patterns in our society. Churches not adhering to their narrow pre-determinist theology are branded as heretics.

Meanwhile, the largest churches in the US are simultaneously hounded with accusations from other Christians of compromising their faith, and by non-Christians of forcing their fundamentalist views on our culture.

Rick Warren from Saddleback Community Church in Mission Viejo, CA received a firestorm of criticism for being too conservative when invited to pray during Obama's inauguration, while also being considered a kind of New Age false prophet by Fundamentalist Christians. In 2011, Rick Warren addressed an Islamic Convention, and embraced them with a kind acceptance. Fundamentalists decried this act as the heresy of "Chrislam."

The largest church in the US, with almost 44,000 attendees, regularly experiences this same tension. Joel Osteen's Word of Faith teaching at Lakewood Church in Houston, TX draws criticism from theologians of all stripes.

These few examples from the many failures of prophecy, breakdowns of moral behavior, and theological tensions give us a picture of religious people holding onto their faith in the face of a sometimes, severe cognitive dissonance. What we believe, and what we experience are not always a match, and individual responses to this discordance are varied.

- I have friends who have rejected Christianity altogether.
- I have friends who have left one church or denomination for what seems to be a safer one.

- I have friends who retain their faith in Christ, but do not attend church.
- I have friends whose once solid doctrinal beliefs have dramatically changed due to the discouragements, the failures, and the abuses they have experienced.
- I have friends (and former friends) who have justified abusive behavior, and false prophecies, and continue to operate under clearly corrupt leadership.
- I have friends who live with a constant struggle of doubt, fear, or confusion and are not sure which way to turn.
- I have friends in church leadership who maintain personal integrity in spite of the dissonance swirling around them. They do their best to model a different kind of faith than that which seeks to undo their nervous flocks.
- I have friends (and former friends) who are part of the dissonance. Through their own behavior they have abused and disenfranchised people.

Non-religious apocalyptic warnings

- 1980's – The Ozone layer was decaying due to aerosol use at a rate, which threatened to give the entire human race skin cancer.
- 2000 – Y2K was going to bring about the end of technology as we know it. Computers around the world would stop working and a technological collapse as the new millennium dawned. Supposedly, there was no way for the computers to transition to the dates they were not prepared for. The possibility that everything run by computers could fall apart, from banking systems to nuclear power plants created a apocalyptic fear for many people who sold assets and sunk their money into silver and gold.
- 1997-Today – Global Warming warnings continue to make headlines. Polling statistics show peak public concern in 2008. There has been a steadily dropping concern since then. The original skeptics in the scientific community were silenced by political, scientific and financial interests, but have begun to speak up once again. Could it be that the global warming is reversing and the heated concern is cooling down as well? Will the issue go the way of the other apocalyptic warnings from the last number of years? The next few years could tell us.

Whether the apocalyptic climate change warnings remain strong or fade away, this one thing is certain. We live in a world filled with apocalyptic pronunciations, and that will not end. If I could make any prophetic declaration it would be this: our fear of the end of the world will not wane. In science, in politics, and in religion we will remain apocalyptic, and the failures of one false prophecy will not deter future prophecies from being announced.

Tales from the Land of Jaw: The Adventures of Gwyn Dee
Peddlers of the One Thing

A short distance down the wide, wide road a festival of hawkers, buskers, and mongers of all sorts filled the road. Its edges were lined with booths, tents and lean-tos. Barkers were barking, and buskers were busking. Hawkers were hawking, and mongers were monging. Jugglers were juggling, and singers were singing. There were fishmonger's carts, tents selling carnival masks, leather bound books on spiritual disciplines, and guides to pilgrimages. There were halo-smiths, hat-sellers, fruit vendors, wine merchants, etiquette teachers, juggling masters, luthiers, brass workers, leather workers, wing-makers, cordwainers, dressmakers, blacksmiths, and a seemingly infinite line of booths with a seemingly infinite set of options.

The wild festival filled the streets, and as Gwyn Dee looked closer, carnival buskers were fighting with other buskers, and singers were singing threats and obscenities at other singers. Hawkers were shouting at other hawkers and stealing their goods, and mongers were sabotaging the booths of other sellers. Fires broke out in the lean-tos and tents, jugglers used their pins and balls as weapons, and fire-breathers chased other performers around the festival spitting fire and curses. And in all the anarchic mess, there were few customers, little audience, but thousands of arguing solicitors.

From under one of the larger lean-tos decorated like a castle with rickety wooden ramparts and a gaudily dressed fat prince on a overly pillowed throne beneath its sagging roof, a group of paper-armor-clad warriors ran out into the wide, wide road with wooden swords and shields. The warriors ran across the road and walloped, and struck, and beat, and thumped, and cracked, and pounded, and threatened, and derided, and castigated, and challenged, and barked at a small group of troubadours singing to a pretty young maiden. The troubadours shrieked, ran in circles, and squealed like greased pigs in a chase at the county fair. The warriors captured the young maiden, lifted her up on their shoulders and ran back to their lean-to castle declaring victory, while the girl giggled and squeaked for joy.

And Gwyn Dee stood and blinked in surprised disbelief, wondering how to navigate the wide, wide road with its violent circus. Taking a deep breath, and stepping down the middle of the wide, wide road seemed as good a plan as any, and on the first step into the festival Gwyn Dee was suddenly surrounded by hawkers hawking their goods.

"Whole wheat bread! If there's ONE THING you need to improve your life and health it's..." and before the bread-wife could finish her sentence, she was unceremoniously shoved across the road by a large toothless fish-wife in a greasy gunny-sack dress and a large cod in her hands.

"Cod it is ye want. We all need Cod. Cod is the ONE THING we all..." and before her rambling repetitive monologue was complete, a group of small boys in top hats pulled on her dress, spun her around, stole her cod, and ran off laughing. She spit and cursed through her toothless scowl and chased them across the road.

A dapper gentleman in a black velvet coat, a bright red ascot, a fine top hat with a bright red feather, and a toothy seductive smile quickly stepped in close to Gwyn Dee with the dashing elegance of a masquerade waltz.

"Our dear deluded friends have offered their smelly fish and their loathsome loaves, but certainly one as sophisticated as yourself and quick of understanding knows that obtaining the ONE THING of greatest importance in life is not a simple matter of loaves and fishes." His monologue was going to last a bit longer than the previous peddlers. The company of 20 to 30 petulant small boys in top hats were scurrying about behind the dapper gentleman, harassing the other dozen or so approaching merchants.

"Life is not meat and drink, but it is peace and joy. I can guarantee that your peace and joy will not be robbed from you..." And Gwyn Dee might have listened to the dapper gentleman's pitch, but was distracted by the noisy confusion created by the band of small boys in top hats picking pockets and stealing goods from the carnival hawkers.

Gwyn Dee finally focused on the dapper gentleman as he pulled a top hat out of thin air. "This is the ONE THING you need. It will protect your..." and before he could finish his sentence, a massive black war horse split the circle of barkers and the thieving top hatted boys, and parted the crowd like Moses with his big stick. A large metal clad man atop the enormous warhorse snatched Gwyn Dee up. Tossed like a rag doll, Gwyn Dee was seated behind the immense warrior before realizing what was happening.

The huge metal clad man spun the gigantic horse around, and they trotted ponderously down the wide, wide road through the festival.

"Don't let anyone tell you what you need to eat, or wear, or rub on your belly to become closer to the ONE THING we all seek. What you need is training and discipline. That I can offer to..." and before the mammoth metal clad man could finish his sentence a troupe of leggy dancing girls blocked the path, formed a chorus line, and kicked up their long legs to the music of an organ grinder and his monkey. The towering metal clad man straightaway leapt off his colossal war horse whooping and hooting like a goony bird in mating season, and ran after the scattering giggling chorus line. The leggy dancers adeptly outran him until both they and giant metal clad man were nowhere to be found.

As soon as they were out of sight, the organ grinder slowly walked up to the brobdingnagian warhorse and addressed Gwyn Dee. "Seems our little warrior could use a little discipline now, doesn't it. Throw a few leggy ladies at him and he falls for it every time. As you can see there are finer ways to connect to the ONE THING we all seek." The organ grinder winked, "If you should..." and before the organ grinder could finish his pitch, Gwyn Dee scooted up into the saddle of the great warhorse, and giving a click of the tongue they plodded down the wide, wide road.

Gwyn Dee hugged the neck of the great warhorse and whispered a thank you.

After nearly 13 hours 7 minutes and 42 seconds, almost 78.119 miles, and approximately 33,791 fighting hawkers, buskers, minstrels, peddlers, mongers and circus troupes offering an equal *number of variations on the ONE THING, Gwyn Dee and the great warhorse finally came to the end of the wild carnival. Gwyn Dee dismounted, and stood on tiptoes to kiss the great warhorse on the nose.*

"Thank you. I suppose if I truly wanted one thing right now, it would be to travel with you on my journey, but you have a master and a home to return to."

The great warhorse threw his great head up high and snorted. Gwyn Dee turned down the wide, wide road and the great warhorse stayed and watched Gwyn Dee disappear over the horizon before turning to head home.

The Preacher's Naked Backside

The cartoon above illustrates our perspectives on religion. The face of religion is clean and charismatic, but the shiny front may at times hide a dirty nakedness. Consider with me the three views represented in the cartoon: The excited crowd who see only the clean charismatic face of religion; the intimately betrayed who stand behind the pulpit in clear sight of the preacher's dirty naked backside; and the confused bystanders whose perspective captures both the clean face, and the dirty naked backside.

These categories are not hard clean lines or complete character descriptions. The average person may vacillate back and forth between these perspectives – at one moment feeling confident in his faith, the next feeling frustration, or doubting the existence of God. The atheist who confidently affirms her atheism may at times yearn for the simple trusting ways of youth, or doubt the bold affirmations of a strictly materialistic definition for the universe in the face of complicated, emotionally charged relational issues, and this is a non-theistic variation of the same intellectual struggle. Guilt haunts the religious person doubting their faith, and fear of losing sanity challenges the skeptic wondering about unseen, immeasurable mysteries.

The Excited Crowd

The excited crowd is made up of wildly divergent classes of people. Simple happy churchgoing families, bullhorn-toting fundamentalists, elderly shut-ins experiencing Christianity by the television set, those who fill the stadium seats in revivals and faith healing campaigns, and hipster neo-Calvinist conservatives are included in this category of the excited crowd. Strange as it may seem, new atheists attending skeptic's gatherings and buying up the latest Dawkins and Harris books are often a non-religious variation of this same classification of people. Every subculture has those who are in an excited state over their own little world, while simultaneously being oblivious to potential weaknesses and abuses within the system they adore.

Think of this excitement as an agitation. One moment it may be joyous and bubbly, but the next angry and aggressive. It is the result of commitment and investment. The greater the commitment – the greater the emotional, financial and time investments, and consequently, the more there is to lose.

This excitement manifests itself in a simple satisfaction with the comfortable little world we find our inspiration in, but in order for this comfortable little world to remain comfortable, it must remain clean and pure. The moment it is broken by unethical practices, criminal actions, lies, or abuses; we are faced with the cognitive dissonance of trying to believe the best while living in a dystopian dream. In reality, cognitive dissonance is something we are all faced with, and all must live with. It is the result of living in a world filled with corruption, violence, and brokenness, but when faced with it up close and personal it can be devastating for many people.

In order to hold our zeal together we may resort to sectarianism. By narrowly redefining our faith, we can identify any discordant action as evidence that the offending parties were truly not "one of us," after all. Sectarianism reduces the size of the space of our faith, but the space appears to remain clean and untouched by evil, because we redefine the offending parties and actions outside the lines of our faith space.

Christianity has a long history of developing small sects, which identify themselves as the only true believers, or the only group with the "fullness of the Gospel." Restorationist Christian traditions are built upon this thinking. It is a natural human response to partition ourselves into groups based upon small details of praxis and/or belief. Yet, people tell stories of sectarianism in religion, politics, and ethnicity as well. A "true American" may be defined according to his stance on gun rights and the 2nd Amendment, or a true Scotsman according to his stance on Scottish independence.

This kind of thinking has been called the "No True Scotsman" fallacy. Scottish Philosopher Anthony Flew[14] developed this informal fallacy with an example of a Scotsman reading a newspaper article, "Brighton Sex Maniac Strikes Again." Brighton being in England, the Scotsman declares that, "no Scotsman would do such a thing!" The next day he reads an article about sexual attacks far more brutal, perpetrated by a man in Glasgow, and he declares, "No true Scotsman would do such a thing!"[15]

The "No True Scotsman" fallacy can be used to isolate bad behavior to a supposedly rejected subclass of my own people group, to establish the boundaries of acceptable behavior and the beliefs of "real" believers, or to fallaciously argue that certain behaviors and beliefs are merely evidence of an individual's disassociation from my tribal identity. Although, there may be unique cases in which the "No True Scotsman" argument is valid, its use as a defense against the supposed disintegration or impurity of my worldview may simply be an attempt to reduce my cognitive dissonance. Yet, as we have seen in the story of Dorothy Martin's flying saucer cult, as I reduce the internal dissonance concerning my own disconfirmed beliefs, I increase my dissonance with the society around me. This is why the more isolated and sectarian the religious group is, the more likely it is to appear disconnected from reality in the eyes of the world around it.

In the Gospel of Mark,[16] Jesus tells a parable of seed planted in the ground. Describing four types of soil and how the seed responds to the soil, Jesus includes seed planted in shallowly tilled ground. It cannot grow deep roots. As a result, its initial growth is all upwards with little sustenance and support beneath the soil. When the sun comes out, the plant cannot sustain the heat and dies. This excited class of people includes those who are illustrated by Jesus' parable. Though they appear to grow excitedly and quickly, when trouble comes their faith,

---

[14] Anthony Flew's life may be a perfect example of our own corporate struggle with cognitive dissonance. As one of the world's most noted atheists, he declared in 2004 that he was a deist, and wrote a book There is a God: How the World's Most Notorious Atheist Changed His Mind, in collaboration with Roy Abraham describing his position. The atheist community quickly responded in defense of their own worldview, and in critique of Dr. Flew.

[15] Anthony Flew, Thinking About Thinking: Do I Sincerely Want to be Right? London: Collins Fontana 1975

[16] Mark 4:3-9

beliefs, and religious affiliation may be burned up in the face of their own internal dissonance.

The Intimately Betrayed

The cartoon's second classification of people, are seated behind the pulpit. All they can see is the preacher's naked backside. The proximity to the stories of abuse and manipulation has made the stories' impact all the greater. Their deep investment in the faith brought them close to the object of their passion – and as we will see when we describe the effects of parallaxis more completely – the closer we are to an object the more impact its influence has upon us, and the more severe trauma we experience. The intimately betrayed are those who have been the backbone of the church and have been abused by the authorities above them. They are the children sexually molested by Sunday School workers or priests. They are the women who have invested their time in serving, but have been relegated to hidden tasks, when their skills, their schooling, and their trustworthiness mandated something greater.

In our media drenched society, the intimately betrayed may include those who read and hear the horrific stories day in and day out. Our senses are jolted with the grotesque over-telling of the darkest abuses. We become excessively traumatized, and are placed into the position of the intimately betrayed, not by actual experience, but by sleight of hand manipulation of a false proximity created by a world of media frenzy.

During 2013 and 2014, a mega-church in Seattle, WA made the headlines for a series of improprieties and abuses by the senior pastor. Stories hit the headlines of plagiarism in his books, buying his way onto the New York Times Best Seller List, and requiring pastors who are fired to sign non-disclosure agreements in order to receive their severance pay and keep their insurance. Websites can be found with former pastors offering apologies for their complicity in the abuses of the church.[17] Both Christian and secular media have been covering the unfolding events. Every story brought Seattle's Mars Hill Church and Pastor Mark Driscoll a little closer to each of us who read about the abuses, the cover-up, and manipulation, and this false sense of nearness traumatizes us. It manipulates and shortens the sense of distance between us, and the abuses. Like those who have experienced the abuses directly, some people similarly feel betrayed by the events merely by reading and rereading about them.

A growing number of people have seen and experienced the dark underbelly of corruption, the moral failures of weak and struggling

---

[17] https://musingsfromunderthebus.wordpress.com/

leaders, or the abuse of power. We have seen the preacher's naked backside, and cannot remember the good for the evil we have seen. We have stopped going to church, and don't care to return, sometimes giving up on our faith, but still feeling the twinge of anxiety at the mention of God.

One evening recently, I gathered with a small group of people I called the "Burn Scars." We met to discuss struggles with our experiences in church life. One of the ladies retold her story of riding in the car with her husband to visit a church for the first time after avoiding it for months.

Along the way, she suddenly blurted out to her husband, "Turn around."

He asked if she was okay, and she responded louder and more aggressively, "Turn around!"

He responded again with a question of concern, and she exploded, uncontrollably screaming, "Turn around! Turn around! Turn around!"

After intimate betrayal, it is too painful to return to the church, and some of us have a violent response to the thought of revisiting anything resembling the spaces of our abuse.

The Confused Bystanders

In 2010, during a season of great stress, I had three incidences of temporary Binocular Diplopia. I was seeing double vision for 30 to 40 seconds. In one instance, I was driving in traffic. Suddenly, there were two roads, and twice as many cars breaking in front of me at indeterminable distances. Binocular Diplopia is double vision created by the inability of your two eyes to adjust and merge their independent images into one image. Excessive tiredness, or drunkenness can set up muscular Binocular Diplopia – and no, I was not driving drunk. There are other causes of Binocular Diplopia, some of them in the nervous system, making the brain unable to merge the two images. Just prior to each instance I experienced, I was focused upon a nearby object, and suddenly looked away to focus on distant objects. In the incident when I was driving, I looked into the rearview mirror, and when I looked ahead to the traffic breaking in front of me, my eyes refused to adjust. It was effectively like crossing my eyes while driving, and I could not uncross them. During those 30 to 40 seconds I was driving in a confusing and unnerving world.

The brokenness of our world, and the double standards of the people and institutions we love have given us all some form of Binocular Diplopia.

Our cognitive dissonance is an intellectual and emotional variation of Binocular Diplopia, and it is not temporary, nor is it simply caused by stress. We live in a double-minded world and we suffer under systems, which feed us an unending supply of double-speak. Whether we are cognizant of it or not, we are seeing double, and it is confusing us.

I use this medical example of Binocular Diplopia to highlight the fact that most of us have seen the two images of the preacher: the clean front, and the dirty, naked backside. It is okay to feel dizzied and confused.

The confused bystander struggling with an intellectual and emotional Binocular Diplopia may be the most honest of our three categories. Your confusion is justified by the fact that you live in an often confusing, and deceptive world. Though your confusion may be justified, many of the images you see cannot be justified. They are irreconcilable, and that is the reason for your internal Binocular Diplopia.

The problem of the pretty exterior and the corrupt interior was given as an ancient warning by Jesus, Who rebuked the religious leaders of His day, as "whited sepulchres" – clean on the outside but filled with dead men's bones.[18]

Like the instability of the praying man James the brother of Jesus speaks of, we have become double-minded in our confusion and doubt, and our double-mindedness is viral and spreading. The two-faced actions of this world are creating a confusing double-image in our minds, and some of us are now vacillating between these irreconcilable images, hopelessly attempting to merge them into one. In James' 1st century world, people were warned against becoming the, *"double-minded man, unstable in all his ways."*[19] They were struggling with an intellectual Binocular Diplopia, and we are still struggling with it today.

---

[18] Matthew 23:27
[19] James 1:8

Tales from the Land of Jaw: The Adventures of Gwyn Dee
The Strange Mass

The wide, wide road stretched across the white, white barren plain as far as the eye could see. After the first day's travel, the road and the plain blended together into one immense barren piece of desert only broken by the distant little hills far away to the north. It had become nearly impossible to tell the difference between the road and the white, white, flat plain. The sparse and tiny tufts of desert grass and the cracked flat ground blended into the road and made the white, white plain and the wide, wide road one. With difficulty, Gwyn Dee followed the road, but at times was forced to simply stay the course of the rising sun in the East. Eventually, the sun rose into the sky, and dropped into the western edge of the white, white plain; and the wide, wide road perfectly camouflaged itself in plain sight under the white, white plain beneath Gwyn Dee's weary bare feet.

Boredom fills the great gaps of the less disciplined minds in spaces such as this barren playa, but one trained from a youth in the ways of the Clown Caste is not troubled by such monotony. The disciplined mind has it own mountain ranges to traverse, and rivers to ford, and Gwyn Dee was well acquainted with these holy spaces.

On the third day, a large, large city filled with small plain white box houses rose up from the white, white plain. Gwyn Dee entered the edge of the city to find rows and rows of the small plain white box houses stretched indefinitely across the white, white plain, and strangely, not a person could be seen – not a sound could be heard.

If it were possible for an egg yoke to be larger than the egg yet still be inside it, or for the sound of a single third chair violin to gulp down the entire orchestra, or if a swallow could swallow the sky and still fly within it, this might begin to describe the strange sight of the large, large city on the white, white plain with its endless rows of empty small plain white box houses.

Gwyn Dee traveled into the heart of the endless rows of small *plain white box houses for three days, and on the beginning of the third day, began to hear a buzzing noise like a distant commotion ahead. As the third day wore on, the noise grew to become the mixed sound of desperate animal groanings, and people conversing happily. It was at the end of this third day that Gwyn Dee came upon the big, big square in the large, large city, and the big, big square was filled with innumerable small people.*

One billion, two-hundred and thirty-four million, five-hundred and sixty-seven thousand, eight-hundred and ninety small men filled the square, with their small wives and their small children in a strange religious festival.

The small people were lined up behind tens of thousands of high, high altars as tall, tall clergymen served a queer mass from behind the altar tables. Billions of live camels were nuzzing behind the tall, tall clergymen, and small fine mesh cages filled with gnats sat on each altar table. The roaring noise of the camels filled the city square, and the small people meanwhile chatted nonchalantly about their children, and Parcheesi.

As each small person arrived before the high, high altar tables, they opened their mouths wide, and the tall, tall priests reached into the fine mesh cages. Saying, "Take this in remembrance of me." Then the tall, tall clergymen placed a single gnat on the tongues of the small people, who swallowed the gnats sputtering, gagging, and complaining. Following the gnats, the small city folk once again opened their mouths as wide as nested baby birds, and the ministers said one more time, "Take this in remembrance of me." Forthwith the tall, tall clergymen forced an entire camel, struggling for its life, kicking, and screaming down the throats of each small person – man, woman and child. The small people swallowed the camels as easily as berries and cream slide down the throat on a hot summer's day. An occasional neophyte celebrant would struggle to swallow the camel, would get kicked in the face, or thrown on the ground by the poor beast fighting for its life, but eventually the neophyte would rise, and just as the rest of the small people, would emerge from the ordeal smiling, and seemingly comforted, albeit bruised.

Gwyn Dee stood agape staring at the spectacle.

A Weathered Old Woman in beggar's cloths appeared. "This is their ritual at every festival." She looked deep into Gwyn Dee's eyes, "As it is written, they strain at a gnat..." and her words trailed off. Before Gwyn Dee could reply, the Weathered Old Woman disappeared in the crowd, and was gone. In Gwyn Dee's mind the sentence finished itself, and then, Gwyn Dee left the city to avoid a certain invitation to the altar tables.

Paralyzed in Parallaxis

Kojin Karatani, the Japanese philosopher and literary critic, who has been called by academia "the thinking machine" used the term "parallax"[20] to define the differences in our perspectives and our understanding of political and philosophical issues when we focus on the same subject from different vantage points.

Parallaxis is the difference in the apparent position of an object when viewed from different points. It is a perceived displacement, but not an actual relocation of the viewed object. Astronomers use parallax lines to measure the distance of stars from the earth. When the earth is on one side of the sun, measurements are made. In an opposite season, on the other side of the sun, more measurements are taken. Distance is determined using trigonometric calculations with the angle created by the inclination of the two lines of sight to the star.[21]

Parallax is used in rifle scopes, binoculars, and optical sensors. Our own two eyes work on parallax, and the fact that we have the two lines of sight gives us this sense of distance we call depth perception.

For Karatani and Salvoj Žižek, the philosophical use of the term parallax is not a tool for the measurement of physical distance. For these social critics, the concern is the gap between points of view, as much as perceived differences in the actual object, and the distance between the lines of sight is assumed as infinite – an un-crossable gap – a zone where *"no synthesis or mediation is possible."*[22]

You and I perceive abstract issues like love, politics or religion from our own intellectual and emotional points of view. My opinion on any potential subject is in parallax with any another person's point of view. Like the straight lines from the outside of a circle into its center, these lines never touch until they reach a center point. To further complicate the issue, we are viewing a different side of an object against a different background, and the face of the object blocks the point of linear intersection.

This complication of the parallaxis existing outside of me (in the disparity of opinions in community), and the parallaxis existing inside of me (in my own disparate and competing experiences) creates

---

[20] In his book Transcritique, Karatani riffs off Kant in using the term parallax. Kojin Karatani;Sabu Kohso. Transcritique: On Kant and Marx, MIT Press 2005
[21] Sorry, for the dramatic oversimplification of the astronomical illustration, but this is one simple and elegant way the distance of stars is being measured. Trigonometric parallax is good for up to 500 light years distance. Further away than that, light measurements are used in what are called spectroscopic parallax or absolute magnitude measurements. http://earthguide.ucsd.edu/virtualmuseum/ita/06_3.shtml
[22] Žižek, The Parallax View, pg. 4.

significant existential complications. You see the exterior of the mask of my opinions, but I see this same fearsome mask upon myself. Even as I become a monster to you, I become a monster to me. The monstrous mask of human experience creates unholy war at every level: within ourselves, with our lovers, with our family, with our occupations, with our neighbors, with our country, with our world, and with our God.

Parallaxis as the Infinite and Impassable Distance

Zeno of Elea was a philosopher in the 5th century BC. He is known only through the writings of others. Plutarch says that Zeno tried to kill the tyrant Demylus, and when he failed, he bit off his own tongue and spit it out into the tyrant's face.[23]

Zeno is known for a set of paradoxes, and is attributed with being the first mathematician to wrestle with the infinite. A variation of Zeno's most famous paradox presents the idea of the space between two points as an infinite, and unreachable distance. To reach my destination, I must first reach the halfway point, yet once I reach the halfway point, I now have a new halfway point to reach before I can reach my destination, and if every move I make takes me halfway from where I begin towards the object, I will never reach the object, because there are an infinite number of halfway points.

Zeno's paradox may seem like an impractical illustration for application to our goals in everyday life, but it best illustrates our disagreements with one another. When you and I argue, you present your opinion, and I may concede to a portion of your argument, but not agreeing 100% I still rebut, but even my rebuttal is rebuted by your "but," and soon, we have 'butted' our way to an unsolvable position. My point of view accounts for facts differently than your point of view, and combined with our misperceptions, the space between our perspectives becomes the impossible space of Zeno's paradox with an infinite number of halfway points. It is the growing argumentation of rebuttals upon rebuttals, and even as we discuss the space between us, we often only discover how deep the gap grows.

Emmanuel Levinas, eloquently described this unnavigable space between us as *"the infinite distance of the stranger."*[24]

In the Biblical parable of Lazarus and the Rich Man, Jesus alludes to the infinite distance in the spaces of human discourse:

"But there was a certain beggar named Lazarus, full of sores, who was

---

[23] Plutarch, Against Colotes
[24] Emmanuel Levinas, Totality and Infinity, pg. 50

laid at his gate, desiring to be fed with the crumbs which fell from the rich man's table. Moreover the dogs came and licked his sores. So it was that the beggar died, and was carried by the angels to Abraham's bosom. The rich man also died and was buried. And being in torments in Hades, he lifted up his eyes and saw Abraham afar off, and Lazarus in his bosom.

"Then he cried and said, 'Father Abraham, have mercy on me, and send Lazarus that he may dip the tip of his finger in water and cool my tongue; for I am tormented in this flame.' But Abraham said, 'Son, remember that in your lifetime you received your good things, and likewise Lazarus evil things; but now he is comforted and you are tormented. And besides all this, between us and you there is a great gulf fixed, so that those who want to pass from here to you cannot, nor can those from there pass to us.'

"Then he said, 'I beg you therefore, father, that you would send him to my father's house, for I have five brothers, that he may testify to them, lest they also come to this place of torment.' Abraham said to him, 'They have Moses and the prophets; let them hear them.' And he said, 'No, father Abraham; but if one goes to them from the dead, they will repent.' But he said to him, 'If they do not hear Moses and the prophets, neither will they be persuaded though one rise from the dead.'"[25]

In this parable, Jesus describes an impassable space in Hell as a "great gulf fixed," which cannot be crossed, and the same fixed gulf is found in the hearts and minds of the rich man and his five brothers. They would not be persuaded to change their ways even if someone rose from the dead to speak to them. The impassable fixed gulf is already fixed inside them. Perhaps it is not the gulf, nor Abraham that is immovably rooted. Perhaps it is the rich man and his brothers who are in fixed positions of prejudice, expectation, economic privilege, and intellectual justifications for oppression and carelessness.

In theology, Calvinism and Arminianism have debated to impassable divides for over 400 years, and the core of the debate finds its source in the first five centuries of Christianity. In American politics, the divide between left and right is so severe as to have almost no commonality in our current age. The party platforms between Democrats and Republicans look like strategic oppositions and battle lines. The polarization of our social interactions into overly simplified lines of left and right, good and evil, and right and wrong is the exteriorization of our internal conflicts.

So I am forced to ask if I am any different than the rich man and his brothers, and I must answer that I am not. The same fixed gulf is in me. It is in you. Like the rich man, we are fixed – rooted in our own

---

[25] Luke 16:20-31

perspectives – even prejudices, which we cannot shake loose, and in these perspectives we become participants in creating the infinite and un-crossable space.

Parallaxis as Isolation

The parable of Lazarus and the Rich Man also highlights the lonely cry of isolation. The "great gap" allows the lonely cry, and only the lonely cry, to pass to Abraham's ears from the burning tongue of the rich man isolated in the place of torment.

The infinite space between our points of reference leaves us on a spot in the universe all alone. No other person can think my thoughts with me. Even the voicing of my thoughts is an incomplete act. How often I struggle to say the right thing in the right way. How often I fight to be heard for what I mean and not what someone else thinks I have said. My point of view becomes the fixed location of my isolation. In this isolation my voice echoes across the "great gap," and it is the only reference others have for my location in this universe of thought.

Zeno's paradox illustrates how our debates with one another exaggerate the infinite distance between us, and we often find resolution to our arguments not by coming to agreement with one another, but by conceding through apologies or agreeing to disagree. Our necessary concessions are the proof that in our worldview we stand alone. We remain isolated from fully understanding others, and others fully understanding us.

When we do not reach gracious concessions, topics such as religion and politics become taboo. Politicians, CEOs, and preachers have made a profession arguing against the evil Other and have often created their own isolation, called "the lonely whine of the top dog,"[26] but neighbors, long time friends, and even family members are handicapped by the impossible struggle of isolation. To relieve ourselves from this tension in family settings we create taboos – untouchable, infinitely distant categories. In these tabooed topics of non-discussion, we have set our boundaries for establishing peace, but the isolating factor always remains – the elephant is in the room and sometimes goes on a rampage. So it is, that we find ourselves dreading the visit to the family. When our hearts desire that family times would be a tension free joy, we discover instead that they are taboo ridden circuses.

Social media provides us with a daily dose of this sense of isolation. On Facebook, people friend and un-friend one another with the speed

---

[26] This phrase has a long history of use, but was more recently popularized in <u>Living on the Ragged Edge</u>, Chapter 8 by Chuck Swindoll

of quickly and poorly written updates and comments. Politics, religion, and social justice issues are primary sources for tension. I have personal friends who are good friends with one another in face-to-face interaction, but have un-friended one another on Facebook, because they cannot contain their apparent need to respond to the objects of their disagreement. I have friends who are married to one another, who have un-friended or un-followed one another on Facebook and Twitter for similar reasons. The quick response, unmediated activity of social media provides us with a 140-character example of the isolation of our points of reference. We cannot even be friends with our friends.

Religion, once the community standard of stability and comfort is now a source of isolation for many people. The face of religion has gazed back at us. At times, it has demanded the impossible – it has betrayed – it has abused, and the comfort we once experienced seems impossibly distant.

Even that which I love most becomes the stranger. It distances itself from me, and gazes back at me demanding the impossible from me. Is this intrinsic to the phenomenon of the deadly Fundamentalism that requires the sacrifice of my own life as the expression of my faithfulness – a faith whose love embraces me with a suicide bomber's vest?

Myself as Subject – enslaved by what I observe

> *"The difference between subject and object can also be expressed as the difference between the two corresponding verbs, to subject (submit) oneself and to object (protest, oppose, create an obstacle). The subject's founding gesture is to subject itself – voluntarily, of course… If then the subject's activity is, at its most fundamental, the activity of submitting itself to the inevitable, the fundamental mode of the object's passivity, of its passive presence, is that which moves, annoys, disturbs, traumatizes us (subjects): at its most radical level the object is that which objects, that which disturbs the smooth running of things."*[27]

Žižek's wordplay on the activity of subject and object in relation to one another describes what happens to us, in our opinions and observations about the objects of our concern and meditation. As we submit ourselves to the consideration of ideas, we are the changed ones. The transformative power of our opinions about God, or religion is observable in the changes our ideas have made on us. I do not so much change the object I perceive in the moment of my perception, as much as the object looking back at me informs and converts me. It

---

[27] Žižek, The Parallax View, pg. 17.

proselytizes me to the degree that I, as the subject, have submitted myself to and identified with it. The actual activities and values of religion do not intrinsically change, because of my opinion of them, until I actively engage with them in word and action. Their history, traditions, and week-to-week activities in the world remain the same. A negative assessment engages me in an opposing manner, but engages me nonetheless. The object challenges me, "annoys, disturbs, traumatizes" me. If I hold a positive valuation of religion, the changed aspect is not in the church but in myself, but immediately my perception of religion calls me toward engagement. Strangely, as seen in the story of Dorothy Martin's UFO cult, our positive valuations of religion may be equally as traumatizing as our negative valuations.

This trauma occurs by creating slavery within us. The stronger our identification, the more we are compelled to engage the matters of our concern. Consider the compulsion, which forces us to use these words, "I just have to say something." How many times have you been caught in the crossfire of the person who says this while you are inflicted by the follow-up of an intrusive, sometimes offensive verbal torrent? These uncomfortable moments are further examples of the unbridgeable space between us, and they are evidence of our slavery to our own opinions.

Love and hate are equally potent examples of the slavery in which the object of our gaze holds us. It engages – it enslaves our passions. We become the servant of what or whom we love or hate, and the returning gaze of the object of our passion may hold our hearts in something more akin to a death-grip than a hug. Former loves hold our attention and betray us, not once, but repeatedly. Long after they have left our lives, they remain behind as the ghosts we serve. History is filled with the stories of those who sacrifice for that which they love, and this is even the story of Christianity – of a God Who loves a wanton fiancée, who cheats on Him – traumatizes Him. Enslaved by His own love He remains faithful to the point of humiliation and death, even in the face of continued unfaithfulness and abuse coming from the object of His desire. But, love leaves no option for God to behave any other way. Christianity is the story of a God whose actions are driven by the object of His gaze, which is looking back and traumatizing Him, and the story cascades through a grotesque, yet, romantic movement from annoyance, to disturbance, to trauma.

Humanity is objectified by the objects it objectifies. We are abused by the systems and the people we abuse. They become ghosts haunting us. They become the demons of our tortured nights.

Is this the traumatizing power of the Person of Jesus? He was tormented in trial, betrayed by a false guilty verdict, and though crucified unjustly, remained silent through it all. Still He looks down the corridors of history with the silent blinking eyes of the lamb led to the slaughter, and traumatizes us with those eyes. Even the communion cup traumatizes us, because the abused God stares back at us through the bread and the wine. It carries the gaze of all the hurting, all the abused, and all the traumatized throughout human history.

Perhaps nothing highlights this reverse objectification, of that which stares back and objectifies us in return, more than the counter-intuitive illustration of the dual oppression of pornography. The attachment to pornography creates the threat of slavery in two directions. The objectification of women through the obscene narratives of them as sex toys, objects of abuse and slaves is one tormenting and twisted half of the story. Yet the paper and pixel ladies stare back, and traumatize the viewer in return. They call back silently from screen and paper in the middle of the night. They keep young and old men (and a growing number of women) up into the witching hours of exhaustion. The pixilated girls call during the day, and government and private sector resources are used for satisfying uncontrollable, unproductive urges. No one is a winner in the isolating and enslaving gaze of pornography. She haunts like a siren and slays many of those who paddle into the surf of her shores. She holds the potential to devour the souls of mistresses she keeps, and the scopophiliacs she titillates.

In Man's Search for Meaning,[28] neurologist and psychiatrist Viktor Frankl begins his story of imprisonment in the Nazi concentration camps of Auschwitz, Kaufering, and Turkheim with the observation that there were captives in the camps who by their behavior demonstrated that they were freer than their captors. The Holocaust is recent history's most hideous illustration showing us that the objects of our gaze captivate, traumatize, and betray us. Even when people look upon their fellow humans as chattel, the face of the oppressed gazes back and enslaves the captors, as though the Stockholm Syndrome were inversed.

Bad News as Hope

If this section on the impassable space between different worldviews seems hopelessly pessimistic, I am sorry if you are troubled by it, but this observation is the first foundational contention of this book: There is an unnavigable space between religion and secular

---

[28] originally published in 1946 under the title Trotzdem Ja Zum Leben Sagen: Ein Psychologe erlebt das Konzentrationslager, meaning Nevertheless, Say "Yes" to Life: A Psychologist Experiences the Concentration Camp. In 1959 it was published in English under the title, From Death-Camp to Existentialism.

society, and furthermore, this is an un-crossable gap that resides in each of us.

The problems of our intellectual and emotional engagement on any subject carry both the danger of isolating others against my opinions, and deeply rooting myself as an existentially isolated lone point in the universe, where no one, not even God speaks into the cell of my isolation.

But, as a pastor in a Christian church, I hang onto my faith with a radical paradox: even while Christianity demands an honest appraisal of reality in my own life, and the world around me, it does not remain in the pessimistic containment of a broken system – it reaches out to the impossible for the solutions to our isolation and brokenness. Consequently, I expect impossible tensions to have impossible but real resolutions. So, as far as the self-immolation I see within my own faith, I paradoxically see a Phoenix-like resurrection, and I hold out hope for navigating the space between the church and world. And this is the ultimate paradox: I believe we can navigate the impossibly impassable spaces.

But, because of the demand for honesty, the adventurous journey toward the impossible does not begin with the determination of the Little Engine that Could. It begins with the acknowledgement of the infinite gap we hold within ourselves. We have been unwitting accomplices to the impossible intellectual, emotional, and prejudicial distances between church and church, between church and world, between nation and nation, between power brokers and oppressed, between one culture and another, between neighbor and neighbor, and between ourselves and our closest friends and family members.

The first step in this journey is not, "I…think…I…can." The first step is to confess, "I am a prejudiced fixed point on one side of an impossibly impassable space."

Dorothy Martin's UFO cult readjusted their conclusions after holding their celestial hitchhiking thumbs out to spacemen who never arrived to pick them up, and there is a new generation of people 60 years later who are still waiting for Dorothy Martin's aliens. Our cognitive dissonance is at its most damaging when we remain uncritically fixed to our own untenable positions. It is when we think we know the answers despite contrary evidence that our cognitive dissonance reaches its proud apex, and we are consequently unaware of our own isolation.

Approaching the Elephant

Perhaps we are the six blind men feeling the elephant in the ancient

Indian tale.[29] One thought it was a tree trunk, and another a rope. One thought it was a fan, and another a wall. Our conclusions, our emotional responses, our beliefs about religion are based upon a perception, which is ours alone. Even when we depend on someone else's work for our opinions, this is based upon our opinion of their opinions. Our views are like no one else's, and in spite of what we are told, we believe something different, and we are feeling our way through the doctrines and the ideas we have been taught.

It was six men of Indostan
To learning much inclined,
Who went to see the Elephant
(Though all of them were blind),
That each by observation
Might satisfy his mind.

The First approach'd the Elephant,
And happening to fall
Against his broad and sturdy side,
At once began to bawl:
"God bless me! but the Elephant
Is very like a wall!"

The Second, feeling of the tusk,
Cried, - "Ho! what have we here
So very round and smooth and sharp?
To me 'tis mighty clear
This wonder of an Elephant
Is very like a spear!"

The Third approached the animal,
And happening to take
The squirming trunk within his hands,
Thus boldly up and spake:
"I see," quoth he, "the Elephant
Is very like a snake!"

The Fourth reached out his eager hand,
And felt about the knee.
"What most this wondrous beast is like

---

[29] The tale of the 5 or 6 blind men describing the elephant has appeared in many eastern religious traditions, but was popularized in the Western world in the poem by John Godfrey Saxe in the 19th century.

*Is mighty plain," quoth he,
"'Tis clear enough the Elephant
Is very like a tree!"*

*The Fifth, who chanced to touch the ear,
Said: "E'en the blindest man
Can tell what this resembles most;
Deny the fact who can,
This marvel of an Elephant
Is very like a fan!"*

*The Sixth no sooner had begun
About the beast to grope,
Then, seizing on the swinging tail
That fell within his scope,
"I see," quoth he, "the Elephant
Is very like a rope!"*

*And so these men of Indostan
Disputed loud and long,
Each in his own opinion
Exceeding stiff and strong,
Though each was partly in the right,
And all were in the wrong!*

MORAL.

*So oft in theologic wars,
The disputants, I ween,
Rail on in utter ignorance
Of what each other mean,
And prate about an Elephant
Not one of them has seen!*
            John Godfrey Saxe, printed in 1873

If we have not seen the preacher's naked backside for ourselves, newspapers, television and popular culture have published it, and we are left with cognitive dissonance in the face of radically different perspectives on religion. The beautiful, the ugly, and our own views may not have anything in common. Yet, these are all opinionated perspectives on the same object. Some of us are paralyzed by the cognitive dissonance of the contradicting perspectives, and for the mystics among us, we are wondering if God has a perspective of this mess we call religion. We are wondering if the Divine perspective is different than our own, and we are wondering what that Divine perspective might be.

Similar to Godfrey's application of the ancient Indian proverb, we are arguing about the God we have not seen, but we are also arguing about the religious experiences we have seen from our different and infinitely distant lines of perception, and we are "partly in the right, and all [are] in the wrong!"

The joke, which is the inversion of the parable of the blind men, describes our paralyzing predicament best:

> *"Six blind elephants were discussing what men were like.*
> *After arguing they decided to find one and determine by direct experience.*
> *The first blind elephant felt the man and declared, 'Men are flat.'*
> *After the other blind elephants felt the man, they agreed."*

Reality is the elephant, and we are the flat men being experienced by it.

Engage: How is your internal dissonance?

The argument for chapter 7 looks something like this: we are trapped in the tension of cognitive dissonance, because what we see and what we believe do not match one another. We are trapped in this less than idyllic world, and our position of beliefs and experiences leave us with an unnavigable gap between what we believe and what others believe. Because of this gap, I am isolated to an opinion all my own, and I often become enslaved to the issues I engage – whether I appreciate and agree with those issues, or despise and reject them.

Where do you fall in the categories highlighted by Naked Pastor, David Hayward's cartoon? Are you excited by your political or religious position? Traumatized by it? Confused? Or, have you traveled through all of these feelings in your lifetime?

Have you seen this struggle happening around you? How do you respond to the person who obnoxiously says to you, "I just have to say something here"?

Interact with the Burning Religion community on the website at www.burningreligion.com.

FLAT FAITH

"You, who are blessed with shade as well as light, you, who are gifted with two eyes, endowed with a knowledge of perspective, and charmed with the enjoyment of various colours, you, who can actually see an angle, and contemplate the complete circumference of a Circle in the happy region of the Three Dimensions— how shall I make clear to you the extreme difficulty which we in Flatland experience in recognizing one another's configuration?"[30]

In 1884, the short mathematical fiction Flatland[31] was published. Edwin Abbott Abbott was an English Headmaster and theologian. The novella did not have much success when first published, but shortly after Einstein's discovery of the theory of relativity the small book was rediscovered, and Edwin Abbott was declared to be a modern day prophet. His short story about a creature living in a two dimensional world, who is led to the discovery of the third dimension is seen as a predictor of the developments in physics, which would occur 30 years later.

In the end of <u>Flatland</u>, the protagonist, the Square, who had tried to share his revelation of a third dimension with his two dimensional world sits in jail with no hope of release, and no hope for success in sharing his knowledge to his own people who are blind to the third dimension.

Like Edwin Abbott Abbott's world of two-dimensional characters unable to envision a third dimension, we tend to see things from the limited perspective of our own little worldview. Perhaps, more conflicting for our own existential trauma, we are like the square seeing something others cannot, and we are trapped in the jail of our own making.

The second section of this book considers this problem with the goal of helping us navigate the space between our worldview differences, maybe even giving us hope in the midst of the tortuous self-immolation of our own personal positions.

---

[30] Abbott, Edwin A., <u>Flatland</u>, pg. 17. Read Books Ltd.
[31] http://www.flatlandthemovie.com/index.html

Engage: Has your world been flattened?

Edwin Abbott Abbott's mathematical tale Flatland highlights the struggle we have in seeing outside the boxes of our limited worldviews. The polarizations within both politics and religion, and the polarization occuring in the interaction between these two different worlds of thought have created a black and white, good and evil bifurcated world. Polarization creates a "flat", two-dimensional worldview. Have you experienced difficulty in getting another person to understand that you had a completely different point of view than the simple two options found in the political and theological debates of our time? What are some of the topics you have struggled with the most in your circle of friends and family?

Have you discovered any principles for breaking polarization and moving beyond the "blindness"?

Interact with the Burning Religion community on the website.

THE SECOND RING
CAUGHT BETWEEN THE RING MASTER AND THE CLOWNS

Tales from the Land of Jaw: The Adventures of Gwyn Dee
The Paper War

*T*he white, white plain finally came to an end, although its end occurred in nearly imperceptible changes. At first, the ragged and few tufts of dry grass became more regular, then the cracked white earth became yellow, then browned as a stray shrub here and there broke the barren landscape. As the scraggly shrubs multiplied, the terrain rose ever so slightly until it became a desert of cactus and scrub brush and random small sand dunes with lizards doing push-ups.

The wide, wide road was occasionally met by smaller paths, and with each merging the wide, wide road grew a little wider. Coming to a sharp rock outcropping along the side of the road, Gwyn Dee heard voices of singing and merriment coming from behind the stubby cliff. Then appearing from behind the rocks, a dozen colorful soldiers singing an unfamiliar anthem stumbled haphazardly from a small merging path onto the wide, wide road. Whether it was marching, or dancing, or tumbling, or a choreographed fight scene, was hard to tell.

Gwyn Dee stood at the corner of the intersection, and the clumsy group would have passed by without noticing the barefoot traveler, but a short round soldier glanced to the side and shouted, "Hey, what have we here? Coming to join the battle? I dare say you'll need some shoes for combat, and a weapon for your hands. Though I think these are the hands of scholar or an artist and not a warrior."

Gwyn Dee looked confusingly into the round face of the gruff portly soldier, only to see the rosy cheeks of a young woman.

"Dare I say, that I know nothing of a battle?"

At this the soldiers all laughed.

"All the world knows of the great battle to protect the Gates of the Kingdom of Jaw. How have you remained ignorant?" The apparent leader of the small gaggle of soldiers was dressed in freshly painted well-dented black armor. A white dove breathing fire like a dragon was the crest upon his breastplate and his shield. Gwyn Dee was more than a bit curious about this strange insignia.

The leader bowed as low as his creaking armor would allow, "We are the servants of Jaw, and the troop from the village of Smallkirk."

"Hear, hear!" The small group shouted together.

"And a fine troupe we are!" A lanky young man with a pointy goatee, bright green armor, and a dozen feathers exploding from the top of his helmet declared.

"A trope made for times such as this." This time a smallish bookworm of a man in untested armor spoke with a voice larger than his diminutive stature suggested was possible.

In short time, and with no actual assent, Gwyn Dee was recruited and the merry clan bumbled along the wide, wide road as the soldiers recited the story of a great and ancient war. The best Gwyn Dee could gather from the tale, this war involved the defense of the Gates of the Kingdom of Jaw against marauders, and an invaluable document connected to the founding of the Kingdom.

They took a short stop at a small trickling of water by the roadside. The leader remained standing and looked down the wide, wide road, "We are nearly there, and shall meet up with our fellow warriors on the battlefield. My hand quivers with excitement upon my sword to serve the Lord Jaw, like my father, and his father before him!"

"Hear! Hear!" The small troop shouted.

Within an hour they arrived at the battlefield. As far as the eye could see armies waged battle against armies. A thousand large armies protected a thousand great sand dunes the size of small mountains. Arrows flew through the sky like flocks of starlings. Great war horses labored up dunes with heavily armored knights. Swords clashed and rang across the dunes with the sound of a thousand dissonant bell choirs.

The small troupe stood dumbfounded with mouths wide open and eyes like surprised deer, that is, all but the battle-tested leader, who scanned the field. After a few minutes of their dumbstruck silence, the leader called his troop together with a shout, "There, on the third hill back and to the right!" He pointed as he called his small trope to arms.

"They are ascending the hill to take the Gates of the Kingdom even now. We shall join our Brethren of the Fire-breathing Dove for the glory of Jaw and of His Kingdom!"

Their leader unfolded a black banner with the dove upon it, and handed it to the rosy-cheeked young woman, "Carry this for the glory of Jaw, and keep us together."

"Little, but brave troop, stay with the banner in battle, and follow me into glory!"

"Hear. Hear." They responded with a little less confidence than usual, but as their leader ran toward the third hill back and to the right, the banner ran after him, and the clumsy troupe followed close along.

Gwyn Dee was standing in the middle of the group, and when they started off, was bumped into the running march with them. Not knowing what else to do Gwyn Dee ran with the small trope.

As they passed the first dunes, Gwyn Dee scanned the armies to the left and to the right. Crosses and lambs, thrones and scepters, rainbows and lions all symbols of the worship of the Lord Jaw were upon their banners, their shields, and their armor.

"Are these all armies of the Lord Jaw?" Gwyn Dee queried aloud.

"Nay, there is only one true army of the Lord Jaw, and we are coming to join it in the moment of victory."

At the foot of the third hill back and to the right a large army with Fire-breathing Doves upon their armor and banners slowly marched up the dune toward its peak. The leader of the small troop nodded to other captains in the large army, and made a few quick greetings.

Gwyn Dee scanned the top of the dune, and saw the desire of the armies. At the peak stood a set of massive wooden doors, closed and leading into no building. Nailed to the doors was a paper document. The army at the top of the hill surrounded the door, and stood in anticipation of an onslaught from below. Their banners were decorated with the crest of a lion with a wind-blown mane. Gwyn Dee looked across the faces of the army at the peak and gasped. There on the hill, in the midst of the army was a small gathering of soldiers

83

with jester's insignias upon their shields. They were from the Clown Caste from Cominkingville.

Gwyn Dee acted without thought and ran. The new friends from Smallkirk shouted after Gwyn Dee, but to no avail. Running around the right side of the great dune, and finding a break in the lines of the army of the Fire-breathing Dove, Gwyn Dee broke through and ran for the peak. Being light, bare-footed and swift, Gwyn Dee ran for the summit and towards the jester crests.

"Friend or foe?" A large knight wielding a broadsword suddenly stood in the path of Gwyn Dee's rush toward the summit.

Spontaneously and involuntarily Gywn Dee shouted in the ancient and holy tongue of the clown caste with a great shout, "Dw i'n dod o'r teulu clown!"

The Clown Caste heard this and shouted for joy, and the great knight stepped aside, "Croeso," he said as he bowed and waved Gwyn Dee on.

Just a few young men of the Clown Caste and a large strong elder were present from Cominkingville. They greeted one another with joy and deep love.

"Your strange travels have not dampened your zeal, I see." The elder looked down at the smaller Gwyn Dee, and stared deeply. "And by Jaw, you have come at the moment of greatest need, as we are set upon by the enemies of truth."

Gwyn Dee quickly described the accidental arrival, and the travels with the little troop from Smallkirk. "They appeared to be lovers of Jaw, just as us. I do not understand this war, and this battle for the gate. This gate does not even stand on the border of the land. What are we fighting for?"

"For the truth, of course, as is ever and always our duty." The elder stiffened, and responded with holy words from the ancient holy book, "Y mae brenhinoedd y ddaear yn barod."[32]

Gwyn Dee flinched at his words, and responded, "Y mae'r Arglwydd yn eu gwatwar."[33]

---

[32] Y Beibl Cymraeg Newydd, Y Salmau 2:2 (Psalm 2:2)
[33] Y Beibl Cymraeg Newydd, Y Salmau 2:4 (Psalm 2:4)

Suddenly a great shout came from the bottom of the mountain, the Army of the Fire-Breathing Doves rushed up the hill. The defenders of the Gates of the Kingdom of Jaw tensed and awaited the onslaught.

Gwyn Dee sat at the steps of the great wooden doors. Nailed to the door was an ancient piece of paper with ninety-five points of doctrine, practices, and complaints. Gwyn Dee sat silently, and sadly reading the ancient paper wondered how its ownership ensured the Kingdom of Jaw. The battle raged. Men and women screamed with anger and with pain. Sword clanged against shield and helmet. Blood flowed like ale in a pub. Bodies fell and rolled down the sandy dune.

In the end of the battle, the warriors of the Fire-Breathing Dove shouted in victory. Gwyn Dee found the soldiers from Cominkingville among the human debris. They were wounded bloodied, and the elder lay dying on the ground.

"You were right my young friend. O that I would have learned before my demise, and avoided these battles at which our Lord Jaw scoffs." And the elder's last words trailed off as he passed away in Gwyn Dee's arms.

The young soldiers of Cominkingville cried. The surviving defenders of the Gates of the Kingdom cowered on the far side of their dune, and the warriors of the Fire-Breathing Dove carried the ancient wooden doors with the ancient holy paper to their own great sand dune mountain a short distance away.

AN APOLOGY

I feel compelled to forewarn you about the next two chapters, and give some apologies.

I am sorry for the dark nature of the next chapter. It is filled with gruesome details of death, torture, abuse, and criminal intent. Yet, it somehow seems necessary to the ongoing direction of the thesis of this book.

I am sorry for the extra-noble nature of the chapter after that. It might give you the idea that perfect nobility exists out there somewhere. Then again, some of us need to begin thinking that things are better than we currently think they are. It might do us a piece of good, and give us some peace of mind.

I am sorry for the fact that as a non-historian, I will be laying out historical vignettes. An intelligent historian might lay these simple chapters out better than I am able. Because history is not my strong suit, I sometimes had to read thousands of pages to write each section of a few measly paragraphs. I am hoping my measliness is somewhat quarantined by this significant preparation.

I am also sorry for the repetition of the next two chapters. The stories I will be telling are a part of a history many of us are familiar with, although, I have attempted to search for information, which is either not part of the common mythos of our culture, or a challenge to these common stories we have taken for granted. In other cases, as will be evident in the latter stories about Communist China under Mao, Pope Pius XII, and the persecution of Witches in our world, I have tried to draw from the most recent work, and/or newly available information.

I am sorry that these chapters are so simple. The kind of writing I appreciate most captures me for its creative and compelling movement, or for its blindingly brilliant scholarship, and intellectual rigor. Yet, in pursuing to develop a thesis calling for a new way of looking at religion, secularism, other individuals, powers that be, and even the nature of our human experience it seemed necessary to state the obvious in grindingly simple terms.

Lastly, I am sorry that you will be assaulted while I attack something you hold dear, but hang in there and keep reading, because I will attack the things I hold dear, and then I will turn it all around and come to defend what you hold dearest. I am sorry for this intentional extremism as well, but there really is a reason for all this extremism, which will appear extremely oppositional one moment, and extremely affirming the next.

Many of us feel as though we've been sold a bill of goods. To many of us, religion at its most dishonest is peddled like snake oil medicine – miracle cures laced with deadly poisons, and at its most benign it feels as comfortable as one size fits all clothing. These vignettes from history are focused first upon the hideously evil elements in human nature, and then upon gloriously noble aspects from the same people groups, and through this simple exercise perhaps we will discover why we feel trapped between radical extremes pulling us simultaneously to love and to hate religion, politics, and sometimes even our neighbors. The following stories are anecdotal evidence of the first basic truth to this second part of Burning Religion: nobility and evil lie in each of us, no matter who we are, where we've been, and to what group we belong. It does not matter whether we think of ourselves as religious or secular, these tendencies still reside within us.

For those of you who are going to trudge through these next two chapters like barefoot hippies lost in a swamp, it is okay to get in the airboat,[34] turn on the fan, and blow over the surface of them, but I should warn you: if you do stop to ponder, some of these stories may tug at your heart and make an activist, or a rebel out of you.

---

[34] "Airboat" is the official name of those wonderfully romantic swampboats propelled by large fans.

EVERYONE HAS IT WRONG

"...repay her double according to her works; in the cup which she has mixed, mix double for her. In the measure that she glorified herself and lived luxuriously, in the same measure give her torment and sorrow; for she says in her heart, 'I sit as queen, and am no widow, and will not see sorrow.' Therefore her plagues will come in one day—death and mourning and famine. And she will be utterly burned with fire, for strong is the Lord God who judges her."[35]

The Christian Wrong
From Denominations to Demon Nations

It was 1985. I began pastoring a small church in Carlsbad, CA on September 1st, 1985. Letters passed from myself to the denominational headquarters two and a half hours north in the City of Angels.

In 1985 spellcheck was not an automated function of my little word-processor, or the Brother typewriter I might have used. My typing skills were much slower then. Yet, as the people in my church will attest, when I write information for the weekly bulletins, I am as inaccurate with my fingers today, even if I am much faster. Consequently, I spelled the word "denomination" incorrectly in a communication to the denomination's headquarters.

Misspellings often go unnoticed, sometimes they are easily spotted, but on rare and embarrassing occasions they are worth being placed on joke lists.

Almost 20 years later, someone remembered my misspelling, and reminded me of it:

D-E-M-O-N-A-T-I-O-N

Whoops.

Thankfully (or, maybe regretfully) I was part of a Pentecostal denomination.

Thankfully, because Pentecostals typically do not believe that their denomination is the only true expression of Christ's church on earth. At least that was true for my little expression of Pentecostalism. Regretfully, Pentecostals can be more than a little superstitious. Some Pentecostals imagine demons around every corner. Accidently referring

---

[35] Revelation 18:6-8, NKJV

to the denomination as a "Demon Nation" is not exactly a way to win friends and influence superstitious denominational leaders.

The misspelling was just a hilarious typo, but there were a couple people who seemed a bit unnerved by it, and the silly typo made gossip rounds at headquarters to be remembered 20 years later.

If you've been burned by the actions of denominational church leadership, you might consider my silly misspelling prophetic or a Freudian finger slip. In our current culture of mistrust, religion is often viewed as the source of oppression, greed, and sorrow - consequently, the activity of churches is viewed as manipulative, or worse – the activity of demons using stupid humans as their puppets. Jeff Bethke's "Why I Hate Religion, But Love Jesus" illustrated how even Christians identify "religion" with false and hypocritical spirituality.

The horror stories of religious oppression and abuse are the street corner discussions of our time. They have made the front pages of our newspapers, the news reports on our television sets, and the trending topics of our twitter hashtags. The 21st century's blazingly swift transference of information brings these stories to us daily, but they are not new news.

Celebrating Easter with Blood

> *Avenge O Lord thy slaughtered Saints, whose bones*
> *Lie scatter'd on the Alpine mountains cold,*
> *Ev'n them who kept thy truth so pure of old*
> *When all our Fathers worship't Stocks and Stones.*
>
> *Forget not: in thy book record their groans*
> *Who were thy sheep and in their ancient fold*
> *Slayn by the bloody Piedmontese that roll'd*
> *Mother with infant down the rocks. Their moans*
>
> *The vales redoubl'd to the hills, and they*
> *To heav'n. Their martyred blood and ashes sow*
> *O're all th' Italian fields where still doth sway*
> *The triple tyrant: that from these may grow*
> *A hundred-fold, who having learnt thy way*
> *Early may fly the Babylonian woe.*[36]

January 1655, the Duke of Savoy ordered the non-Catholic sect – the Waldensians (aka the Vaudois) to attend Catholic Mass, or move to

---

[36] John Milton's Poem On the Late Massacre in Piedmont.

the upper Piedmont Valleys. The Duke gave the people 20 days to sell their land and move, or attend Mass. The Waldensians had suffered hundreds of years under the brutal oppression of Catholicism, and viewed the Catholic Church as an idolatrous false expression of faith. Celebrating the idolatry of the Mass (as they considered it) was not an option. Men, women, children, elderly and the sick all moved together into the high alpine valleys of Northern Italy in the middle of winter. They waded across freezing rivers, climbed frozen peaks, and were graciously received by their poorer brethren living high in the Piedmont Mountains.

The Duke was dissatisfied with the results. His goal was the conversion of the Waldensians. In April 1655, Irish, French, and Italian Catholic forces under his command besieged the Waldensian upper valleys. The Waldensians having been accustomed to centuries of abuse at the hands of Catholic backed military forces had easily defensible mountain positions, and drove back the significantly stronger, and larger forces of the Duke.

When the Duke's forces saw they could not win an outright battle, they played a ruse. Under a deceptive guise of having mistakenly attacked the wrong people, the Duke's forces apologized and claimed that they had been pursuing rebels in the mountains. They asked the hospitable Waldensian people to house the soldiers for a few days during the week preceding Easter. Despite warnings against trusting the Duke's forces, the generous and forgiving Waldensians took the soldiers in.

For three days the soldiers lived and ate with the families, but early in the morning on the third day, April 24th, 1655 a watch fire signaled from a nearby hill. The soldiers rose up and slaughtered the families.

Pastor Jean Leger survived the massacre. Twenty-five years later he wrote about it in Histoire General des Eglises Evangeliques des Vallees de Piedmont. Below is an excerpt from J.A. Wylie's book The History of the Waldenses published in 1860, quoting Pastor Leger's accounts of this horrific day:

> *"From the awful narration of Leger, we select only a few instances; but even these few, however mildly stated, grow, without our intending it, into a group of horrors. Little children were torn from the arms of their mothers, clasped by their tiny feet, and their heads dashed against the rocks; or were held between two soldiers and their quivering limbs torn up by main force. Their mangled bodies were then thrown on the highways or fields, to be devoured by beasts. The sick and the aged were burned alive in their dwellings. Some had their hands and arms and legs lopped off, and fire applied to the severed parts to staunch the bleeding and prolong their suffering. Some were flayed alive, some*

were roasted alive, some disembowelled; or tied to trees in their own orchards, and their hearts cut out. Some were horribly [mutlitated], and of others the brains were boiled and eaten by these cannibals. Some were fastened down into the furrows of their own fields, and ploughed into the soil as men plough manure into it. Others were buried alive. Fathers were marched to death with the heads of their sons suspended round their necks. Parents were compelled to look on while their children were first outraged, then massacred, before being themselves permitted to die. But here we must stop. We cannot proceed farther in Leger's awful narration. There come vile, abominable, and monstrous deeds, utterly and overwhelmingly disgusting, horrible and fiendish, which we dare not transcribe. The heart sickens, and the brain begins to swim. "My hand trembles," says Leger, "so that I scarce can hold the pen, and my tears mingle in torrents with my ink, while I write the deeds of these children of darkness—blacker even than the Prince of Darkness himself"

1,700 people died that day. It became known as the Piedmont Easter. This massacre incited anger across Europe. Sanctuary was offered the Waldensians by various countries. Oliver Cromwell (ruling England at this time) raised money to provide for them, and sent forces to rescue them. The Swiss and Dutch Calvinists established an underground network to protect them, and the Dutch sent 167 Waldensians to their Colony in the New World (Delaware).

"Milton's Sonnet 18: On the Late Massacre in the Piedmont" reminds us of this cruel, dark, and hideous moment from religious history.

The Waldensian movement gained its momentum under the leadership of the merchant Peter Waldo, in Lyon, France in the 12th century. Eighty of those first Waldensian laymen were burnt at the stake in Rome by edict of the Pope for preaching the Gospel without church sanction. In 1997, the Roman Catholic Church issued an apology for the persecution and death of these eighty. This apology was 700 years late, but perhaps it was a beginning. The Piedmont Easter itself may not have happened by direct edict of the Pope, but it stands among the great atrocities of European history incited by Catholic fervor.

The Piedmont Easter was so cruel and shameful that it should have marked the end of the Catholic oppression and slaughter of the Waldensian people, but it would not be the end of it.

Parts of this book were written in Asheville, NC. An hour's drive to the east on Interstate 40 is a Waldensian community. The city of Valdese was settled by Italian Waldensian immigrants from the Piedmont region in 1893. In Valdese, you can visit the Waldensian Trail of Faith[37] with replications of famous Waldensian locations in the

Piedmont Valleys. It includes a house, which was used as a Waldensian seminary, and a cave replicating the now (in)famous hiding place where they once held their illegal church services.

Anthony Collins was the director of the Trail of Faith while I was researching the Waldensian history. He took time out of his day to discuss the history, and the persecution of the Waldensian people with me. Milton's sonnet highlighted and made the Piedmont Easter notorious and noxious in the eyes of all Europe, and remains as a reminder today, but to Anthony this was just another heinous crime in a long list of cruelties.

A mere eight years after the Piedmont Easter, the Waldensians were once again declared to be heretics, were condemned to death, and had to fight for their survival. Then in 1686, Catinat's war would kill 9,000 Waldensians, and imprison another 12,000 men, women and children. Most of them would die in prison before their eventual release.

Denominations Abusing the Most Innocent

Shortly after I moved to the north shore of Boston in 1999, the Catholic priest sexual abuse scandal broke out in January 2002. It seemed that the Boston Globe had the story on the front page every day for the next two years. The Globe received a Pulitzer for breaking and covering the story.

People were mad. People were hurt. Ex-Catholics soon were speaking of themselves as "Recovering Catholics." The church attempted to hide behind the separation of church and state, and their First Amendment protections. Years of abuse, and cover-up, secretly moving offenders from one parish to another, were uncovered in court cases, and hearings. Papers from the diocese revealing the depth of the problem were slowly and with great difficulty released.

It is thirteen years later as I finish this book. Cardinal Law, the Archbishop of the Boston diocese resigned one year after the story broke. He was called to Rome, and received a very nice job as archpriest of Saint Mary, a major basilica in Rome, where he stayed until his retirement in 2011. Many people viewed this as evidence of the lack of repentance on the part of the church itself. Lawsuits remain active not only across the US, but now across the world. The world's largest denomination of Christianity looks like a Demon Nation to some of those who have been abused by it.

---

[37] Mitchell Garabedian - January 24, 2012 NPR interview

Mitchell Garabedian a lawyer for victims in suits against the Catholic Church went on a vocal rampage during a January 24, 2012 NPR interview:

> *"When the priest molested the child, the priest would threaten the child to keep the matter a secret or, for instance, their mother would burn in hell. Then, the supervisors when they receive the report of the sexual abuse by a parent would tell the parent - and this is all documented - to keep this matter a secret. So you have this secrecy within an entity that has started to circle the wagons, and they play upon people's faith and morality. You have purportedly the most moral institution in the world acting the most immorally and using for leverage the fact that they tell little children if you tell anybody your parents are going to burn in hell."*

Stories such as this are kindling for the fire to those who believe that God is anti-denominational. This is understandable in the face of the abuse, and the hypocrisy by the leaders of organized religion, but this is not limited to the Catholic Church. Abuse has been reported across all denominational boundaries.

And this heinous story only scratches the surface of abuse and oppression at the hands of religious leaders in our world.

Priests burn with lust, while the abused burn with rage. And the walls of the church are crumbling in the ashes of our distrust.

Could it be that there is hope outside denominations?

Forced Child Labor in the Church

In 1972 former child evangelist Marjoe Gortner released the documentary simply named "Marjoe." At 4 years old, Marjoe became America's youngest ordained minister. Twenty-five years later, at 29, he went on his final evangelistic crusade with a film crew, and although he preached as he had always preached, and shouted Hallelujahs like he had always shouted them, he revealed in the documentary that he had never truly believed in God. Rather was forced into the preacher's life by his domineering parents.

> *"I remember my mother going through very, uh, correctional activities, you might say, to get me prepared to say the wedding ceremony, because I would have to say the whole Episcopal ceremony verbatim and write my name on the certificate... As I child I'd want to go out and play and we'd have to spend hours and hours, you know, memorizing and my mind would slip and finally my mother would begin to lose patience with me and she would put a pillow over my head maybe and smother me for a little bit, other times she would hold*

me under the water faucet, but she never wanted to put any marks on my body, because she knew I had to be in front of the press and so she never hit me or anything."

— *Marjoe Gortner from the film "Marjoe"*

The film was a disgrace to the independent Pentecostal churches and Pentecostal denominations visited during Marjoe's final crusade. Of course, the Pentecostal Churches treated Marjoe Gortner as the offender and the disgrace for telling his story.

The film Marjoe is a documentary every Christian professional (pastor, evangelist, missionary or church secretary) should watch, if for no other reason, because the abuses of the church are now winning awards.

Marjoe won the Oscar for Best Documentary of the Year in 1972.[38]

Keeping up with the Joneses?

In 1955 an American of Welsh and Scottish descent started a church in Indianapolis, Indiana based upon a concept called "apostolic socialism." Early in the development of the church they created an ethnically integrated congregation at a time when denominations kept themselves strictly divided by ethnicity. By 1959 the church had increased its African-American membership from 15% to 50%.

In 1959 the church joined the Christian Church (Disciples of Christ), but with a strong socialist leaning and anti-organized-religion stance this may have been nothing more than a move to establish cultural legitimacy in the Midwest.

In 1960, the church started a soup kitchen serving 2,800 meals a month.

Over the course of the next decade and a half the influence of the church increased as politicians lauded their social work, but increasingly the church distanced itself from orthodox Christian theology. The church began to vacillate between what appeared to be atheism, apocalyptic warnings of nuclear holocaust, and declarations that the divine principle was love expressed through socialism.

The church moved to California during these years and eventually created a number of satellite locations across the state. With increased paranoid conspiratorial concerns about the US government developing fascist tendencies, the church leased land in South America's only English speaking country, Guyana, in 1974. Behind the scenes of this reactionary momentum, dangerous signs were appearing. Suicide pacts

---

[38] You can order Marjoe at http://www.sarahkernochan.com/documentaries/

were discussed, and critics published these warning signs. By 1978 the number of people living at The People's Temple Agricultural Project grew to over 900.

On November 18, 1978 Jim Jones, the founding pastor of The People's Temple, and 918 members committed suicide by drinking a concoction of cyanide laced grape Flavor Aid. Until September 11, 2001 this would remain the largest non-disaster loss of American civilian life in US history.

These are the kind of stories we tend to bury, and hope to forget. There is no memorial to this tragedy (yet) in Guyana. There is no memorial in San Francisco, where most of the people came from; but there is a memorial on Evergreen Cemetery in Oakland, CA. 412 unclaimed remains from this tragedy are buried at Evergreen. In August 2014, the cremains of 9 more people who died in Jonestown were found in a defunct funeral home in Dover, Delaware.[39] Perhaps, because our minds bury the tragedies, it has taken all these years to finally bury the last of the Jonestown victims.

Denominational oversight of The People's Temple might have saved the lives of almost a thousand people. To this day Jim Jones and The People's Temple remains the gruesome poster child of the negative power of non-denominational cultic pseudo-Christian influence. Strangely, the group did not end their days under a Christian cult leader, but rather under a communist-atheist-apocalyptic fearful man.

Witch Hunts in the 21st Century

I am still a Pentecostal by my beliefs – for the most part. It may not be true if the reference point is tradition, and praxis. I don't look like a typical Pentecostal, but that's a distinction to be made by those who know the finer points and would even care. Of course, the finer points are important to me.

I believe in what is called the Baptism with the Holy Spirit, and I believe that God is still in the miracle making business.

I believe that Pentecostalism (and her little sister, the Charismatic revival) has given more to the world of Christianity in the last hundred years than almost any other religious movement. This point would be difficult to disprove considering the phenomenal growth of the movement (which has grown to over 500 million in its short 100 year history), and the help it has offered to the poor.[40]

---

[39] http://www.usatoday.com/story/news/nation/2014/08/07/jonestown-massacre-victims-ashes-found-delaware/13725725/
[40] http://www.pewforum.org/2006/04/12/the-new-face-of-global-christianity-the-emergence-of-progressive-pentecostalism/

What it has given, unfortunately, falls into the categories of both good and evil.

Enter stage right: The witch children of the Congo – La Sorciers. And, if this is Pentecostalism, I am not Pentecostal. I do not regularly practice yelling at devils, because my prayers and spiritual communications are reserved for God. I do not pretend to know the names of evil spirits as some people. I do not map out cities with designated areas of spiritual intensity, because this is something some of my friends in Salem, Massachusetts and the UK who practice Witchcraft have been doing for decades, and I am not convinced it is accurate or helpful for Christian ministry. I do not assume that every difficulty in life and every stubborn habit is the fault of an evil spirit. These are not the trappings of my faith.

Steven Pinker outlines the history of Witchcraft accusation and the tragic tortures during the early modern times.[41] Today's Witches and Neo-Pagans call this season of history in Europe the Burning Times. Throughout the 1980s and 90s it was commonly declared among Neo-Pagans that millions of women died in these persecutions. Historian Ronald Hutton has given us a more reasonable number. The estimate has been more accurately adjusted to 35,000-60,000 people who were executed during the Witchcraze of the Burning Times.[42] A much smaller number. Still tragic.

Pentecostalism, and some of her Neo-Pentecostal stepsisters sometimes practice a superstitious folk magic syncretism. This has made itself most evident in the cities, the villages, and the slums of Africa. So called "deliverance ministries" with their emphasis on spiritual warfare and exorcism are far too common to be considered a passing phase, or a mere nuisance.

In the slums of Kinshasa, children as young as four years old have been accused of being witches. People claiming to have spiritual power to cast out demons charge money to perform exorcisms on the children. Often the so-called deliverance does not work the first time, and more money may be required to finish the supposedly long and difficult deliverance. Parents who cannot afford to pay the cost of these

---

[41] Steven Pinker, The Better Angels of Our Nature: Why Violence Has Declined, 2011 by Viking Penguin. I believe Pinker wrongly attributes the Burning Times to late medieval superstition, a kind of last gasp of Dark Age thinking. Most of the worst of the Burning Times is planted solidly in early modernity. There is strong evidence to suggest that many of those involved were not simply superstitious, uneducated people. If early modernity gives us some of the strangest and most brutal tortures and prejudices, it may significantly challenge Pinker's general thesis on the reason for the decline of violence.
[42] http://en.wikipedia.org/wiki/Witch-hunt - Execution_statistics

deliverance services are drained of the little money they have. Yet they press forward in hopes of ridding their lives of calamity and poverty. When the parents are told that the exorcisms did not work, parents may be encouraged to cast the child out of the home. These children are blamed for the ills of the household, and perhaps the whole neighborhood. Sick animals, sick people, drought, the loss of father's job, or the lack of food and water are all blamed upon curses the Witch Children supposedly bring to the village. When the community forces these children out of their homes, they are left to fend for themselves to survive.

Those who are beaten and chased away to survive on their own are sometimes the more fortunate among the Witch Children. Children have died during deliverance rituals. Parents have tried to saw the top of their children's heads off to release the demons residing in them. Others have had acid poured down their throats to chase away the evil spirits. They have been burned with fire, and skewered with hot pokers to "save" them from demons.

Are these children the offspring of Pentecostal doctrines on spiritual warfare? Have superstitions of American Pentecostals merged with the extended generations of African folk-magic to bring us "God-fearing" parents who torture, and then throw their own children out on the street? Are these the children of American Neo-Pentecostal superstition? Are we, am I somehow responsible?

These may be inflated numbers, but it has been estimated that there are 20,000 to 40,000 Witch Children, called La Sorciers, in the slums of Kinshasa alone.[43] The Congo is not the only nation accusing children, old women, and social outcasts of being Witches.

Helen Ukpabio is one of Nigeria's most famous women ministers. For years now, she has been at the heart of the witchcraft accusation craze, emphasizing the need for deliverance of children. Firstborn males are declared to carry a curse, like that of Cain, the firstborn of Adam and Eve; and Reuben, the first-born of Abraham. Although she denies abusing children who are accused of being witches, her sermons, exorcisms and even movies on the subject of child witches are evidence of an aggressive and superstitious approach. Her influence foments the already roiling fears and superstitions of a struggling continent. While editing this section, I revisited the website of her Liberty Foundation Gospel Ministries. On the front page was a banner linking to an event on November 11-17, 2013 called "Witches on the Run."[44]

---

[43] Mike Davis, Planet of Slums pg. 191, published by Verso 2006
[44] website homepage - http://www.libertyfoundationgospelministries.org/history.htm
The links have since disappeared and Helen Ukpabio had been hiding in the UK until recently. The primarily atheistic Ethical Society and similar organizations

The stories of ritual abuse, and even murder at the hands of so-called Christians who fearfully attempt to rid their neighbors and even their own kin of evil spirits is not limited to Africa. These terrors have been occurring in Asia, Oceania, and for the last dozen years – even in the UK as well.

This superstition has played into the hands of modern day slave traders who have taken advantage of the children cast out of their homes on accusation of witchcraft. Child witches are being taken off to labor in the cocoa fields, or are being sold into prostitution.

Denominational Pentecostal Christianity has been a partaker of these offenses. The eccentric and eclectic Pentecostal/Charismatic movement is often denominational, often non-denominational, and sometimes anti-denominational. The fact that the burgeoning Pentecostal movement has been responsible for some of the worst atrocities on the 20th century religious landscape highlights this point: denominations are not the only problem with Christianity.

Perhaps the Burning Times have not ended. They may be as severe today as any time in human history. These times of burning are burning our children, our grandmothers, the disenfranchised poor, and our hope for creating religious institutions of hope and trust.

The Non-Christian Religious Wrong

In the United States of America, September 11th is our yearly reminder of the connection to religion and violence. Images of the Twin Towers falling in massive clouds of smoke and dust are burnt upon our corporate retinae. We imagine troubled young men acting on the utopian promises of 72 dark-eyed virgins awaiting them in paradise. From the warrior-prophet who brought us Islam, to the holy wars in the times of the Crusades, to the recent growth of Al Qaeda, the American mind makes a quick connection to violence and Islam. These connections hardly need be reiterated. But, this connection to violence and abuse certainly cannot be found in the peaceful Eastern religions – can it?

Buddhism and Violence

> *"I've told my story more than a 100 times. More than a hundred times. What's the point? What has changed? Nothing has changed. Nothing."* – Ha Sang-Suk (Korean Comfort Woman)[45]

---

worked to have her removed from the country, and never be allowed to return. In April, 2014 she was apparently deported from the UK. For a screen shot of the advertisement go to http://burningreligion.com/2015/07/27/witches-on-the-run/

Chinese Scholar on the Japanese Comfort Women, Dr. Su Zhiliang believes (contrary to popular belief) that there were over 400,000 women forced to work as sex slaves for the Japanese army.

Japanese religion is an ancient amalgam of Shinto and Buddhism. Some historians believe that Buddhist practices were introduced to Japan as early as 538. Coming from the distant Nepal where Guatama Siddhartha was born in 5th or 6th BC.

As we weave forward through history 1,500 years, we find Zen Buddhist monks in Japan apologizing for the part Zen Buddhism played in WWII. Brian Victoria, a former Methodist missionary turned Buddhist priest and historian on the wartime activities of Japanese Buddhist leaders compiled the stories of atrocities in his book Zen at War. Victoria has been challenged on his scholarship in respect to the part Zen master D.T. Suzuki played during the War, but his books on the subject have given us a backroom view into the violent underpinnings of a Buddhist system, which supported and trained warriors for some of the worst atrocities of the 20th century.[46]

Ha Sang-Suk is a Korean living in China. When she was 12 years old she was kidnapped and taken to China to work as a sex slave offering "relief" to the Japanese military fighting in China. When the war was over, she remained in China due to her shame, and rebuilt her life there. Now, in her closing years she is part of the last remaining "Comfort Women" who were abused by Japanese military during the wars. Former Filipino, Korean, Chinese, and even Dutch women still await an apology and reparations from the Japanese government. Every Wednesday, Korean Comfort Women stand outside the Japanese embassy in Seoul, Korea awaiting the Japanese response. They have been holding this vigil every week since 1992. Their numbers are dwindling as they pass away, as of this writing only 55 remain, but the echoes of their pain will continue to haunt the corridors of history. It is not the Comfort Women, but Japan itself, and the Buddhist leadership of Japan who truly carry the shame.

While North America and Europe was necessarily focused on Germany's aggression and evil in World War II, Japan raped Nanking, forced children into sex slavery, and committed some of history's worst violence under the guiding hand of Buddhist masters.

I am finishing this small section on December 7th, the anniversary of the Pearl Harbor attack. It is shortly before 1pm in Asheville, NC

---

[45] Arirang Special: "Comfort Women" One Last Cry, March 1st, 2013 on Arirang TV, Korea: https://youtu.be/5yHHfYOGumI
[46] http://www.thezensite.com/ZenEssays/CriticalZen/Question_of_Scholarship.pdf

where I am writing. The Pearl Harbor Memorial Anniversary Tour is playing live in the background as I type. It coincides with the attack upon Pearl Harbor at 7:55am. I watch the moment of silence as it is observed. A ship, the USS Halsey, passes the USS Arizona memorial. The Captain salutes. The survivors of the Pearl Harbor attack salute back. A Buddhist reverend offers a prayer for peace and forgiveness as a representative for the Japanese Religious Community.

Attempts at reconciliation are noble, but some crimes have no limit to the cost of reparation. They stand as a grave reminder of the evil of religious self-justification.

If even the "peaceful religions" fail the test of goodness, what hope is there for religion in the future of humanity?

Are we left to assume that our only hope is secularism? Is humanity better off without God or religion in our future?

The Irreligious Wrong

Richard Dawkins recently suggested that being raised Catholic was potentially worse than sexual child abuse.[47] Some of the above stories make this accusation seem almost reasonable. Well, no, not really. Perhaps Dawkins has mistaken bizarre cruelties from history with the average Catholic parent living in his neighborhood.

With such a remarkably absurd position, I could not help but jokingly question on my Facebook page if being raised listening to Richard Dawkins was worse than child abuse.

Religion has its problems, but the lack of religion will not erase the world's woes. A look back at the 20th Century, and into contemporary social ills ought to make this fairly obvious.

What's so great about the Great Society?

Perhaps some day it will be taught in schools, that Pol Pot and Hitler killed their millions, Stalin killed his tens of millions, but Mao has exceeded them all.

Since the middle of the first decade in the 21st Century, the archives of the regional records from the reign of Mao Zedong, and the statistical data of his "Great Leap Forward" have begun to be released. From the years 1958 until 1962, Chairman Mao pressed the Chinese people into greater production in every respect possible with the goal of exceeding the production of Great Britain within 15 years.

---

[47] Interview by Al Jazeera interviewer Mehdi Hassan with Richard Dawkins, www.aljazeera.com/programmes/general/2012/12/2012121791038231381.html

According to the public records from the central government, an estimated 20 million people died during these few short years of the Great Leap Forward. The large part of the tragedy was blamed upon famine induced by natural disaster. Mao's hidden kingdom, isolated from the rest of the world and moving at breakneck speed toward innovation worked to increase production of food, steel, power, and goods of every kind.

In an attempt to do what Stalin could not, Mao believed he could create the most powerful socialist revolution through his communist ideals. All across the country, people were herded into communes. All personal property became the property of the state. Farmers were sent off to build massive dam projects for power and for irrigation of the arid land, and women and children were forced into the fields to do the work of their husbands and fathers. While the Chinese government lauded the successes of the Great Leap Forward, production of food dropped, the amount of arable land decreased and famine ensued. Mao pressured his leaders for more, for larger, for better results. As production dropped, expectations rose, and the people suffered. Turning a deaf ear toward the suffering of the people, force became the answer for better results. Pots and pans were taken from homes and melted down to increase steel production, and the villagers were fed in undersupplied community canteens.

During the Tiananmen Square massacre in 1989, Chen Yizi, a senior official for the Central Party fled to America. Chen claimed that unpublished investigations from the late 70's and 80's revealed between 42 and 46 million people died during this time. The preponderance of evidence now shows that disasters were primarily manmade, the result of poor planning, substandard building, and forced evacuations of people from their homes to establish this Great Leap Forward. During the great famine, not everyone died from starvation. People were beat to death by cadres for not performing up to expectation. Suicide dramatically increased due to sheer terror, and to the public shaming of those who were too weak to perform. Those who starved to death were often forced into starvation. As they became sick or weak, food was withheld for the stronger workers.

People sold their children to survive. As the government-created famine increased, cannibalism began. The dead were exhumed and cooked. Meanwhile China hid this force-fed tragedy from the world.

In Mao's Great Famine, Frank Dikötter ends with an estimation of death by famine, violence and other unnatural means at 50-60 million people between 1958 and 1962. These numbers do not include Mao's violent rise to power, or the rampage of purging from 1966 to 1971, which was benignly called the Cultural Revolution in which millions more would be persecuted, and millions more would die.[48]

A 1967 propaganda poster showed a Chinese Red Guard swinging his sledgehammer to crush a crucifix, a Buddha and classical Chinese texts. The poster reads, "Destroy the old world; Forge the new world."

Through the wild technological advances of the 20th century, if we have learned anything, perhaps it is that among other false panaceas for a better world, secularism is not the answer. Polpot, Stalin, and Mao are the most infamous Wanted Poster faces of secularized atrocity. Like organized and non-denominational religions of all sorts, secularism holds an abysmal record in its oversight of humanity. Our hope in secularism was burned with the same cruel torch that burned our hope in religion.

But at least science, and technological advance will give us the answers we need, right?

The "Opium War" on our Children

For a handful of years I worked in group homes for children. For a short season I was a liaison between a group home and the state.

I have sat with psychiatrists, and acted as the group home voice for children being prescribed psychotropic medications. I have sat on the opposite side of a half-door to the drug room dosing out morning and evening drugs to children from 8 to 18.

I have read the reference guides listing purposes for giving psychotropic drugs and the resulting side effects. I have seen these side effects take hold on children. I have seen psychiatrists prescribe drugs upon drugs to counteract the side effects, knowing they were attempting to modify behavior problems, while simultaneously creating physical and emotional side effects.

According to the laws of my state, a child has the right to refuse medication. In contradiction to this right, if a child did refuse medication, it was required to be written up as an "incident report." A certain number of incident reports, and a child would be sent away from the group home – typically to a psychiatric hospital, where medication was enforced.

Medication as behavior modification was regularly discussed at group home meetings. What we could not control was chemically altered into submission with drugs – drugs, many of which have not been tested and approved for use on children. Not all group homes appreciated this process, but they did all feel pressured by the state to

---

[48] Frank Dikötter, <u>Mao's Great Famine</u>, Bloomsbury Publishing Plc.

support the system driving it. Does the state become party to drug companies using children as test animals for their products? We have yet to see the full apocalypse of the results from years of chemical behavior modification. An inability to apply self-control to our own lives will certainly be a result, but perhaps not the only one.[49] Meanwhile, there are children who are being poisoned in the name of so-called science, and under the supposedly caring supervision of the medical community.

This same medical/psychological community is excessively careful to isolate religious content and extricate it from the places it might influence children. Religion, after all, is still considered by some to be the "opiate of the masses."

Have we come far enough to believe that actual opiates[50] are better for us than religion? Have medicine and science become false, cruel, and capricious gods demanding our allegiance at the hands of money hungry corporations with their agents acting as priests who offer us Paradise and give us Hell?

In the name of Science

It hardly seems necessary to list the experiments on human test subjects performed in the name of science, but the mention of a couple scientific tortures and killings should be evidence enough that scientists and doctors are not immune to evil tendencies. This further highlights the fact that education by itself does not evoke nobility, and science in the hands of broken people is not the panacea for the betterment of the human race.

The Aversion Project

From 1971 to 1989 the South African military attempted to cure homosexuals with electro-shock therapy. When this did not work, soldiers were treated with chemical castration, hormone therapy, and many were given gender reassignment against their will.[51]

Unit 731

---

[49] Psychiatric drugs and violence review of FDA data - http://www.psychologytoday.com/blog/mad-in-america/201101/psychiatric-drugs-and-violence-review-fda-data-finds-link
[50] I understand that not all drugs are opiates, but I could not resist this play on words. Chalk this one up to poetic license.
[51] http://www.mrc.ac.za/healthsystems/aversion.pdf

General Shirō Ishii was the chief medical officer of the Japanese army during World War II. His unit, called Unit 731 is responsible for the some of the most heinous experiments on human subjects in history. From 1939 to 1945, Unit 731[52] set up camps in the occupied territory of Manchuria, and from these camps conducted experiments on Chinese, Russian, and Korean prisoners of war and civilians. Prisoners were infected with diseases and plagues. The effects of the infections were monitored, and when the prisoners died, they were dissected for information. In some cases, the prisoners were dissected without anesthesia while still living. Other prisoners had body parts frozen, and tests were made on methods for treating frostbite. Weapons were tested on live subjects, who were tied to stakes. The effects of germ bombs, chemical weapons, and explosives were tested on the live targets at various distances and different positions. Women were infected with venereal diseases via rape, and serum, and were vivisected to measure internal reaction to the diseases. They were forcefully impregnated to determine the transmission of the diseases to the children.

In order to anesthetize the sensibilities of the soldiers, doctors and nurses involved with the experimentation, prisoners were called "maruta", meaning "logs." They were treated as though they were simply fuel for the fire.

At the close of the war, General Ishii was granted immunity by the United States (under the leadership of General MacArthur), in order to gain access to the results of these trials, which the US knew they would never be able to conduct themselves.

Today, we use the information from General Ishii's frostbite studies on patients with severe frostbite cases in our hospitals.

In the name of science, history's worst criminals became the leaders of a generation of pioneers in the field of science.[53]

None righteous, no, not one

Whether it is denominational Christianity, non-denominational Christianity, other religious expressions, secular societies, or science and medicine, this one thing should be obvious: the great evils do not necessarily rise from the systems themselves, but from the individuals who control the systems. The power of evil appears to be less inherent to organizations, and more intrinsic to the individuals who manipulate the systems. In saying this, I am not making observations on specific

---

[52] https://en.wikipedia.org/wiki/Unit_731
[53] http://www.unit731.org/

philosophical and theological tenets. I am making the simple observation that grand evil resides in every form of human community, belief, praxis, and worldview.

If there is systemic evil, it resides in human hearts and minds. It rises up in an inharmonious cacophony among people who band together to suppress others. It is not intrinsic to religious, secular, or scientific communities. That, at least is my conclusion, and if it is true, it may be that the early Christian Church Fathers Irenaeus and Augustine had a point when they formalized the doctrine of original sin.

Tales from the Land of Jaw: The Adventures of Gwyn Dee
The Heeling Stones

*T*he small village of Heeling sat alongside the wide, wide road. Tucked into the tight crevice of a small oasis in the rocky desert, surrounded by the sharp red granite cliffs and tumbled stones amidst scrubby oaks it looked like a piece of hidden paradise. Heeling was sheltered in the shade of its valley, and welcomed passersby with a peaceful, earthen Gargantuan smile.

Gwyn Dee stared into the valley. The days of slow trudging journey since the battle for the Gates of the Kingdom, and the death of the elder of the Clown Caste all wore together until Gwyn Dee could not remember if it had been a few short days or a fortnight. How many suns and moons had passed were lost in the haze of grief, confusion, and weariness.

Another traveler passed by quickly, silently and glanced at the valley with the eyes of a small rodent sneaking behind the cat. Before Gwyn Dee could speak to the traveler, a jovial well-dimpled woman with smiling eyes and a soft soothing voice appeared almost magically from the little valley.

"Welcome. May we offer you refuge from the weary labors I see upon your countenance? A cool drink? A little respite from your travels?" The jovial well-dimpled woman smiled a little larger, "We are a watering-hole and rest stop for many a weary traveler. In fact, some have found a new home here, and have never left."

Gwyn Dee followed like a tired lost puppy as the jovial well-dimpled woman led the way into the sheltered oasis. The narrow entrance to the valley was covered with overhanging oak trees, gentle dripping water from the red rocks, and a subtly hidden, but comfortable wooden house spanning the valley entrance from cliff edge to cliff edge, acting like a homey gate to the valley behind it. The doors to the house seemed to open of their own accord, and the jovial well-dimpled woman escorted Gwyn Dee inside.

A cool sweet drink was handed to Gwyn Dee, and as it passed from lip to tongue to throat to belly it came with a gentle, unnatural euphoric calm.

"Sit for awhile. Put your feet up. We will escort you through our peaceful home when your weary bones are ready."

A large well-stuffed chair with a well-stuffed ottoman in the corner looked out to falling water and soft ferns growing from the cliffs. The pattering sounds and cool air drifted with Gwyn Dee to a long, dark, and restless sleep.

It might have been an hour. It could have been days. Gwyn Dee woke with a start. Somewhere deep in a dream, a scream, which indeterminably could have been in ecstasy, or could have been in pain, snapped Gwyn Dee out of the deep dark sleep.

Still feeling the fog of slumber, Gwyn Dee looked around to find the jovial well-dimpled woman smiling nearby. Before words could be formed on the lips, tea and dried fruits appeared. In a short time, Gwyn Dee felt awake and nervously excited about nothing in particular, and wondered about this strange feeling.

The jovial well-dimpled woman led Gwyn Dee out into the valley of Heeling. What had appeared from the road to be a narrow valley suddenly opened up into a wide and wonderful oasis trapped in a round valley of high red stone cliffs, and trickling streams and waterfalls falling into cool clear pools.

"Welcome to the Valley of Heeling, Gwyn Dee. Many of the Clown Caste have been here for restoration over the years." Gwyn Dee wondered how the jovial well-dimpled woman was privy to this information, but was quickly diverted by the next words. "Our healing stones have been a resource of blessing and restorative power for generations now. Perhaps it will be the same for you, in your short visit."

The mention of stones, and the reminder of the stone shoes of Cominkingville stirred dark memories from the not so distant past. Gwyn Dee glanced upward to the cliff faces all around, and saw a network of small caves with access by ladders and wooden walkways.

"Yes. Those are the famous caves of Heeling. This is where people re-find themselves, discover wholeness, and their true destiny." Her

words wove through Gwyn Dee's mind like the fingers of a masseuse kneading a knotted back.

A thin prematurely grayed middle-aged man sat by a large deep pool stirring the water with his fingers, and staring into the broken reflection. The jovial well-dimpled woman gently cleared her throat, and the thin prematurely grayed middle-aged man looked up, and smiled a genuine, but slightly hollow smile.

"This is Gwyn Dee, of high nobility from Cominkingville. Perhaps your story of hope and peace could serve to introduce our little valley to this most notable visitor."

Gwyn Dee grimaced at such a regal introduction, but the thin prematurely grayed middle-aged man responded as though his mind had suddenly snapped to attention with the discipline of a soldier on duty. He smiled a large smile, queerly like the jovial well-dimpled woman, and began to tell his tale with the skill of the best storytellers of the Clown Caste. He wove a tale of sorrow and loss, of abuse and injury, and of an eventual discovery of the Valley of Heeling and the healing stones, but before his tale could come to an end a piercing scream echoed through the valley. Gwyn Dee recognized the scream as the same from the dream and the first waking moments.

Responding with the quickness and grace of a gazelle, Gwyn Dee ran for the caves and the direction of the still echoing scream. The excited fogginess had suddenly disappeared as Gwyn Dee ran to help the screamer.

The jovial well-dimpled woman shouted with the joviality lost in her voice, "Let them be! The healing stones must do their work!"

At ground level, a small cave held the prisoner. "Prisoner," is at least, the best way to describe the visitor to the famous Caves of Heeling. A young man wearing only a loincloth and a pair of sandals was on his knees doubled over with his face to the ground, and a heavy stone yoke around his neck. Over the young man, a large robed man with a wooden staff stood.

"Heel!" the large robed man shouted, and swung the staff to beat the back of the young man in the loincloth.

Before the staff could strike, Gwyn Dee caught it, twisted it out the hands of large robed man, and spun around cracking his head and knocking him cold. The formerly jovial well-dimpled woman appeared at the door of the small cave, gasped in horror, and prepared to shout for help. Gwyn Dee quickly poked the formerly jovial well-dimpled woman in her ample belly, and sent her butt first into a small pool sputtering, and coughing.

Pulling the stone yoke off the young man in the loincloth, Gwyn Dee shouted, "Run! Run for your life!" and the young man in loincloth ran for the house and the exit from the Valley of Heeling.

Gwyn Dee climbed to the next cave to find a wrinkled old woman under a heavy yoke. Gwyn Dee entered the cave, and began to lift the yoke off her neck. The wrinkled old woman screamed, "What are you doing? How dare you steal my stone of healing!"

Perplexed, but undaunted, Gwyn Dee went from cave to cave searching for prisoners in the famous Caves of Heeling, but in cave after cave people young and old were in stages of groaning caught between pain and ecstasy refusing to be released. One under a pile of weighty stones, another bowed over by the stone yoke, one walking painfully about with stone anklets, another with large stones chained to his body, and yet another wearing a massive stone hat clamped with iron straps to her head – they all refused help.

The formerly jovial well-dimpled woman had now extracted herself from the pool, and was calling for help. Strong men from all the over the Valley of Heeling came running, but none of them were quick enough for Gwyn Dee, who scrambled across the wooden walkways, leaped to the roof of the house at the entrance of the valley, and swung through the trees to safety. Coming to the wide, wide road Gwyn Dee looked back to see the formerly jovial well-dimpled woman, and her strong men standing at the door of the house scowling.

Gwyn Dee turned down the wide, wide road and a mile down came to a Weathered Old Blacksmith. He held a chisel in one hand and sledgehammer in the other. The young man in the loincloth sat exhausted and panting in the scraggly grass beneath a lone oak tree, carefully sipping water from a water-skin.

"I see you've escaped the Valley of Heeling unburdened." The Weathered Old Blacksmith smiled. "Most people arrive needing their Heeling Stones removed."

Gwyn Dee joined the young man in the loincloth, and promptly fell asleep under the lone oak.

EVERYONE HAS IT RIGHT

> *"It was the best of times, it was the worst of times, it was the age of wisdom, it was the age of foolishness, it was the epoch of belief, it was the epoch of incredulity, it was the season of Light, it was the season of Darkness, it was the spring of hope, it was the winter of despair, we had everything before us, we had nothing before us, we were all going direct to Heaven, we were all going direct the other way - in short, the period was so far like the present period, that some of its noisiest authorities insisted on its being received, for good or for evil, in the superlative degree of comparison only."*
> – Charles Dickens, <u>A Tale of Two Cities</u> *(but you knew that, didn't you?)*

Dickens opening words to <u>A Tale of Two Cities</u> is one of the most famous opening paragraphs in literary history. It seems fitting to use these words as I open the second chapter in the second section of this book, and close out my grindingly simple segments of historical examples of evil human behavior and look toward the noble side of humanity. Dickens seems to have conveyed the entirety of my thoughts to this point in his brilliant opening. His words resonate through history and reach our ears today. They still ring true today as they did for the French Revolution, "in short, the period was so far like the present period".

After having run through the history of atrocities committed in the name of many different groups, I had to hunt more vigorously for the compassionate, self-sacrificing noble side behaviors among the same people groups.

I desperately want to misquote Dickens and say, "These were the best of people, these were the worst of people," and I want to attach those words to you, and to myself.

Follow me as I look away from the litany of our evils, and search for glowing gems encrusted within the dark underbelly of our history.

When The Right is Right

During my short writing sabbatical in Asheville, North Carolina I jump ahead to study for this chapter. It is a few days after Thanksgiving. Yesterday, I attended the First Baptist Church of Asheville. During the offertory, the pastor highlighted the number of meals the church served on Thanksgiving. 270 meals were served, and 20 more families received food supplies to hold the Thanksgiving meal in their home. This was one of at least four churches serving free meals in Asheville during the week.

In Robert Putnam's book Bowling Alone, he describes his analysis of the 1996 National Election Survey with these words,

> *"In one survey of twenty-two different types of voluntary associations, from hobby groups to professional associations to veterans groups to self-help groups to sports clubs to service clubs, it was membership in religious groups that was most closely associated with other forms of civic involvement, like voting, jury service, community projects, talking with neighbors, and giving to charity."*[54]

In other words, actively religious people are on average the most active givers, doers, and volunteers in the community. The most common factor among people, who served and donated to voluntary associations of all kinds, whether religious or secular, was membership in a church, a synagogue, or a mosque.

Small, and personal social action is the strength of a local religious group. Faith communities find a way to give, and teach and help in their community, but there are times the Christian church and its people have stretched out their hands in large and noble ways to help those suffering under the cruel hammer of history.

A Short Reprieve for the Waldensians

Although oppression and poverty have been used by the rich and powerful as a means of suppression of the smaller peoples of this world, there are noble leaders who have given up everything as protectors for those they rule.

Francois Rabelais was a medieval French scholar, and would become one of what would be called by Francois-Rene de Chateaubriand, "the mother-geniuses" of the world's writers.[55] Rabelais' wild, bawdy, and grotesque tales in Gargantua and Pantagruel are among the most influential writings in French literature. What Shakespeare was for English, Dante for Italian, and Homer for Greek, Rabelais was for the French language. Rabelais lived during dangerous times. Yet his tales poked fun at the rich and powerful as well as the common man on the street, but through all his biting and typically crude satirical wit, Rabelais hid great praise for one leader inside the tales of his carnival stories.

---

[54] Robert D. Putnam, Bowling Alone (Kindle Locations 1027-1030). Simon & Schuster. Kindle Edition
[55] Mikhail Bahktin, Rabelais and His World, pg. 123.

Rabelais' survival during the tumultuous Reformation times was most likely due to the protection of his employers – the powerful brothers, Cardinal Jean Du Bellay and the statesman/military man Guillaume du Bellay (aka Seigneur de Langey). In 1542, Rabelais followed Guillaume du Bellay to the Piedmont region in what is now Northern Italy, and was a witness to Bellay's great kindness and generosity towards the persecuted Waldensian people who made the remote mountain region of the Piedmont their home. Bellay was a strict disciplinarian and demanded that the military forces under his care treat the people of the region well. During a famine, Bellay spent his own fortune having grain shipped into the Piedmont to feed the people.[56] The Catholic Bellay became the protector and benefactor to this religious sect, which had suffered for three centuries under intense persecution by the Catholic Church.

Guillaume du Bellay died only a year later in 1543, and Rabelais stood by his deathbed. Bellay was a rich man who died poor, with debts greater than his assets. There was very little left for his heirs, and not enough to pay Rabelais the pension, which had been willed to him.

The Piedmont Easter, and the following wars against the Waldensians were still to come, but during the rule of Guillaume du Bellay in the Piedmont, the Waldensians had a short reprieve under a Catholic protector who spent all of his own fortune to ensure their safety, their health, and the benefit of their local economy.

The normally satirical and famously critical Rabelais would memorialize Guillaume du Balley in the third book of <u>Gargantua and Pantagruel</u>. Though Bellay is not listed by name, his actions as a leader are praised in these passages. Pantagruel acts as a wise and kind leader, even spending all his money to help a conquered people. Today we know these words are a memorial to the kindness of Guillaume du Balley the Seigneur de Langey, who, when assigned the duty of overseeing the troubled Piedmont region and the persecuted Waldensian people, treated them as though they were his own family.

> *"Like a child, conquered people must be allowed a new freedom to suckle at the breast, to be rocked and soothed in their cradles, to play and enjoy themselves. Like newly planted trees, they need to be supported, made secure, defended against all storms, and injuries, and disasters. Like someone rescued from a long, threatening illness. And just entering convalescence, they must be fussed over, treated with infinite kindness, restored."*[57]

---

[56] Mikhail Bakhtin, <u>Rabelais and His World</u>, pg. 450.
[57] Francois Rabelais, <u>Gargantua and Pantagruel</u>, translation by Burton Raffel, 1990 W.W. Norton and Company, Book 3, Chapter 1, pg. 248

The Abused and Forgotten Hero

A dilapidated mansion, looking like a set for a ghostly Disney mystery movie, sits on a corner in the Portuguese village of Cabanas de Viriato. A sign on the corner points to Cristo Rei, the monument of Christ the King with outstretched arms. The King of Belgium gifted this statue to the community. It looks down upon the once stately 19th century mansion.

In 1954, a penniless man died in a Franciscan Hospital in Lisbon. Because of his traitorous actions during World War II, he lost his job, and was denied the ability to practice his trade. His family was spurned by the nation, and his 15 children were denied access to higher education. Eventually they left their homeland and scattered across the globe in shame. His family's troubles had begun 15 years earlier.

In November of 1939, Circular 14 was released by the Portuguese leader, António de Oliveira Salazar – during the early days of World War II. Circular 14 directed diplomats to deny passage into Portugal for Jews, Russians, and people who for any reason could not return to their state of origin. Circular 14 placed Portugal on the side of Germany during the Great War, but a Portuguese diplomat stationed in Bordeaux, France refused to follow orders.

Citing his Catholic faith as the reason to disobey Circular 14, Portuguese consul Aristides de Sousa Mendes addressed his staff. They documented these words, "I cannot allow all you people to die. Many of you are Jews, and our constitution clearly states that neither the religion nor the political beliefs of foreigners can be used as a pretext for refusing to allow them to stay in Portugal. I've decided to be faithful to that principle, but I shan't resign for all that. The only way I can respect my faith as a Christian is to act in accordance with the dictates of my conscience."[58]

Europeans began to flee their countries for safety from the coming Nazi onslaught. Mendes set up a production line for creating visas, and in a two-week period in June 1940 issued 30,000 visas. Then he personally stood at the border to ensure passage for these same people.

Of the 30,000 visas, 12,000 were to Jews. The entire Belgian cabinet, Hollywood actor Robert Montgomery, and artist Salvadore Dali were also among those offered sanctuary through Mendes' sacrificial disobedience to the dictator of his own country.

The thousands of families who were saved by his heroic actions – actions driven by his Catholic faith – are questioning how Schindler's

---

[58] The Independent, Sunday, October 17, 2010
http://www.independent.co.uk/news/people/profiles/sousa-mendes-saved-more-lives-than-schindler-so-why-isnt-he-a-household-name-too-2105882.html

List of 1,100 people got a blockbuster movie, and the Mendes' family home still sits forgotten in ruins. In 2009 Joël Santoni directed the film Désobèir[59] about Mendes.

After all these years, the home is back in the hands of the Mendes family, and there are plans to raise the money to restore it. The goal is to turn it into a museum, and a memorial for this Holocaust hero, whom we can imagine in an eternal mansion in a better place today.[60]

Portuguese dictator Salazar ostracized and severely persecuted Mendes and his family for their father's actions, and the hero died a silent and ignoble death in 1954.

While Aristides de Sousa Mendes worked feverishly in Bordeaux in 1940 to grant asylum to the fleeing, fearful masses, a new Pope in Rome appeared to remain silent about Hitler's policies toward the Jewish people, or at least that's what we've been told.

Pius or Impious?

In 1943, Der Fuhrer devised a plan to kidnap the Pope and bring him to Germany. According to evidence outlined by Gordon Thomas, Hitler was obsessed with kidnapping the Pope, and was hindered by his own people in Italy who viewed the idea as madness. Hitler ranted in July 1943 that he intended to go into the Vatican and "clean out that gang of swine."[61]

Pope Pius XII has been called Hitler's Pope and has been demonized by his detractors as just another silent authority refusing to speak out against the atrocities committed upon the Jewish people. The stories from the Vatican appear to contradict this demonization of Pius XII, and the sealed Vatican records from WWII are now coming to light. Vatican records are released 75 years after their date, which means that in 2014, records from 1939 were newly being released. And here are some things we know about the work of Pope Pius XXI during the war:

- Pope Pius XII assigned Irish priest Monsignor Hugh O'Flaherty, who was set up in the Vatican throughout the war, to create and communicate with a network of monasteries concerning the care and protection of the persecuted Jews.

---

[59] trailer for the film Désobéir: https://youtu.be/cZQFjBi7Eio
[60] You can donate to the cause of helping rebuild the mansion and spread this story at http://sousamendesfoundation.org/how-can-i-help/
[61] Gordon Thomas, The Pope's Jews: The Vatican's Secret Plan to Save Jews from the Nazis, pg. 146). St. Martin's Press. Kindle Edition.

- He personally hid a small number of Jews in his own residence, and when they were granted visas to escape the persecution, he gave each family $1,000 from his personal account.
- He was trapped between open and public denouncements of Hitler, which would potentially condemn all German Catholics to Hitler's wrath and ensure the German invasion of the Vatican, and remaining silent while establishing a secret network of help behind the scenes.
- After the war, even Israeli authorities like Golda Meir praised the Pope for his work helping the Jews.

There were some rogue priests who helped German officers evade the hand of justice following the war, but a wholesale demonization of the Catholic Church during WWII is not supportable by the evidence. Secretly, plans were enacted during the war to create a network of safety for the Jewish people. It may never be fully acknowledged that the leader of the world's largest church stood in solidarity with the Jewish people during the most dangerous time in European history.

Ion Mihai Pacepa, a defected Romanian 3 star general alleged that in the early 60s, Krushchev set up a secret plan code-named "Seat-12" to portray Pope Pius XII as a Nazi sympathizer.[62] This supposedly led to the 1964 stage play in New York City entitled "The Deputy, a Christian Tragedy." It was translated into 20 languages, and began a sixty-year struggle for truth concerning the work of the Pope Pius XII during WWII.[63]

The Pastor and the Imam

Pastor James Wuye has one hand. The other hand has been replaced by a plastic replica. He lost his right hand fighting his Muslim enemies. He is a Nigerian Pentecostal Pastor in the embattled city of Kaduna.

Imam Muhammad Ashafa is a Muslim cleric in the same city. He lost his mentor and teacher to the violence of Christian soldiers attacking his Muslim people, and Pastor James was a leader among those Christian fighters.

Once they were sworn enemies. For three years, Ashafa was looking for a way to kill Pastor James, and Pastor James held a deep bitterness in his heart, because of his injuries at the hands of Muslim fighters. Today, they are sworn friends. In 1995, they established the Muslim-

---

[62] This information about the Russian connection is disputed, but in active debate. See https://en.wikipedia.org/wiki/Seat_12
[63] Gordon Thomas, The Pope's Jews, pg. 286.

Christian Dialogue Forum. In 2002, they helped craft and sign the Kaduna Peace Declaration with other Christian and Muslim leaders. Together they represent the dangerous position of living as men of peace in regions filled with violence. Their wives regularly worry that their husbands may not return home after an outing to foster peace. Yet, these men view their mission as necessary to the survival of a generation.

"Dialogue is all about talking to the person 'across the red line'", says Pastor Wuye. "Talking, talking, and talking some more."[64]

You can watch the trailer to a movie about these two heroes.

Heroes in Scarves

Islam suffers under severely bad press today, perhaps more than any other religion in the world. The violent outbreaks across the globe, which have occurred in the name of Allah, have biased a generation against the Muslim people. Islam struggles from within for stability, but beneath the violence, there are heroes emerging from the midst of tragedy.

Somalia had become a violently out of control country. Humanitarian non-governmental organizations (NGOs) were fleeing the country. Their workers and volunteers were being killed and kidnapped. In October of 2008, 52 NGOs still working in Somalia wrote a letter about the rapidly increasing humanitarian crisis, and called for help from the international community.[65] Over 30% of the total population was displaced due to ongoing civil war. 1.1 million people out of the 3.25 million in the country were in need of emergency aid.

Heroes wear uniforms, or capes. They carry weapons, or vanquish their foes by brute force – or so we've been taught by history and fantasy literature. But in the midst of this violent crisis, the hero of the disenfranchised Somali people wore a scarf and was armed with a stethoscope.

During the famine in the early 1990s, Dr. Hawa Abdi formed a camp for refugees. Women and children were pouring into her family farm. A hospital was built, and soon thousands were coming to the camp for help.

---

[64] See more at: http://www.kaiciid.org/news-events/news/voices-dialogue-co-founders-nigerias-interfaith-mediation-centre-share-their-story - sthash.vuId1xif.dpuf

[65] http://www.oxfamamerica.org/press/statement-by-52-ngos-working-in-somalia-on-rapidly-deteriorating-humanitarian-crisis/

By 2010 insurgents controlled the area surrounding Mogadishu, and Dr. Hawa Abdi found herself standing against a rebel army. Early in the morning in May 2010, a group of teenage gunmen from an Islamist militia came to the camp of refugees, and demanded control of the camp, "Because you are a woman," they said.[66] She stood up to them, and surprisingly they backed down, but only long enough to return with 750 angry armed soldiers. The hospital was looted and destroyed, and Dr. Hawa was held hostage in her own home, but soon her home was swarmed with thousands of women who had been helped by the doctor. They slept on her floor, and all around her house as a protection against the insurgents. Community support was so strong that the Islamist militia backed down, but in doing so they demanded strict Islamist rules be kept. Recognizing that this represented a step backwards for the rights of Somali women, Dr. Hawa refused the demands, and instead made her own demands upon the army. She demanded an apology. A woman brandishing a headscarf demanded an apology from an army with guns, and with the power of her popularity, she got that apology.

Today Dr. Hawa's family farm is home to 90,000 displaced people. She and her two daughters run the hospital and manage the camp. They have only two rules for managing the camp: 1) There are to be no clan or political distinctions, and 2) men cannot beat their wives. The men who do beat their wives end up in a jail Dr. Hawa had built for that very purpose. During a TED Talk Dr. Deqo Mohamed, the daughter of Dr. Hawa, described their daily workload as, "300 patients, 20 surgeries, and 90,000 people to manage."[67]

When Salvation Came from the Atheists

Harrowing times create heroes, and perhaps give us the clearest evidence that there is something innately good in people. Responses seem automatic during the darkest hours. A hero may not even be able to tell you why they did what they did. They may not be able to express the thoughts going through their minds in the moments of crisis, because their responses are automatic.

The Righteous Among the Nations title given by the State of Israel has been awarded to more than 10,000 non-Jewish people who helped save Jews during World War II. An archive of information tells the stories of regular people doing heroic things. A database created by Yad Vashem retells the tales of heroism for all of us to hear and see.[68]

---

[66] Griswold, Eliza (2010-08-17). The Tenth Parallel: Dispatches from the Fault Line Between Christianity and Islam (p. 141). Farrar, Straus and Giroux. Kindle Edition
[67] www.ted.com/talks/mother_and_daughter_doctor_heroes_hawa_abdi_deqo_mohamed

Studies by Paul J. Zak at the Center for Neuroeconomics Studies at Claremont Graduate University suggest that telling stories may chemically alter our brains.[69] If this is so, heroic stories may help create heroes, and Yad Vashem is helping make heroes out of regular people.

Tineke Buchter is one of those stories. She was born in Holland in 1920 in a socialist atheist family. She and her mother would be named "Righteous Among the Nations."

Tineke (aka Dr. Tina Strobos) and her mother helped shelter over 100 Jews in their home in Amsterdam, during the Nazi occupation of the Netherlands. Tina Strobos died in 2012 at the age of 91. When she recalled the years of the War, one captures a sense of the automatic heroic goodness of Dr. Strobos. There was no question in her mind as a young woman whether she should help the Jewish people escape from the Gestapo's search through Amsterdam. There was no thought in her mother's mind whether they should open their home to fleeing Jews. Over the course of the five years of Nazi occupation, Tina worked with the Dutch resistance to find homes to temporarily house fleeing people, and supply money and food to those in need. Meanwhile the Gestapo regularly visited them to threaten and search their house.

Tina Strobos lived only a few blocks from the house where Anne Frank and her family were hiding. She spoke of feeling guilty for years for not knowing that Anne was in hiding nearby, because she was sure she could have used her network to get Anne and her family to safety.

The obvious inherent heroic goodness in this atheist family bleeds through the simple words of Tina Strobos, and it reminds us that in a world of great evil, there are people who will respond with automatic self-sacrificing heroism when they are needed. These people come from every nation, every belief system and every ethnic group. This ought to remind us that good and evil are not inherent to religion or to secular society.[70] Rather the potential for great good resides within the people in the systems, and someday you may owe your life to someone who is radically "other" than you. You just might get saved by an atheist.

Generosity from Every Tribe

Dobri Dobrev is a centenarian, who at his ripe old age, travels by train every day into the city of Sophia to beg. He is known as Elder Dobri, or the Saint of Bailovo. He gives away all his earnings to the

---

[68] http://www.yadvashem.org/yv/en/righteous/index.asp
[69] http://greatergood.berkeley.edu/article/item/how_stories_change_brain
[70] Dr. Tina Strobos tells her story:
http://www.ushmm.org/wlc/en/media_oi.php?ModuleId=10005185&MediaId=2962

church. This humble beggar has been the largest supporter of the Orthodox Cathedral in Sophia.[71]

Wang Zhiyou is known in China as the generous beggar. For over 15 years, he has traveled, begged, and given away the money he earns begging to people he deems more needy than himself. December of 2014, Wang could be found in Mengcheng raising money to pay the bills for a three-year-old with cancer.[72]

Where Nobodies are Somebody: Postman's Park

A quaint park is hidden on Saint Martin Le-Grand not far from the Museum of London. It is not easy to find. I knew what I was looking for, and still had a difficult time spotting the small gate leading into the park, which is sandwiched between the tall buildings. Because the civil servants ate their lunch at this location over a century ago, it is named for them. Postman's Park is also home to the Watts Gallery. Fifty-four tiles tell sad but heroic stories of common people who lost their lives in the act of trying to save someone else. Men, women and children who ran into fires, fell victim to drowning, or were hit by trains, while saving or trying to save others are listed on these tiles.

George Frederic Watts was the painter/sculptor/philanthropist who dreamed of this Memorial to Heroic Self-Sacrifice, and after years of lobbying it finally became a reality in 1900, when he was too sick to attend the opening.

120 spaces were laid out against a wall at the park for the placement of memorial tiles commemorating the sacrificial acts of common people attempting to save the lives of others. By 1931, fifty-three of these spaces had been filled. Then the wall stood silent and unchanged for seventy-eight years. The fifty-fourth name was added in 2009. The latest memorial tile reads,

> *"Leigh Pitt, Reprographic Operator, Aged 30,*
> *saved a drowning boy from the canal at Thamesmead,*
> *but sadly was unable to save himself.*
> *June • 7 • 2007."*

In the movie "Closer", Natalie Portman played a woman who took one of the names on the tiles at Postman's Park, and created a false identity for herself around the name of Alice Ayres.

The real Alice Ayres was a hard working young housemaid, who lived and worked for the Chandler's – her older sister's family. They

---

[71] http://saintdobry.com/elder-dobry-from-baylovo/
[72] http://www.chinadaily.com.cn/china/2014-12/16/content_19093183.htm

lived together above the oil and paint store owned by the Chandlers. On the night of April 24, 1885 a fire broke out in the shop, and trapped the family upstairs. Alice appeared at the window while a crowd below formed, and they shouted for her to jump, but instead she disappeared into the flames to try and save the children. Alice Ayres was twenty-five. Her death would gain national attention in the UK, at a time of growing concern over conditions of the common worker during the Industrial Revolution.

Her story would help create the momentum for George Frederic Watts' passion to develop the Memorial to Heroic Self-Sacrifice. In 1887, Watts wrote about Alice Ayres in a plea to create the memorial space:

> *"The roll would be a long one, but I would cite as an example the name of Alice Ayres, the maid of all work at an oilmonger's in Gravel-lane, in April, 1885, who lost her life in saving those of her master's children.*
>
> *The facts, in case your readers have forgotten them, were shortly these:— Roused by the cries of "Fire" and the heat of the fiercely advancing flames the girl is seen at the window of an upper story, and the crowd, holding up some clothes to break her fall, entreat her to jump at once for her life. Instead she goes back, and reappears dragging a feather bed after her, which, with great difficulty, she pushes through the window. The bed caught and stretched, the girl is again at the window, a child of three in her arms, which with great care and skill she throws safely upon the mattress. Twice again with still older children she repeats the heroic feat. When her turn comes to jump, suffocated or too exhausted by her efforts, she cannot save herself. She jumps, but too feebly, falls upon the pavement, and is carried insensibly to St. Thomas's Hospital, where she dies."*[73]

Seventy-six spots remain open on the memorial wall. It is not difficult to find the names to fill those spaces. There are some people who are pretenders, trying to take on the persona of a self-sacrificing hero, but others are made of the simple stuff from which real heroes are crafted. Famous people, rich people, unknown people, and poor people from every tribe, religion and non-religion under the sky have self-sacrificing heroes among their numbers, and there are not enough memorials in the world to memorialize these micro-saints around us.

> *No soldier nor sailor by land or sea*
> *In the bed of honour laid.*

---

[73] George Frederic Watts, Another Jubilee Suggestion, 5 Sep 1887

> *Was ever more great of heart than she,*
> *That simple serving maid.*[74]

It would be a shame to wait for heaven in order for us to see the canonization of the common man and woman to occur.

Saved by Scientists

Stories from modern science seem like miracle cures when seen in the light of centuries of human suffering, and poverty. The development of anesthesia in 1846 helped make surgery safer and more effective. Pasteurization discovered in 1863 has helped to stave off food poisoning, and has lengthened the shelf life of products, thus increasing food supply. Electricity was harnessed in the late 19th century, and our world will never be the same. Communication began its rapid innovation in 1876 with the telephone, and today we can communicate almost anywhere in the world in what we now call "real time." Manned flight developed in 1903 made our world a smaller and more accessible place. Penicillin (1928) and the Polio vaccine (1952) have helped eradicate disease.

These wonderful inventions and discoveries from the realm of modern science have changed the world for the better and saved millions of lives. This fact is used by some people to declare that religion's usefulness in the world has come to an end, if indeed, they surmise, religion had any good purpose ever.

Arguments against religion, using tragic examples from religious leaders abusing their power are contrasted with the successes of modern science, but such comparisons are not equal. As shown in the previous chapter on the evil activities from the past, science and religion are similar to one another in a fundamental sense: They are nothing without people to activate their resources. Religion is nothing without its practitioners. Science is nothing without scientists and laborers. Both religion and science are dumb and silent without practitioners of their arts. Sometimes they have worked together to help change the world, as when science gives us medical innovation to heal the sick and infirmed, and religion builds and staffs a hospital to accommodate the resources of medical science. Other times they seem to be at odds with one another.

It is my contention that science and religion (as generic categories) are neither good nor evil, but the people who wield power in the respective fields determine the quality and nature of the outcomes.

---

[74] Alice Ayres, Poem by Emilia Aylmer Blake, 1886

Josef Mengele and General Ishii's Unit 731 show us the most repulsive side of the use of science. The atomic bomb, and biological weaponry show us some of the most devastating uses of scientific advances. Thus the accurate comparisons between religion and science require comparisons and contrasts of religious people and scientists. As observed in the previous chapter, neither science nor religion offers a panacea for a better world. The corruptibility of both systems could kill us, but as seen in this chapter, people of great nobility reside in the religious community, and sacrificially offer themselves for the sake of saving others. Can we also find this nobility in the scientific community?

The complexity of looking for nobility or evil actions within the scientific community is that people of all worldviews work in the scientific community. Although the stories represent science correcting itself through the sacrificial actions of individuals, it does not distinguish the worldviews of those represented.

Whistleblowers: Public Safety versus Private Safety

Roger Wensil was a pipefitter. He was not a scientist with academic accolades. He had no published papers. He was just a pipefitter in the Savannah River Plant, a nuclear reservation in South Carolina.

In 1984, Roger Wensil began working at the Savannah River Plant and grew concerned about the open drug use occurring at the facilities. Workers were sharing drugs, buying and selling drugs, and using them during working hours. The situation seemed out of control, and irresponsibly dangerous, in the sensitive nuclear weapons facility. So, Roger did what a concerned employee should do, he went to his employers. Instead of looking into the problem, Roger was demonized, fired, and his reputation was ruined. After being fired, no one would listen to Roger Wensil for quite some time. He sent letters to the Department of Energy, to Nancy Reagan, to local Senators and Representatives. When Roger finally found attorneys to represent his case, they found his complaints were accurate, and he was eventually ordered by the court to be allowed back to work in 1987.

Back at work, Roger was treated terribly again. He was placed in work situations with high levels of radioactivity without proper protection. Roger wrote to the Secretary of Energy concerning his abuse, to no avail. He eventually left the job. He developed lesions on his legs. He required reconstructive surgery on his nose due to the carcinoma he developed from the contamination. While his personal case was still in appeals, Roger Wensil died in 1993. At the moment I am writing this, you will not find a Wikipedia page on Roger Wensil, but you will find one on the Savannah River Site, and it will not include the story of Roger Wensil and his sacrifice for your safety on their page. There are still too few people taking up his case.

He may not have been somebody important in the schemes of national plans, but his case changed federal law in respect to the rights of Department of Energy whistleblowers.[75]

Whistleblowers like Roger Wensil represent the sacrificial edge of science and technology. They are the people who are willing to sacrifice their reputations and their personal safety for the safety of us all.

---

[75] www.whistleblowers.org/index.php?option=com_advancedtags&view=tag&id=18&Itemid=108

Engage: Do you see good and evil in all groups?

The last two chapters highlighted the evil and the noble deeds of individuals in a variety of religious and non-religious systems. The cursory glance anecdotal evidence from these different groups is meant to highlight that good and evil resides in every system. Secularism does not have the lead in either nobility or evil over religion, and this appears true in reverse as well. Do you agree, or disagree with this assessment? Why? Is there another way of looking at this issue?

Interact with the Burning Religion community on the website at www.burningreligion.com.

WHERE ADOLF HITLER MET MOTHER TERESA

Quora is a website for questions and answers. It initially started with a group of intellectuals who were invited to participate in answering questions on their expertise. Quora has long since expanded to the general public, and the questions are growing in their general appeal.

A few years back, the question was asked, "Life: What surprised you the most about growing up?"

I answered this question succinctly:

> *"That Hitler and Mother Teresa aren't anomalies. They are simply potentialities in all of us, and I have been surprised by miniature versions of both throughout my life."*

In concluding these thoughts on how every people group has shown evidence of great evil, and yet, somehow each of these same groups show evidence of deep and beautiful self-sacrificing nobility, I am led to conclude that inherent to each of us is a little bit of Adolf Hitler, and simultaneously, a little bit of Mother Teresa.

Our tendency is to look at the actions of history from an either/or perspective. Hitler is wholly evil, and Mother Teresa is wholly saintly, and so people become one or the other in our eyes, but in fact, we know this is not true. Hitler loved children, and animals. He was an artist. Mother Teresa devoted herself to a life of service, and yet, she spoke openly of her doubts. Christopher Hitchens claimed she should be arrested.[76] Life does not fit nicely into an either/or scenario.

And so, we are tempted to say that neither pure evil, nor perfect saintliness, can be attributed to any person. This skepticism of modernity is unsatisfying. It moves from the black and white world of either/or to the gray dullness of a lost romanticism. A neither/nor world is a world without heroes, a world without sacrifice, a world without knights on white horses, or black and white cowboy hats. There are no 'happily ever after' endings. We are left with something less in the neither/nor world. There is no hopeful prophetic momentum.

---

[76] Christopher Hitchens on arresting Mother Teresa: https://youtu.be/4_piZ3Gmf7U

I find myself rejecting the simple and polarizing either/or approach to good and evil, because I find both tendencies in myself: at one moment noble, the next selfishly destructive. I also reject the idea that true nobility and deep evil do not exist, that as humans we are somehow void of the tension between the divine and the demonic. History and experience seem to cry out and tell us that the balance of good and evil in humanity is not an either/or proposition, and it is not a neither/nor proposition. Rather, it appears to be both/and.

BOTH Adolf Hitler AND Mother Teresa live inside of me.

And you.

This is where they met.

FOUR-YEAR SENTENCE

My friend Brian O'Mearlaigh is a passionate Irish-American Chicagoan and urban artist. His art and his rebellious streak scream for justice, and demand understanding of the underprivileged youth in America's inner cities. His best friend was shot and killed by a Chicago policeman. Brian's friend was mistaken for holding a gun, when all he had was a spray paint can in his hand.

Brian moved away from Chicago. Living in Maine, he joined a church and began working with the youth. The pastor, who was a former cop, told Brian that his urban art was an offense to God, and that he could go to Hell for it. This drove Brian away from church. By the time I met Brian, he hadn't cracked the door of a church in a number of years.

When Brian puts his work to canvas it is often an urban declaration of his passion for justice, and among these works he has a painting entitled "Four Year Sentence."

From the distant horizon a long line of people wait along a barren road to enter a building. The square, non-descript, Soviet-era styled concrete building has a sign saying "Voting Booth." The line of disinterested, subservient looking people emerges from the near side of the building dressed in black and white prison stripes.

Politics in America is suffering from a lack of perspective, and consequently from a lack of true choice. Many people feel that their experience of religion similarly lacks depth and choice. Brian's social commentary on our limited choices highlights the imprisonment of our situation, and this imprisonment is just a part of the problem with our limited worldviews.

In our passion to simplify our world into sound-bite sized talking points with directly opposing positions on every subject, we have surprisingly complicated our lives. We have right and left, which correlate to our sense of right and wrong/good and evil. It is a supposedly simple world, but it has created an, 'us vs. them' approach to life. Like Cubist art, we have deconstructed political, theological, and philosophical positions into their simplest forms, and these simple forms seldom look like the original design.

In the 1907 Salon d'Automne exhibit in Paris, the latter works of the recently deceased Paul Cezanne influenced a group of young and upcoming artists. In a few years, Picasso, Braque, Metzinger, Gris and others would lead the way for modern art schools through the radical and influential Cubist movement. Cezanne's breakdown of nature into the simplicity of the "cylinder, the sphere and the cone" preceded the coming complication of our world brought about by our deconstruction of everything we know. Cezanne died in the dawn of incredible changes to our world. In a few short years, Einstein and new mathematics would turn our thinking upside down.

Picasso, Braque and the Cubists sought to break from the perspective painting of realism. They embraced the two-dimensional aspect of the canvas by incorporating simple geometric forms. Yet, they sought to simultaneously utilize multiple vantage points of an object and layer them on top of one another in hard two-dimensional simple patterns. Thus, a cheekbone in a face might be a triangle shape, as if viewing the face from the side, and an eye might become a parallelogram when looking at the face from the front, and these shapes would be placed one upon another to create the abstract images we know today. And so, Marcel Duchamps' 1912 "Nude Descending a Staircase" has the futuristic movement of motion pictures, with broken imagery of simple geometric forms indiscernible as a "nude."

Is Cubism the ultimate artistic expression of our struggle with parallaxis? We see complex things like human behavior, corporate interaction, and political, theological, or philosophical viewpoints from our flat perspectives, and our limited capabilities to understand them. The best we can accomplish is a deconstruction of these complex images into a few simple shapes perceived from a few different viewpoints. In our attempt to define a whole person, a political position, a corporation, or a church by a few broken parts, we reconstruct a new image in our minds and create a monster.

Complication through an attempted multi-perspectival simplicity is the order of our day. Systems and organizations take the place of relationships. Complex contracts replace the shake of the hand, and the good of our word. Hard fast rules are our protection, yet they have also become our demise, as only lawyers seem able to determine what is really meant in the law, or in a contract.

The number of components we discover in a hand or the face of friend can be broken down to innumerable smaller parts. In the work of the doctor, the lawyer, or the mechanical engineer working on new prosthetic limbs this complexity is the essential information of the specialist. In my relationship with my friend, the familiarity of a face is a simple and comforting sight. His or her face is something I feel as much as see. I feel relief. I feel something like the comfort of home. I feel safe. Once I dehumanize the face as gingivitis, a quizzical look, a bad hair day, and a momentary scowl, I begin to read deeper things into the relationship – deeper, potentially more sinister things, unreal things, complex story lines that may not have existed when the face of a friend was simply the face of a friend and not a series of broken components.

Has our experience of one another and of religious life become a Cubist work - out of a place, disjointed and inhuman? Has it lost the comforting sense of a friend's face? Is it a complex deconstruction of a body, now disjointed and thrown together as layered patterns of geometric forms no longer recognizable as a body?

In writing about the nature of blogging, Mark Phillips makes this observation about parallaxis in his blog post "Blogging as Cubism":

> *"Modernist parallax was about multiple subjectivities perceiving events within their individually flawed points of view. Postmodernist parallax is about bringing multiple orders of text into relationship."*[77]

I love the quote. It highlights the nature of apparently random blog posts drawn together to create a fuller picture of life and the blogger, but I might add to it that, "Postmodernist parallax is about bringing multiple [flawed] orders of text into relationship."

Whether we are dissecting things to discover their individual parts, or putting disconnected things together to create a greater 'je ne sais qua', we have begun the process from the same place: we are looking at parts, and the complicated interconnectedness of them with imperfect observations.

Giovanni Papini wrote an interview of Pablo Picasso (who is recognized as the primary founder of Cubism) in 1951. In it is what has become one of Picasso's most famous quotes:

> *"From the moment that art ceases to be food that feeds the best minds, the artist can use his talents to perform all the tricks of the intellectual charlatan. Most people can today no longer expect to receive consolation and exaltation from art. The 'refined,' the rich, the professional 'do-nothings', the distillers of quintessence desire only the peculiar, the sensational, the eccentric, the scandalous in today's art. I myself, since the advent of Cubism, have fed these fellows what they wanted and satisfied these critics with all the ridiculous ideas that have passed through my mind. The less they understood them, the more they admired me. Through amusing myself with all these absurd farces, I became celebrated, and very rapidly. For a painter, celebrity means sales and consequent affluence. Today, as you know, I am celebrated, I am rich. But when I am alone, I do not have the effrontery to consider myself an artist at all, not in the grand old meaning of the word: Giotto, Titian, Rembrandt, Goya were great painters. I am only a public clown - a mountebank. I have*

---

[77] http://www.markphillips.com/blog/blogThatAtePacifica.html

understood my time and have exploited the imbecility, the vanity, the greed of my contemporaries. It is a bitter confession, this confession of mine, more painful than it may seem. But at least and at last it does have the merit of being honest."

The problem with the quote is that Picasso never said it. Papini wrote the interview as a spoof, one of a number of spoofs, which he wrote about Kafka, Freud, Picasso and others.[78] This quote is still making the rounds on the internet, as though it were a direct quote from Picasso. Yet, the falsely attributed quote highlights something many people already believe about modern art. They view it as simple, childish, not worthy to be called art, and the mocking actions of mischievous jesters, as Papini farcically attributed to Picasso calling himself, "a public clown – a mountebank."

Papini appears to have used the term "public clown" as a derision of Picasso, but perhaps there is no greater observation on the subversive, and revolutionary power of Picasso than this descriptor.

The brilliance of Cubism just might be that it is the ultimate artistic expression of our problems in parallaxis. It is both an observation about our modern and our post-modern perspectives of life, and a simultaneous carnivalesque critique. We see complex things like human behavior, corporate interaction, and political, theological, or philosophical viewpoints from our limited capabilities to understand them. The best we can accomplish is a deconstruction of these whole images into a few simple shapes, and then we attempt to reconstruct them with the result of monstrous and fearful images.

We play God and create in our minds a Frankenstein people, Frankenstein churches, and Frankenstein nations by pretending to comprehend what we perceive. We perceive only disjointed pieces and we rebuild them into a monstrous whole. Then like Victor Frankenstein, we reject the monster we have created with our own hands, and chase it to edges of the earth to destroy it.

<u>Mary Shelley's Frankenstein</u> has the monster as an intelligent creature whose desperately violent and lonely existence comes to an end by jumping overboard in arctic waters. James Whale's 1931 film adaptation has the grunting unintelligible monster trapped and burning in a tower.

The film version ending may more aptly illustrate how many people feel about religion and politics today. Religion is a confusing

---

[78] http://www.independent.co.uk/arts-entertainment/art--picasso-and-that-famous-interview-the-identity-of-jack-the-ripper-look-no-further-than-the-poet-swinburne-or-the-artist-sickert-or-wossisname-and-shakespeare-he-was-really-marlowe-right-or-was-it-bacon

deconstruction from its original intent, which we have rebuilt in our own minds into the unintelligible monster we perceive it to be. Now it is trapped in the tower, and it is going down in flames.

Engage: Have you seen the monster in you?

In the chapter on Hitler and Mother Teresa, we look for the evil within ourselves, and the goodness in others. We have a monster within us. Is this a helpful perspective, when we are in dialogue with others?

Cubism becomes the model for describing how we deconstruct other people and their worldviews with our arguments, and when we put them back together, we create monsters out of them in the same way cubism expresses different two-dimensional views of the object it represents from many different perspectives. These perspectives when pieced together create a monstrous image. What are your thoughts about this point in respect to how others have treated you? and likewise how you have viewed other people, other religions, and other political views?

Interact with the Burning Religion community on the website at www.burningreligion.com.

Tales from the Land of Jaw: The Adventures of Gwyn Dee Red Faced in the Valley of Decision

"One plus one is two! Yea? or Nay?" A large squarish man with the voice of adolescent thunder shouted. One moment his voice rolled like a great deep storm, the next it squeaked like arguing titmice.

A great crowd filled the wide, wide road making it impossible to walk on the road between the two long hills, but at the shout of the large squarish man with the voice of adolescent thunder the great crowd suddenly jumped and scattered to the hills in an unruly and unseemly manner. Mothers grabbed their children, fathers herded their families together, teenagers outran their screaming parents going in the wrong direction, families split up and screamed at each other as they argued violently concerning which way to run, and the older folk tottered off the road as far up the hill as they could manage. When the running stopped, half the crowd stood on one hill, the other half on the opposite hill across the wide, wide road, and they all settled into a complete, yet uncomfortable silence.

Gwyn Dee stood at the entrance of the valley beside the large squarish man with the voice of adolescent thunder, and looked up to ask about the strange crowd and their strange behavior, but before the question could be formed, the adolescent thunder squeak-rumbled once again.

"Declare your decision."

He held his left hand up, and the people gathered upon the left hill shouted with one monstrous voice, "Yea."

Holding his right hand up, the hill to the right rumbled with a great, "Nay."

"Choose your elders." The adolescent thunder squeaked and growled.

After a short noisy confusion, two men half a mile down the center of the long valley stepped into the wide, wide road – one from each hill. They faced each other like boxers in a prizefight. The crowd cheered and hooted then returned to the eerie silence. The large squarish man with the voice of adolescent thunder walked the long, slow walk toward the two men.

The adolescent thunder squeak-rolled a fourth time.

"Prepare your arguments!"

The man from left hand hill disappeared into his half of the hill, and returned with two large ripe tomatoes.

"One tomato plus one tomato is two tomatoes! Tell me that it is not so!"

On the left hand side of the hill, the yea team cheered wildly. Across the wide, wide road the nay team stood nervously while the wild cheering subsided, then suddenly, nearly a quarter of the nay team ran to the opposite side of the wide, wide road. Fleet footed young, and tottering older people fled as fast as their feet would take them. Mothers cried as their children ran, and fathers shouted angrily. Some whole families fled together, and as they did, the nay team hurled large ripe tomatoes with deadly accuracy at their deserters, and no one reached the other side without looking like a freshly baked pizza. The yea team cheered their new members, and greeted them with big, happy tomato sauce hugs.

The nay team elder stepped over to his now diminished hillside with the strutting confidence of prize rooster at the cockfight. He returned to the road with two families: a father, a mother and two young children in one family; and a father, a mother and six children in the other.

"One father plus one mother equals a family of four, or perhaps a family of eight! One plus one is indeterminable! Tell me that it is not so!"

The yea side of the wide, wide road looked nervously around as the nay side jumped up and down with violent excitement, and when the excitement died down, people young and old, whole families and individuals fled the yea hill for the opposite side of the wide, wide road. Some people already covered in tomatoes returned to the nay team, and others ran across for the first time. With the same pinpoint precision tomatoes from the yea team met their mark, and no one reached the other side without being covered from head to toe like a sauce-drenched Eggplant Parmigiana. The nay team thundered with applause and cheering and red-stained squeaky hugs. Fathers happily received their prodigal children, and mothers kissed their tomato soaked faces.

"Before the battle begins, we have one last point of order," said the large squarish man with the voice of adolescent thunder. "Stranger! Enter the valley and tell us your decision!"

He pointed at Gwyn Dee as he rumble-squeaked.

Time stands still for decisions – even for silly decisions.

'Choose this day whom ye shall serve.' The simple words from the great scroll of Jaw ran through Gwyn Dee's head. Gwyn Dee's sore feet, and tired legs trudged slowly – yet, almost involuntarily toward the large squarish man with the voice of adolescent thunder, and the great crowd buzzed like a droning hive.

"I am Gwyn Dee from the Clown Caste of Cominkingville. I come bearing no ill will – only greetings from my little village."

A kindly sigh rose from both sides of the valley, and the older people smiled and shook their heads in pleasant agreement.

"I am only passing through on my journey, and come briefly with nothing but peace."

The smiles increased, and the people from both sides buzzed with solidarity.

Now Gwyn Dee, well worn from an arduous journey, sought to avoid a tomato pelting over a decision on one plus one, and so, magnanimously and diplomatically declared "I have heard wisdom from both sides, and have come to this conclusion: that you are all people of great wisdom…" and the crowds cheered as Gwyn Dee paused, "… and I deem that you are all correct, and so I take no side."

The great mass of people from both sides of the wide, wide road dropped to a deadly silence.

The large squarish man with the voice of adolescent thunder grumble-squeaked impatiently, "You have not chosen well," and stepped slowly away from Gwyn Dee.

Before he could back away ten paces the sky was filled with tomatoes like the arrows of Welsh archers in a medieval battle. If a tornado could throw a billion hailstones down a single chimney, or if a thousand angels could simultaneously crash land on the head of pin it would not have been as accurate as the rain of tomatoes. Gwyn Dee ducked low with arms overhead, and was quickly covered six feet deep in squashed tomatoes.

When the storm of tomatoes had subsided, Gwyn Dee swam carefully to the top of the tomato pile. Nervously poking above the mountain of Italian sludge, Gwyn Dee looked out to find both sides of the valley cheering, and dancing, and hugging, and congratulating each other.

Dragging a sloppy red body out of the mush hill, Gwyn Dee sloshed down the wide, wide road to the far end of the valley making a trail the spaghetti monster would be proud to leave behind.

Beside the road at the end of the valley a stream gently passed under the oak trees, and Gwyn Dee knelt on the grass beside a calm pool in the stream. Preparing to plunge into the water, Gwyn Dee saw a kindly face in the reflection, and looked back to find a Weathered Old Woman, smiling and offering a cup in outstretched hands.

"Tomato Juice?"

Gwyn Dee's eyes became as large as a deli plate.

"Sorry. Bad joke."

Gwyn Dee rolled into the water, and the two laughed hard and long before settling down to bread and wine – without the spaghetti.

LEX REX, OR WHEN RULES RULE

Rules rule.

In 1644, Scottish Presbyterian minister Samuel Rutherford wrote the book Lex Rex, and in the eyes of the monarchs he unleashed a monstrous super villain. He argued against a commonly held position of "rex lex" (the king is the law) and was part of a growing opposition to royal absolutism. Sovereigns would not be pleased with this governmental theory, because after all, the definition of "sovereign" includes, "having supreme or ultimate power," otherwise, to be a true sovereign is to be above the law. "Lex Rex" (the law is king) would prove to be fightin' words, and would form the basis for revolutions.

Rutherford was cited for high treason for writing the book, but died before he could be tried. Lex Rex was burned by the authorities in Edinburgh, St. Andrews, and at Oxford, where in 1683 it became the last official book burning in England.

As a foundational concept behind the American Revolution, America's 2nd President John Adams would describe the infant country as "a government of laws and not of men."[79] The 17th century was filled with governmental theories, which would turn monarchial systems on their head in the 18th century. Rutherford helped popularize a newly developing dream – that laws should be the ruling power, and that they should preside over all persons equally. No man, not even the ruler, should be above the law according to Lex Rex.

Samuel Rutherford and his fellow rebels were latecomers to this theory of law. Aristotle laid out the concept of the sovereignty of the law over man in Politics, "Rightly constituted laws should be the final sovereign; and personal rule..."[80] But, if we should think that Samuel Rutherford and his contemporary thinkers like John Locke were latecomers to the view that laws should be sovereign over humans, it appears that even Aristotle, in the 4th century BC, was a late bloomer to this idea as well.

When Rules were Written in Stone

---

[79] Massachusetts Constitution, Part The First, art. XXX (1780)
[80] Aristotle, Politics 1287b5-8

A thousand years before Aristotle, a nomadic tribe and some of their Gypsy-like[81] friends struggled with living together as a small wandering nation. Like the greater Boston area, or the nation of Wales going on a 40-year camping trip, they numbered perhaps as many as 3 million during the years of their wandering through the Sinai wilderness.[82] Moses, their prophet-rebel leader, became the mediator of laws, which were passed down from God to the people of Israel. In the attempt to establish a theocratic form of rule over the people, the abstractly visible, generally inaudible God needed to set some guidelines for living.

Ten commandments, and 603 other laws later,[83] the nation of Jews had the law for living laid out on chiseled stone, inked on animal skin parchments, and passed on from generation to generation by oral tradition. Now this God, Whose leadership consisted of communicating through a single man, and directing movement through a slowly migrating pillar of cloud and fire had spoken and placed His desires for human behavior and social interaction into an easy to understand set of rules: Don't steal or murder each other, don't be getting all romantic with your neighbor's wife (or his sheep), keep the edges of your crop un-harvested so the poor will have food, accept the stranger who visits you… Of course, there were the more peculiar, and challenging laws: capital punishment for the kid who curses his parents, illegalization of delicious foods like bacon and lobster, or the surrender of your passport and citizenship if you touched a dead body and didn't spend seven days in a purification ritual.

These laws have a well-established history of influencing the governments in the lands of the Abrahamic religions, but until the enlightenment and the beginning of the challenge to the status quo of the divine and sovereign Right of Kings, rulers were not always subject to their own laws.

---

[81] When the Romani people first arrived in England in the 17th century it seems that it is was wrongly believed that they had come from Egypt, and people used a slang term from the Middle-English "egypcien". It is typically considered offensive by the Roma today. Perhaps the term "Gypsy" just as aptly applies to these nomadic Jewish people and the "mixed multitude" of Egyptians who joined them after they left the land of Egypt.
[82] Numbers 1:49 gives the number of men as 603,550. Adding women, and children to the mix could multiply that number by as many as 5.
[83] Rabbi Simlai mentioned 613 laws in the 3rd century AD, and this number is attributed to him. But, of course, as with any good rabbinical system, the Rabbis have not all agreed on this number. This is the most accepted number. It probably helped that Maimonides used these 613 when compiling the Mishnah Torah in the 1170s.

This was not the case for Moses, or the people of Israel though. Moses may have given the law, but He, like the children of Israel, was subject to its commandments.[84] When 40 years of wandering ceased and Israel came into the inheritance of the land of Canaan, Joshua became their new leader. Joshua was commanded by God to "meditate on [the law] day and night."[85] Joshua's knowledge of, and obedience to the Mosaic Law would ensure his success.

Through the following generations, and until the eventual demise of the autocratic system of kings in the nations of Judah and Israel, the kings would be evaluated and judged by God on the basis of their adherence to the Law of Moses. The king was not supposed to be above the law, but like all the people, under it. [86]

Prophets were the voice of the oppressed people when the king was ruthless, but the rebel prophets were also subject to the Law of Moses. The prophet who sided with oppressive or disobedient kings was subject to the same punishments and judgment from God as the kings, and it appears that a whole cast of false prophets was acting as court jesters for the kings just before the Babylonian captivity in the 7th and 6th century BC.[87]

So it was, that for nearly 700 years a nation of people attempted, but failed, to live under the system of lex rex - the law is king. The invisible, inaudible God made His desires known through His law, and what we call Theocracy (rule by God), was in all practicality a Theocratic Nomocracy (the fancy word for "rule of law"). The overwhelming percentage of 3 million nomads, and their descendents in the land of Canaan, never saw or heard from God personally. Instead, the law and the rituals of the tabernacle were their interaction points with deity. Effectively, they were ruled by rules and by the religious servant rulers who defined and enacted the rules.

Rules ruled.

Sometimes though, rule-breaking rulers ruled.

Some things never change.

Meanwhile, the pillar of fire occasionally wandered away, and they, like we tend to do, gave frantic chase.

---

[84] Exodus 4:24-26 gives us the most obvious example of God's expectation for Moses to keep the laws. It is the strange story of God coming to kill Moses on the way to fulfill his call to deliver the children of Israel out of slavery. Moses' neglect to circumcise his own son got him into a heap o' trouble with God.

[85] Joshua 1:9

[86] I realize this will meet some challenge when we consider some of the actions of David and Solomon, but something like that will have to wait for another time, another day, maybe a face to face, or, hey! Email me.

[87] Jeremiah 14:14; 28:1-17

Is the Bible a Book of Rules?

Many people perceive of the Bible as a book of rules, and in light of the Pentateuch this is a completely sensible observation. Consequently, the religions born from the Bible are understood as religions of rules. Is this an accurate assessment of these Holy Scriptures? Let's take a brief tour through the Bible (New and Old Testament), with an eye on the actual laws established by God for human behavior control and modification.

The first story in the Bible tells a tale of our primeval parents, and the first rules are embedded into this ancient story in the first 3 chapters of Genesis. To begin with, a commission was given to Adam and Eve – "be fruitful and multiply."

So, God started the big communal world experiment by telling Adam and Eve to do the baby-making dance – and do it often. That was His first command to the human race. Most of us could cross this off the list of laws, and categorize it as the fabulously sexy Woodstock of prehistory.

But, shortly thereafter the heavy hand of God came crashing down, and the Big Man in the Sky established the first oppressive rules. He nonchalantly strolled into the garden one afternoon, and announced a meeting, and the complete staff of earth appeared for this momentous event. There was God, and Adam, and Eve, and…and…and that was it, because there wasn't anybody else on staff yet.

Thunder rolled across the sky, because that's what happens when God clears His throat.

Adam said, "Cooooool, I love it when you do that. When are you going to show me how to do that trick?"

Eve was a little more reserved than Adam, and whispered across the soft bed of Scottish Moss growing at the foot of the official meeting rock, "Adam! Shhhhh."

Adam responded like he always did when Eve got slightly perturbed, "Wow! you are so cute when you do that. Wanna…"

"Adam!"

Thunder rolled across the sky again.

"Cool."

God smiled, because that's what God does when God is happy. The clouds cleared, and sun broke across the fields of Eden, because that's what happens when God smiles.

"I have an important set of rules to establish for our society."

Adam and Eve looked around the garden. The groundhog was scuttering away with the Echinacea flowers, and the squirrels were digging up the Tulip bulbs again.

"Hey! Stop that!" Adam shouted at the squirrels. "Can we make a rule about squirrels and Tulip bulbs?"

Eve wondered what was meant by 'society.'

"Uhm, what's a society?"

The thunder rolled again. God likes clearing His throat, because it sounds pretty awesome. "Society is us getting together and hanging out in the garden, and when there are more of us, it will be important to have some rules." Thunder rolled again for a little exclamation point.

"Cool."

"Adam! This is important." Eve looked concerned, "What are the babies going to look like when we have them? Will they be like kittens?"

"No! I want puppies. Puppies, puppies, puppies." Adam just didn't like the kittens quite as much. "Or Hippos."

"I don't think so! I am not having Hippos."

The thunder rolled, and the sun broke out from behind the clouds again.

"So here are the rules…"

Adam and Eve sat up a little, and Adam pretended to pay attention to God, but he was staring at Eve, because that's what Adam did most of the time anyway. She was wearing a little string of purple and white pansies low around her waist. He couldn't help himself so he whispered, "I love your outfit today."

"What? ADAM!"

The sun broke out bright and warm, and then the thunder rolled extra loud.

"COOL!"

"Rule number one: Do not eat the fruit of that tree over there in the middle of the garden."

Eve looked across the fields, "Which one? The purple one? Or the one with the long yellow fruit?"

"No, no, the one where the snake sits in the shade." Thunder rolled super loud this time.

"Whoa! Cool!"

Eve was a little perplexed, "Why is it bad to eat from that tree?"

Thunder rolled, and lightning cracked this time.

"Wow!"

"Because you will die."

Eve scrunched her nose a little. Adam raised his eyebrows.

"Dude, that sounds bad."

145

Thunder again and a little sun peeked out, "I think you understand. Thank you. And now for the next rule."

Adam was paying serious attention to the sky. He was expecting a good light show now.

"Rule number 2…"

Eve leaned forward. Adam stopped looking at the sky and peeked at Eve.

"Rule number 2…"

And there was silence.

"Rule number 2…O darn, I just can't think of anything else important. Just be sure to keep rule number one, and keep trying to make babies."

"Oh yeah!"

"That's it? Just one rule about that one tree where the snake hangs out?" Eve looked a little confused. "That doesn't seem like enough rules to run an effective, what did you call it? Society?"

Thunder. Sun. "Yep, that's all. By the way, Adam's correct, you have a nice outfit on today."

"God!" Eve blushed.

Thunder and bright Sun. "Go on now. Make some babies, and take care of the garden. Oh, did you name the little guy with the black and white stripes yet?"

"No, he's kind of skunky smelling, we have to wait until he's not too excited to name him." Eve didn't like the cute little guy when he was squirting and showing off as the king of the garden.

The meeting ended, and Adam thought that it was a pretty good deal. All they had to do was keep one easy little rule – and make babies. Eve wasn't quite as sure. She thought maybe a few more rules might have been helpful.

And this is the absurdity of the garden story: not that it was about the seemingly arbitrary rule involving fruit prohibition, but that the Biblical story of the creation of the first social order in human history had only one rule. What was God thinking? Did He seriously expect the future of humanity to live in peace, love and understanding with one weird little law about one singly peculiar tree with a snake lying under it?

It worked for a short season. These primeval parents were perfect hippies. They ran around wearing nothing but flowers in their hair, worked on making babies, named a few animals, ate lunch, worked on making more babies, snacked on mangoes, tried making babies again, snacked again, finally named the smelly little black and white guy, did some more baby making… and then they did what all, good hippies do

– they stuck it to The Man. Like true hippies they practiced a little peaceful resistance – they ate the prohibition fruit.

What were they thinking? I totally would have worked on making more babies.

In this primeval story, God saw that the Utopian experiment wasn't working. He expelled the young hippies from the garden, because He thought they just weren't utopian material, and of course, God was right. It didn't take long before the children Adam and Eve had been working on making started getting really nasty. Brothers were killing brothers, and it got all bloody.

After the false start, God would eventually find someone else to restart the social experiment, but this time God was not starting with a perfect prototypic scenario. The world had been a mess for a long, long time.

Abram was a Pagan in the land of Ur. God spoke to Abram and told him to travel to a land, which would be given to him. It seems to have been a rather non-specific command. So Abram took his family, and they traveled till they bumped into the land of Canaan. There God promised the land to him and his generations, but Abraham (now renamed) never got a chance to inherit the land. It took 400 years of traveling, getting abducted into slavery, fighting off a few enemies, and escaping Pharaoh, but eventually the family moved back toward Canaan, and along that return journey they received a new set of laws.

"Moses, do you know why I called you to this meeting on the mount?"

"I am having a bit of difficulty with the family down there. I'm sure it has something to do with that. Any advice is welcome."

Thunder rolled across the valleys and mountains of the desert, and dark clouds filled the sky. God had cleared his throat, and then He sighed. The dark clouds typically roll in when God sighs. "Oh boy, I wish I had some advice for you. I've been dealing with you stubborn knuckleheads for a few millennia now, and it's becoming quite difficult."

God and Moses had a silent moment. Moses understood God a lot better in that silent moment.

"Okay, so I've got an idea. We are going to give them a law, and perhaps set them on a safer and more prosperous journey."

Moses scratched his head, "But didn't you try that back in the Garden?"

The dark clouds rolled onto the mount.

"Sorry. I didn't mean to bring up a sore point."

"Okay, so here's the rules I will give you to give to them. I am going to give you 10 commandments on a stone tablet. The first three will be about how the people relate to me. The fourth commandment will be about taking a day off from work, and the next six will cover some rules about how to treat each other. I'll follow up with some other rules later. Maybe a couple hundred of them."

"Hundreds of laws? That seems like a lot to remember, can we condense this somehow?" Moses scrunched his face in concern.

"You're such a guy Moses. I think maybe Eve was right and we needed just a few more rules to make this work properly." The clouds parted for a moment and the sun broke out. God smiled for the first time in the meeting.

After forty days with God, Moses went back down the mountain with two stone tablets and the 10 Commandments. This experiment took less time to mess up than the first social experiment with Adam and Eve. Part way down the mountain Moses heard the noise, and it didn't sound good. This enormous campground of desert hippies didn't do any better than their primeval parents. They built themselves a large ugly golden cow to worship, held a massive debaucherous bonfire party around it, and started doing that baby-dance with someone else's baby and even with some of the sheep. Moses didn't even make it down the mountain, before he got mad and broke the stone tablets.

And so, Moses trudged back up the mountain for another 40 days with God. When he returned to the bush, it was dark and crackling, spitting out an occasional small flame burst.

Moses and God didn't have anything to say to one another for the first few days. Moses finally broke the silence.

"So, what do we do now?"

Dark clouds rolled in, and Moses wondered if God's burning bush was going to get extinguished. "You don't know how many times I've thought about getting rid of them all and starting over." And after a long pause God asked, "What do you think?"

Moses thought about it, "Uhm, not a bad idea."

"Yea." The clouds lightened up a bit.

"Naw." As if on cue, Moses shook his head and God shook His bush as they spoke simultaneously.

God called jinx first.

It was a couple more days before they spoke again.

God gave them repeated chances to work it out – over millennia. At some point a dude named Maimonides, who seemed to be working a little harder at this social experiment than most of his fellow Jews, counted up the laws, and listed them all. It was a whopping 613 laws.

613 laws.

I tried to find out how many US laws (State and Federal) were on the books, but they are so plentiful that no one knows. New laws are being added daily to the already over-stuffed tomes. Besides the important things like theft, and murder, we also have regulations on where you can walk barefoot, where you can distribute your spit, where you can show your breasts, where you can blow smoke, and how many bug parts can be processed into your canned peas.

Once again, God seems to have under-regulated societal order. His whole legal code was 613 laws. And guess what? Yep, you guessed. Those desert hippies kept trying to stick it to the Man by breaking the laws.

So, God thought it might be a good idea to send His Hippie Son, because certainly the desert hippies would listen to Him. Right?

It turns out that by the time Jesus arrived the desert hippies had grown up, and now they were Yuppies. They were concerned about looking good and making money. And when the Hippie Dude from Heaven arrived, He told the Yuppies that all those crazy 613 laws could be condensed into two simple laws.

Say what? Didn't they try something like that back in the primeval utopian Woodstock garden? But, the Hippie Dude from Heaven was sure they could capture these two simple rules:

1. Love God with all your heart.
2. Love your neighbor as yourself.

But, the Yuppies didn't like this Hippie Dude from Heaven, because He messed with their sweet banking deals in the temple, and challenged the status quo. So, they off'd Him, and it seems humanity has been unable to keep those two simple rules ever since.

Fortunately the voice from the Hippie Dude from Heaven was not to be kept down. He is still speaking down the winds of human history, and He retells His story through people who are trying to keep the two simple rules. It turned out after all this rebellion and sticking it to The Man, that The Man was kind of a Hippie to start with. All He wanted was love.

So you might ask, "How many rules are there in the Bible?" Well, here's the answer:

In the beginning: 1
Under the Mosaic covenant: 613
Under Jesus: 2

Total number of rules[88] in the Bible: 2

I know, it looks like new math, but Jesus describes these two rules as the basis for God's expectations for all human behavior. All other laws are simply a sub-category of those two laws of love. Those two laws were already embedded into the 613 laws of the Mosiac Covenant, and Jesus was the person Who pointed this out most clearly. Could it be that He was helping us to discover what religion, and what life itself might look like if a simpler set of rules ruled our lives? Apparently, Jesus wasn't advocating lex rex in the same way we have done.

Caritas Rex

"Love will not be held by mastery. When mastery comes, the God of love beats his wings, and farewell – he is gone."[89]

Caritas rex means love is king, and we might think of this as "love rules." The law of Jesus is love, and this love is meant to be the ruling guideline for our lives.

Jesus reminded us that the most important laws passed down from Moses called us to become lovers - lovers of God, and lovers of other people. These two laws comprised the totality of God's expectations for us. In Jesus' philosophy, these laws covered everything in the laws of Moses, and all ethical behavior for all humanity regardless of the times, nationality, social class, age, or sex. And they bear repeating over and over again.

- Law #1 – Love God unreservedly
- Law #2 – Love others at least as much as you love yourself

And Jesus really thought it was that simple.

Oh, how subtle is the distinction between God's love and God's law. Yes, the law rules. But that ruling law is a law of love. Making the mature personal and holistic transition from "lex rex" to "caritas rex" is critical and foundational to both Judaism and Christianity. In the Jesus

---

[88] there are other rules in the New Testament about how to gather, and how to treat one another, but these are descriptors and extended practices of what it looks like to keep the two Great Commandments.
[89] The Canterbury Tales, Geoffrey Chaucer, from The Franklin's Tale

Way these are not separate concepts. Lex rex is caritas rex, because the law is love. The person who does not make this transition does not understand the simple and liberating focus of those words, which were at the front of our church, "A Christian church which is short on rules and long on relationships."

For many of us, it seems far too simple, and hopelessly impossible to condense the laws of God into two lines. Like the story of the Fall in the Garden of Eden, we wonder how the world can possibly survive under such unlegislated freedom? How can people benefit society with this loose and simple approach? Where are the constraints keeping people from random immorality and violence?

Externalities to Internalities (and back again?)

When rules rule our lives, external factors too easily become our focus. We are discouraged by our inability to keep up with the performance standards, whether these are hard standards like the Ten Commandments, or the soft but more dangerous unspoken standards of corporate expectations. And this is where our cognitive dissonance reaches its most intense levels.

In the History of Sexuality, postmodern philosopher Michel Foucault challenged the idea that the transition of morality and ethics from Pagan Greek philosophy to Christian theology was a movement from external force to internal influence.[90] He outlined the components of self-regulation called for by the pre-Socratic and Socratic philosophers in ancient Greece. In other words, Pagan Greek leaders were enjoined by the philosophers to be careful about their behavior: their generosity, their influence over others, their ethics, and their passions. They were called by the philosophers to a self-regulated life, and were held accountable.

In sexual practices, ancient Greece was known for behavior we arrest people for today, but the philosophers were not unanimous in their approval of aberrant behavior such as the sexual attraction to young boys. The leader who could not control his passions was not fit to be a leader in the eyes of Plato, and it was expected that ethical and moral men would lead the city. To be driven by one's own passions was to fail at the first and most important battle in life – to overcome oneself. This discipline of moderation, and the warfare against one's own passions, was also a focus of Jesus and the writers of the scripture.

Paul spoke of an internal warfare in much the same way Socrates did,[91] and he called us to the necessary hard work of mastering

---

[90] Michel Foucault, The History of Sexuality, Vol. 2 The Use of Pleasure, pg. 63
[91] Ezekiel 23:26-27

ourselves. Jesus pointed out the failures of the religious leadership, and called the average person to a righteousness that exceeded the religious leaders.[92]

The brilliance of the early Christian call to righteousness cannot be overstated. Christian morality took the expectations of the Greek leader to a new level, and applied those expectations to all people. In Jesus, in Paul, in James, in Peter, and in John we find a higher calling for the average person (male and female alike, regardless of age, class or race) than we find for the ancient Pagan Greek rulers of state. The early Christians were referred to as kings and priests. They were told that one day they would sit in judgment over the nations. They were identified as ambassadors of Christ. The expectations of the average Christian toward one another were higher than the expectations of the Pre-Socratic philosophers toward the rulers of the Greek democracy, and the internalization of morality to a self-regulating and a self-psychologizing way of life was an expectation of the embryonic Christian community.

You were a king or queen. You were a priest or priestess. You were an ambassador in the early Christian church, and your behavior was expected to be an example of such high nobility, because it was believed that this was the inheritance of the followers of Christ.

In a world of class distinctions, with high expectations for the ruling class, and low expectations for the ruled, this was a liberating theology. To expect as much self-regulation from the lowly, as from those of high pedigree is to recognize that we all come from one source, and we all end up in the same grave with the same post-life evaluation. The playing field of life is leveled when noble behavior is recognized as the realm of all people. In a social order like this, bread and circuses are powerless as a form of manipulation against the poor.

When we see Christian morality as a controlling agent enforcing fear upon the poor and underprivileged masses, we have lost sight of the original liberating force of Jesus' message. The Good News has been cut from the heart of the Gospel, and we are left with an external set of rules mandating our every thought, word and action, rather than the simplicity of the two principles of love.

The original call from Jesus, from Paul, from Peter, from John and from James was a call to come up to a higher place. It was not the mandate of oppression, but the expectation of nobility. The call was not to be bound by the rules with a fear of judgment and Hellfire, but it was a call to behave oneself as someone who is fit to rule the world.

---

[92] Matthew 5:20

All along, this was the expectation during the years of the 613 laws of Moses. The internalization of the ethics of God was emblazoned on the psyche of the Jewish people. Those who understood this found joy in their faith, those who did not only saw the ugly signs of oppression.

Somewhere along the way, the followers of Jesus appeared to have lost sight of the internal nature of the two laws, which commanded them to love others. They saw the minutiae of specifics in the commands of God, the lists of sin, and the expected "fruit of the Spirit." In these details, they saw their own failings, or the failings of their fellow Christians. They divided themselves up into camps of doers and non-doers, of the anointed and the disobedient, of the chosen and the sinners, and soon their hearts grew cold and hard. The flame of the commandments of love was extinguished, and replaced with the coldness and inflexibility of the stone tablets.

Strangely, we are often deceived by cold hardness. The zealous hardness of legal demand mimics the flame of holy passion. Could it be that some of our leaders shout, debate and persuade with a passion that is more akin to smoke and mirrors than burning passion of an ancient mystical faith?

In our passion to understand right from wrong, and to feel comfortable with the complexities of life, we set guidelines, we form our lists of dos, and don'ts, and the comfort of a prescribed action for complex situations soothes our discomfort.

Working with alcoholics and drug addicts in rehab programs, we would establish a strict set of guidelines to live by. The brokenness, and deception of the addict in need of a fix often does not process the simplicity of how the two simple commandments impact the intense momentary need. A list of rules defined every moment's decision, and navigated life's uncertainties. The drug addict has spent most of his life in feeding a destructive habit. Many simple social skills and ethical values were never unpacked and tried on. The same procedure held true when I worked in group homes for children who were wards of the State. We raise our own children in a similar prescribed manner of rights and wrongs until they grow mature enough to make wise decisions. The experience of religion for many people in the 21st century has been a similar list of rules, and we feel as though we've been treated like immature children – or social outcasts.

In an interview with Biola's Center for Christian Thought, Pentecostal theologian Amos Yong speaks about the Great Commission – the call by Jesus to share his teachings across the world. He describes the pressure of Pentecostal/Evangelical motivation to fulfill the Great Commission as a "rule based theology" enforcing the preaching the Gospel, and says that in the moment of being faced with meeting a new person, this theology, "doesn't give [the Pentecostal] much room not to do it."

Amos Yong goes on to ask, "What if we had another kind of theology that said something like this: 'Life in the Spirit means that we have to discern in every encounter in every relationship – what is the appropriate thing to do?'"[93]

Somewhere the ancient prophet Ezekiel is looking on and asking the same question. Perhaps he weeps. The promise God gave to him appears to be reversing itself.

> *"I will give you a new heart and put a new spirit within you; I will take the heart of stone out of your flesh and give you a heart of flesh. I will put my spirit within you and cause you to walk in my statutes, and you will keep my judgments and do them"*[94]

Unlike the promised heart of flesh, we sometimes chisel the law into hearts of stone, and we wonder why the passionate fire of religion appears to be nothing but the noisy chisel sparks of steel on stone.

Iesus Rex

If I could make an appeal to the Christians of the world, it would be this: Please rediscover the truth that "God is love." Many who do not share the name of "Christian" are rediscovering this truth, and are wearing it better than we do.

I believe that the same Jesus, who came to teach the rules of love, is the King of the Universe. He is both the lawgiver, and the law. This law made itself most obvious at the cross, when Christ gave His life.

Iesus caritas. Jesus is love.
Caritas rex. Love rules.
Iesus rex. Jesus rules – but He rules by love.

I do not believe that there should be any effective difference between these three statements: Lex rex, caritas rex, Iesus rex. The law is love, and love is a Person.

---

[93] https://youtu.be/yS2vBPf9KvU this point starts at about 21:50 in the discussion
[94] Ezekiel 23:26-27

Engage: How do you feel about the power of law?

When things get out of control, we add laws. Law seems to be a good and necessary thing, but the biblical story shows this process of legal additives in the stew of our life, and the conclusion appears to be that adding laws does not necessarily make things better. In fact, it often seems to compound the problem, by giving us leaders who take advantage of the rules for their own purposes, and suppress others with those laws. How do you feel about the conclusion, which simplifies law into two simple things – both having to do with love?

Interact with the Burning Religion community on the website at www.burningreligion.com.

Tales from the Land of Jaw: The Adventures of Gwyn Dee Dancing in Salvatown

*T*raveling the wide, wide road for only a short distance, a worn out sign, barely legible from the years of hot winds and sand storms, pointed down the hill to the south. The sparsely vegetated desert still stretched as far as the eye could see. Gwyn Dee was tired to the bone from the previous days of trial.

'Salvatown' read the weary sign.

The dragging barefoot traveler turned south down into the valley of Salvatown. Trepidation is not a long enough word to describe the feelings of visiting another village, but tiredness outweighed the fear. Turning a corner around a large outcropping of rocks, Gwyn Dee was pleasantly relieved to see a grove of oaks in the valley below hugging the winding stream, which crossed through the scattered village of Salvatown.

Gwyn Dee stopped and sighed, and because of the hopeful weary relief did not see the Weathered Old Man seated beneath the shadow of the overhanging rocks.

"Greetings wayfarer." A deep resonant voice startled Gwyn Dee.

Large white teeth sparkled behind the leathery brown face.

"Sit here in the shade for a moment. Have some cool water from the stream in the rock, and tell me your story. I see it weighs heavy upon your brow."

Gwyn Dee was too exhausted to question. The old man sat on the ground with a light blanket covering his legs. He gently handed Gwyn Dee a cool water skin, and it was drawn dry in a long slow squeeze.

He laughed. Gwyn Dee apologized. He laughed again, and waved the apology and the exhaustion away like a disappearing card in a sleight of hand trick.

Before the Weathered Old Man could ask, Gwyn Dee poured out the story of life in Cominkingville – being born at the solar eclipse, living with stone shoes, of a passion for the adventures of Jane Foole, of the stone shoe race, of the lost shoes, of joyously flying like the wind, of the brutal ostracism and injury at the end of the race, of training for the Clown Caste, and now these years later leaving to find the borders of the Land of Jaw only to be disappointed by the state of the land. The old man's eyes glinted with the sparkle of early forming tears.

"I hope you shall find some small peace in our little valley, even if only for a short season. It will be a short season, of course. I see the unshod feet of a traveler are with you." *He smiled, and the little forming diamond-like tears leaped from his eyes to his wrinkled face.*

The Weathered Old Man stood, and as the blanket fell off his lap he said, "Please do not be afraid."

Still sitting, Gwyn Dee now saw the old man's feet, and they were shod with the same stone shoes of Cominkingville.

There are moments when the mind screams louder than words can voice, and a stone frozen silence suppresses all reaction. This was one of those moments.

From a bag on his side, the old man pulled out a pair of stone shoes.

Gwyn Dee recoiled in horror.

"These are for you to wear while you are with us. You cannot enter our village without them. It is the law. But, if you will take these, I think you will find that not all things are as they appear." *He smiled. Gwyn Dee blinked the blink of terror.*

Somehow Gwyn Dee's hand reached for the stone shoes. As the shoes passed from hand to hand, they seemed to float with the lightness of a bird on wing in a gentle breeze, and as Gwyn Dee began to speak in wonder the Weathered Old Man shushed, and put his finger to his lips.

This would be their secret.

The short trip down to the village of Salvatown was as light as running barefoot for the first time.

The sun was setting over the nearby hills. A bonfire was being set in the center of the village. A carnival of food, and art, and music was beginning to emerge from the small huts of the village, and the festival exploded as lively as fireworks on a holiday and nearly as quickly. As the last shadows of the day faded into the black of night, the people danced, and Gwyn Dee danced, and everyone danced with a lightness of foot uncommon for stone shoe wearing people. The dancing went late into the night, and when it ended, Gwyn Dee was full, refreshed, and happily tired.

For three nights Gwyn Dee danced, and leapt, and sang, and shouted, and hooted for happiness, and ate, and drank, and overate, and over-drank, and laughed, and howled at the moon, and lifted hands to the multitude of the stars, and stained the earth with tears of joy, and slept like a baby for the few short hours till the rising of the dawn.

And on the rising of the third sun after the third night Gwyn Dee knew it was time to travel on in search of the boundaries of the Land of Jaw. Feeling as relaxed as a fortnight of holidaying, Gywn Dee walked to the edge of the wide, wide road with the Weathered Old Man and removed the magical stone shoes, handing them to the wizened saint.

"There is hope then?" Gwyn Dee asked.

"Keep the shoes. You may need them again soon." He smiled and winked. "Hope? I can only hope so. Sometimes it seems like an old magician's trick to keep the hope alive, but perhaps even our secret mockery finds some happy glimmer of hope."

The Weathered Old Man turned and walked back toward Salvatown. Gwyn Dee watched him disappear around the outcropping of rocks, and heard his deep gentle voice on the wind, "Fare thee well barefoot traveler. We shall meet again."

BETWEEN THE CIRCUS & THE CARNIVAL: FROM CONTROL TO REVOLUTION

"It must be very fragile, if a handful of berries can bring it down."[95]
— Katniss Everdeen

The Hunger Games, by Suzanne Collins, spotlighted the theme of what the Roman playwright Juvenal called "Bread and Circuses" with all its social implications, and placed it on the stage of popular youth culture. She challenged us to consider the possibility that this same manipulation is going on in our world today. The first person perspective of the books initially merely winks toward the machinations of political powers behind the development and running of the games involving young people playing a survivalist battle to the death. The last one standing is the champion, and the 12 districts of the empire watch helplessly as they cheer and mourn their children, who are pitted against one another in a gladiatorial death match, which reminds us of the duel characteristics of oppressive cruelty and public enthrallment found in the Roman Coliseum.

The movies present the third person perspective, and periodically cut away from the heroine Katniss Everdeen to openly show the dark government manipulation playing behind the scenes of the games. The country of Panem developed the Hunger Games as a means of reminding the people that they would survive only if they were wholly subservient to the government. Of course, this lesson was couched in terms of maintaining the peace, and remembering the history of an apocalyptic war out of which the distopian empire of Panem had emerged from the ashes.

Panem is the Latin word for bread, and with children fighting children in the Hunger Games the books call us to remember a quote from the Roman playwright and poet Juvenal.

> *"Already long ago, from when we sold our vote to no man, the People have abdicated our duties; for the People who once upon a time handed out military command, high civil office, legions — everything, now restrains itself and anxiously hopes for just two things: bread and circuses."*[96]

---

[95] Collins, Suzanne (2010-05-28). Catching Fire (The Second Book of The Hunger Games) (p. 22). Scholastic Books. Kindle Edition.
[96] Leisure and Ancient Rome, By J. P. Toner, pg. 69

Juvenal simultaneously satirizes the common people and the ruling elite. The common folk were satisfied with food in the belly and grotesque entertainments. Consequently, they were numbed to the more noble passions for truth and civic duty. The ruling elite of Rome took advantage of need and sensuality based instincts to manipulate the masses to their will. It worked like an anesthetization against the pain of injustice and oppression in a poorly run government, and that anesthetization was a form of rebellion suppression. Keep the masses addicted to cheap food and wild entertainment and they will not have time or interest to rebel against a poorly run, self-serving government.

Julie Clawson looks at Suzanne Collins' trilogy in her book The Hunger Games and the Gospel, and points out the similarities between governmental manipulation in Panem, in Rome, and in the world today.

> *"Our world is much like Panem, where the wealth and comfort of the few in the Capitol is provided through the oppression of the districts. Where having the latest toys, instant everything, and the fashions of the moment (at the cheapest possible prices) are more important to some than the lives of the people who suffer to supply them. Where protecting a political ideology and hoarding one's wealth are higher priorities than feeding the hungry. Such a world is obviously not a realization of God's dreams. And sadly, Christians, especially in countries like the United States, are often seduced into living in the ways of the world that devalue the image of God in others."*[97]

The ancient Roman Bread and Circuses manipulation is insidiously woven into the weak fabric of our culture. It holds our economy, the sociology of the way we gather, and our political decisions together in a subtle stratagem designed to direct our choices, our movement, our spending habits, and our sense of fulfillment. It is at the heart of the marketing that bombards our senses and our sensibilities daily.

The Three-Ring Circus of Capitalism

Advertising appears to be leading us into a dystopian future of little blue pills, the trendiest fashions, chemically and surgically sustained prescriptions for eternal youth, and entertainments supposedly designed to further our evolutionary transformation. Those of us seduced by the Madison Avenue circus and its playful gimmickry are being drawn to find meaning in the meaningless, and to chase

---

[97] Clawson, Julie (2012-03-05). The Hunger Games and the Gospel (Study Guide Edition): Bread, Circuses, and the Kingdom of God (Kindle Locations 176-180). Patheos Press. Kindle Edition.

experiences of short-lived and shallow fulfillment, and this cycle of short-lived experiences spins with ever-increasing speed. The sales pitch promises to provide even the most benign joys with products designed to wear out in abbreviated seasons as they break, or become obsolete or un-trendy.

Sociologist C. Wright Mills called the automobile an overdeveloped commodity.[98] When its fundamental goal is our speedy transportation from one location to another, it has become a temporary home with a climate-controlled environment, communication devices, high quality entertainment systems, seats more comfortable than our own beds, and a look designed in the best art schools. C. Wright Mills made this observation in his book The Sociological Imagination. It was published in 1959. He died in 1962 and never even saw the advent of cassette tapes, let alone iPods, satellite radio, computer driven climate-control systems, built-in GPS devices speaking to us in sexy voices while guiding us from one location to another, or hands free blue-tooth connected phones allowing us to talk to people anywhere in the world while we drive. All these luxuries are being hawked as needs, and the days of the Ford Model T coming in only one color, or the inexpensive Volkswagen Beetle are long gone.

Hedonism and overt sensuality are sold as high points of personal experience, and we have proven our susceptibility to the ringmaster's call at both ends of the age spectrum. On the graying edge, erectile dysfunction drug sales peaked at over $5 billion annually in 2010, and since has dropped only slightly. Visits to the emergency room related to MDMA abuse (Ecstasy and Molly) increased 128% between 2005 and 2011 among people younger than 21.[99] Steve Pasierb, the CEO of the Partnership at Drugfree.org, calls the emergency room statistics "a wake up call for everyone." Perhaps, unknown to us, our children have already woken up. They've discovered what we were doing, and like us, they started dancing with the monkey to the squealing pitch of the same organ grinder.

The advertising in our television sets and on the columns of our Facebook pages leads us to the titillating circus of capitalist fulfillment. Drug enhanced eroticism and automobiles built to stroke our egos are only two obvious examples in our world of circus-like activities. Purchasing stuff and spending our "disposable income" has become such a part of the American economy that following the attack on New York City's World Trade Center on 9-11, the President included shopping as a wartime action response. With the public fearing terrorist

---

[98] C. Wright Mills, The Sociological Imagination, page 10
[99] Ecstasy Use on the Rise Among US Teens: Report by Dennis Thompson, HealthDay Reporter. Dec. 3, 2013

attacks coming to local malls, theaters, and festivals; the possibility of a luxury, entertainment and service based economy spiraling into severe recession leading to job losses was looming over the nation, and the President of the United States was forced to say the now infamous words, "I encourage you to go shopping."[100] Abercrombie and Fitch, Victoria's Secret, the Apple Store and Starbuck's had now taken their place alongside the Marine Corps, the Coast Guard and the Air Force as branches of service to the nation.

President Bush's call to shop following the terrorist attack says less about the Bush administration, than it says about the people and the economy of America. Has America already reached a position similar to the latter days of Rome, or the fantasy obscenity of Suzanne Collin's collapsing Panem? Is the strength of the nation built upon an economy of sensuality, status and greed? If the circus tent burns, and the capitalistic ringmaster is silenced will it mark the beginning of the end?

In a radical socialist critique of American capitalist-democracy and its search for freedom, Žižek recalls America's mocking observation about itself in the opening salvo of his book Living in the End Times.

> *"The people wanted to have their cake and eat it: they wanted capitalist-democratic freedom and material abundance but without paying the full price of life in a "risk society"; that is, without loosing the security and stability once (more or less) guaranteed by the communist regimes. As sarcastic Western commentators duly noted, the noble struggle for freedom and justice turned out to be nothing more than a craving for bananas and pornography."*[101]

Given the history of communism in the 20th century, Žižek has a long way to go to show that the communist dream is somehow less prone to Bread and Circuses oppression than capitalistic democracy. Irrespective of our ideology, the whole world seems to be trapped in this tension between our passions and our oppression. We are like the beautiful young woman whose reluctant and seemingly only option for income was to sell her body. We are on the inside of the cake of our own making crying, while we wait for the music to play and the stripping to begin.

Let them Eat Cake

The attribution of the phrase "Qu'ils mangent de la brioche" is famously attached to Marie Antoinette, but is highly unlikely to have

---

[100] http://thinkprogress.org/politics/2006/12/20/9281/bush-shopping/
[101] Slavoj Žižek, Living in the End Times, introduction page vii

ever passed from her lips in regards to the plight of the common folk during the French Revolution. It first appeared in Rousseau's Confessions written in 1765, when Marie Antoinette was nine years old and had not yet have arrived at Versailles from Austria.

Whichever "great princess" Rousseau was speaking of in his Confessions, the phrase landed in Marie Antoinette's lap along with her head, and the cruel thoughtless comment concerning the plight of the poor has been attributed to her for centuries.

It seems as applicable to the plight of the poor in the 21st century as it did in the 18th century. Julie Clawson's social commentary on the Hunger Games highlights our first world obsessions, and the direct connection they have to third world suffering. Often, our inexpensive cocoa, coffee, and tea is harvested by people working in slavery conditions on the other side of the world. Stories from the far east tell the tale of enslaved young women, sold by their parents, working the mills and factories pumping out our luxury commodities under brutal conditions. Some of this has been wildly exaggerated, as proven by the lies of the journalist who fabricated the story of the suffering of the people working in the factories making Apple products,[102] but there is enough truth to many of the tales of woe to deserve our full attention, and warrant the sackcloth of mourning for our greedy lifestyles.

Meanwhile, at home in the first world, the food we eat has driven us into class warfare. Inexpensive overly processed, fat heavy, carb heavy and sugar heavy foods have been the staple of the middle and lower classes for two generations now, and we show our diet choices on our waistlines. America topped the UN's list of obese nations until 2013, when it was surpassed by Mexico.[103] The problem of obesity is most prevalent among the poor, who despite often eating more than enough calories are still classified as under-nourished. Lots of cheap, fattening food – little nutrition. Someone at the top of the food chain is still responding to the problem of poverty, with a flippant, "Qu'ils mangent de la brioche."

Recently, a friend of mine who spent four years studying in the United States began her doctoral work in Geneva. We spoke on the phone, and she was nearly ecstatic to tell me she had lost weight, and was now jogging every morning. "There are not as many good

---

[102] See the NPR blog post "Retracting "Mr. Daisey and the Apple Factory."" NPR was forced to retract the story when they learned that it "contained significant fabrications." Unfortunately, Mike Daisey continued to take his one-man show, called the "The Agony and the Ecstasy of Steve Jobs," on the road even following this discovery and public retraction.
http://m.thisamericanlife.org/blog/2012/03/retracting-mr-daisey-and-the-apple-factory
[103] http://www.cbsnews.com/news/mexico-takes-title-of-most-obese-from-america/

restaurants here, as there are in Boston. Now I am cooking at home again and exercising. I lost 13 kilos!" This food war is not only a struggle for the poor, but for those with heavy workloads and strict time constraints, who have relied on the service industry to serve them their every meal.

For many people, keeping up with a lifestyle, which has become the norm in America has become a parade of Bread and Circuses, but it is often cheap bread and expensive circuses.

The Disappearing Face of 21st Century Gathering Patterns

> *"...among several dozen potential predictors of malaise (including self-described physical health, financial anxiety, frequency of exercise, use of cigarettes, religiosity, various forms of social connectedness, and all standard demographic characteristics), the top four, far above all other factors, turned out to be physical health, financial insecurity, low education (a proxy for social class), and TV dependence. Not surprisingly, physical health was the strongest predictor of malaise, but the other three were essentially equal in predictive power."*[104]

Perhaps the question is not how we gather, but rather if we gather at all. Social interaction has diminished in the last 40-50 years, according to the statistics gathered by Robert Putnam. We belong to fewer groups, and the groups we belong to have less impact upon our lives, and fewer instances, sometimes no occurrences, of face to face contact.

Putnam's evidence points to television viewing as the greatest factor leading the loss of social capital (a term used to describe the variety of benefits when people gather together in social groups). In 2009, Benjamin Olken (now professor of economics at MIT), published a study on the impact of the introduction of increased television and radio signal coverage, and the growth in the number of private television channels in rural villages in Indonesia. For each additional channel added to a community there was a decline in the number of social groups by 7 percent. The conclusion was that there was a measurable negative impact on social capital with the introduction of television. Perhaps more telling was a self-reported drop in trusting other people, which also came with the increased television usage.[105]

---

[104] Putnam, Robert D. (2001-08-01). Bowling Alone (Kindle Locations 4191-4195). Simon & Schuster. Kindle Edition.
[105] "Do Television and Radio Destroy Social Capital? Evidence from Indonesian Villages" by Benjamin Olken. American Economic Journal: Applied Economics 2009, 1:4, 1–33, http://economics.mit.edu/files/4120

With 70% of the households in the rural villages in the study group in Indonesia owning a television, the picture being painted is that the negative impact upon social capital may be most deleterious in developing countries, and among the poor. Satellite dishes dot the low-lying rooftop landscapes from the slums of Mumbai to the favelas of Sao Paulo. The expensive, but lonely entertainment of the television is somehow making the world a smaller place, while simultaneously increasing the distance between next-door neighbors, and perhaps even family members.

Robert Putnam's anecdote from a Detroit newspaper experiment in 1977 makes television usage seem like an addiction.

> *In 1977 the Detroit Free Press was able to find only 5 out of 120 families willing to give up television for a month in return for $500. People who do give up TV reportedly experience boredom, anxiety, irritation, and depression. One woman observed, "It was terrible. We did nothing—my husband and I talked."*[106]

The impact of television upon our world in the last 60 years brings the circus seats to our home. Now, we are entertained in private. Even the communal laughter we experience has been pre-recorded for us in canned laugh tracks. We experience the laughter without laughing, and the community of people who get the joke with us are digitally produced and mastered. We are living in a virtual circus, which further increases the dissonance and isolation of our world. Žižek regularly speaks of canned laughter as the most brilliant invention to come out of America. [107] I hope he's joking, but I'm not sure. The canned laughter may temporarily alleviate our stress with a sense of having laughed with the crowd, but the most brilliant, and the darkest manipulative social engineers could not have designed a more anesthetizing tool to stupefy the common man against joining a revolution.

In 2000, when Bowling Alone was published, it was too early to tell if internet usage was helping to alleviate this problem or exacerbate it, but the scant evidence at the time suggested a combination of both benefit and harm to social capital was occurring. The debate over internet usage and social capital continues. It appears to have both positive and negative impact.

---

[106] Putnam, Robert D. (2001-08-01). Bowling Alone (Kindle Locations 4175-4178). Simon & Schuster. Kindle Edition.
[107] Žižek on canned laughter: https://youtu.be/JE9bE1wiHdw

Religion meets Bread and Circuses

On YouTube, there is a mashup of televangelist Benny Hinn performing at a crusade synched with the song "Bodies" (popularly called "Let the Bodies Hit the Floor") by the band Drowning Pool.[108] Benny Hinn shouts and waves his hands, pushes people to ground, and swings his coat like a warrior with a battleax felling his enemies. Bodies fall in ecstatic twitching piles, and conservatively dressed businessmen in suits and ties flop on the floor like gasping fish. Beneath the surface of a hilarious, mocking video is a rather dramatic social commentary. The song lyrics of "Bodies" represent the internal conflict of someone who has been bullied, and responds with deadly Columbine-like violence. The bullying of big religion is a common theme in our skeptical culture, and the rallying call for the end of religion is often a violent abusive kneejerk response. This kneejerk response is clearly visible in the comments under the YouTube video.

The video mix of Benny Hinn with the Drowning Pool song illustrates the Bread and Circus issues at force in Christianity. The adoring eager crowd wait like nested baby birds for a touch from the God they cannot see, and trusting the man who supposedly speaks and acts for God, they respond willingly to the wild ecstatic circus of spiritual experience. Skeptics cry foul seeing cheap crowd manipulation at play, and mock both the performer and the gullible followers.

Although far more is occurring behind the curtain of the tangible screen of material reality, the critiques are accurate, and both Pentecostal and Evangelical Christianity too often look like the Pagan Rome we supposedly rejected. We offer the bread of cheap intellectual content, and a sad outdated circus of spiritual gimmickry. In doing so Christianity has adopted the modus operandi of centuries of Caesars and dictators who have waved Bread and Circuses before us. This Bread and Circuses approach to running a nation, a corporation, or even a church is seductive. It simultaneously creates a sense of adoration and fear in the heart of the followers, but for leaders desiring such respect, it is reminiscent of the story of Lucifer's fall, whose aim was to sit upon the throne of God.[109]

The end game of the Bread and Circuses approach to controlling and containing society is the same duel characteristics we find in the Roman Empire, and in the <u>Hunger Games</u>: cruel oppression, and public enthrallment. It should be no surprise that in a world enlivened to social justice the thinking person finds Bread and Circus religion

---

[108] YouTube mashup of Benny Hinn and Drowning Pool: https://youtu.be/5lvU-DislkI
[109] Isaiah 14:12-15

uninviting, and in some cases downright oppressive. The warning of Jesus concerning the manner of religious leadership still rings true after three millennia:

> *"Ye know that the princes of the Gentiles exercise dominion over them, and they that are great exercise authority upon them. But it shall not be so among you: but whosoever will be great among you, let him be your minister, and whosoever will be chief among you, let him be your servant."*[110]

Willow Creek Community Church in suburban Chicago, one of the largest and most influential churches in America, released the findings of a multi-year study of their congregation in the book, Reveal: Where Are You? By Greg Hawkins and Cally Parkinson. Willow Creek had been the center of what was called the "seeker-sensitive" church model. It was a high quality, performance based church model designed to attract people who did not normally attend church. The study revealed that although they were able to put butts in the seats, the model did not make the attenders better people – neither their love for God, nor their love for other people appeared to be growing significantly, and so, Willow Creek embarked on a new way of doing things. They had not intended to develop a Bread and Circuses model of leadership, but they discovered they had been offering cheap bread and expensive circuses for 30 years, and it had not accomplished the desired results.

Senior Pastor Bill Hybels said it this way, *"Some of the stuff that we have put millions of dollars into thinking it would really help our people and develop spiritually, when the data came back, it wasn't helping people that much."*[111]

The Willow Creek example shows clearly how well intentioned people doing great work may still resort to this style of leadership passed down to us since ancient times. Throughout the millennia of the life of the Christian Church, the Roman style of Bread and Circuses oversight has come and gone. We desire an easier way of living and learning, and settle for less nutritious bread and receive more expensive circuses.

Fortunately, this Bread and Circuses approach to ruling carries an inherent weakness – it is highly susceptible to revolutionaries.

The Carnival Flip:
Philosophers, Artists, Revolutionaries, and Preachers

---

[110] Matthew 20:25-27
[111] Christianity Today article "Willow Creek Repents?" October 18, 2007. http://www.christianitytoday.com/parse/2007/october/willow-creek-repents.html?paging=off

"A people who dance before their gods are generally freer and less repressed than a people who cannot."[112]

In the late 1920s, during the fury of Stalin's takeover in the Soviet revolution, a group of philosophers and literary critics met in small enclaves and discussed issues, which had a counter-revolutionary critique of the ongoing socialist/communist revolution. Some of these scholars were religious voices concerned with the growing persecution of Christianity in the still young Soviet Union. Others simply critiqued the development of socialism as they saw it forming. The young Mikhail Bakhtin was near the center of this movement. In a few short years, some of these scholars would be killed, others would flee, and Mikhail Bakhtin would be sent into exile. During his time in exile, Bakhtin would lose a leg to ill health, and yet maintain his scholarly work from the distance of the "rehabilitation camp." Rabelais and His World would be written during these years, and yet would not see publication until the 60s. When Rabelais and His World hit the scene of scholarly literary criticism in Western Universities in the 80s, it would become popular among film critics and theorists, and literary scholars. What Bakhtin brought to the table of discussion in the film and literary world were two unique theories, which he called Carnivalesque, and the dialogical. It is the intersection of these theories that the following thoughts on the "Carnival Flip" are dependent, and owe their genesis.

There is an inherent and fundamental difference between the manner in which I am using the word "circus" in this book, and the Bakhtinian definition of "carnival." The circus is an entertainment performance meant to woo and wow the crowd. The circus performer lives in the world of "go big or go home." The performer must dazzle the audience. The ticket price covers the large infrastructure supporting the line between the performer and the spectator. The carnival, at least in Bakhtin's idealized medieval sense, is a radically participative event. The high regard for rulers is erased in the mocking festivities of a fantasy world. Each person comes to the carnival to act out – no, to live for a day – his/her mythic hopes and dreams. Costumes become a skin of temporary transformation, and the wearer expresses his interior passions with greater freedom from behind the mask. In this world, everyone is an actor, everyone has a part to play in directing the festivities, and I am empowered. I am King for a day.

"Goethe correctly stressed that carnival is the only feast the people offer to themselves; they do not receive anything and have no sanctimonious regard for

---

[112] Feast of Fools, Harvey Cox, Harvard University Press, 1969, page 48

anyone. They are the hosts and are only hosts, for there are no guests, no spectators, only participants."[113]

Examples of the participative carnival are found all across our culture. Mardi Gras in New Orleans is a festive event with a king picked from among the commoners who floats through the streets in high regalia with his attending court, while the local leaders look on from the sidelines. The structure of power is mocked and turned upside down, and the city comes alive with a wild expression of common people pretending to be kings and queens displaying their creativity in the grandest ways. Burning Man and the host of smaller "burns" around the world have developed a set of 10 principles outlining the ethic of their wild, often hedonistic expression. Among these principles are included radical self-expression, gifting, communal effort, and participation. Everyone is asked to be a giver, a participant, and a co-worker in the event. Ideally, there are no pure spectators. Perhaps even the rise of Halloween as a major holiday is a mark of our innate desire to be players on the stage of life and not spectators only. We dress up, we show off, and we become actors and actresses for a night.

This participative nature of the Carnivalesque is the rip in the fabric through which the light of day shines into the darkened tent of Bread and Circuses, and it is the artists, the philosophers, the revolutionaries, and the preachers who poke their heads through the hole. Mikhail Bakhtin intimately connected his theory of Carnivalesque and its revolutionary power of a participative, mocking, ambivalent festivity with what he called the "dialogical." The dialogical is related to a multi-voiced (polyphonic) artistic style Bakhtin saw in Dostoevsky's novels. The dialogical is not a closed ended monologue with all the questions answered and nothing left to say, rather it is always open for response and dialogue between parties – this is true even within our own minds as we struggle with ourselves. The dialogical is not limited to literature though. It is the way of community involvement in the wild and interactive medieval carnival, and it is inherent to the nature of the relationship between God and humanity. As Ruth Coates observed,

> *"What Bakhtin often used to call the 'philosophy of dialogue' lay at the basis of all his literary-critical works: all of life is a dialogue, a dialogue between person and person, person and nature, person and God ..."*[114]

---

[113] Mikhail Bakhtin, Rabelais and His World, page 249
[114] Ruth Coates. Christianity in Bakhtin: God and the Exiled Author (Cambridge Studies in Russian Literature) (Kindle Locations 151-152). Kindle Edition.

The multi-voiced, open world of the Carnivalesque is inherently revolutionary. It is given to speaking its mind, asking questions, fostering tomfoolery, and challenging authority. It is mocking. It is a pimply, stubborn, yet talented and brilliant youth standing angrily in the face of unquestioned and meaningless rules, and it despises status quo for the sake of status quo. Although a multi-voiced world also includes conservative law abiding citizens, fearful law keepers, and even micro-managers; the wildness and the challenge of the rebels brings the party to the circus and transforms it into a wild interactive carnival by changing the rules. This is where the philosopher, the artist, the revolutionary, and the preacher create a world of trouble for us, but we would live a suppressed, manipulated, meaningless existence without them. It is they who call us out of spectatorship in the grandstand seats of the darkened Bread and Circus tent and out into the festive open market of the Carnival.

On April 13th, 2014 three British spies surrounded a telephone booth in Cheltenham, UK. They hugged the wall behind the phone booth and listened in on conversations with their electronic surveillance equipment. The spies were the stenciled graffiti work from the UK artist known only as Banksy. Cheltenham is the home of Government Communications Headquarters and the work was a humorous critique on the British government spying on their own people.

Banksy is the most famous urban artist in the world today. His work is often a dark, laughing social commentary, and paradoxically, if your wall gets tagged it could be worth a lot of money. Although now a world famous artist, Banksy still represents the subversive side of graffiti art, where poor urban youth illegally create a voice for themselves, because it is perhaps the only way they can be heard in the suppressed life of an impoverished cheap bread and expensive circuses existence. Through graffiti artists like Banksy and the Parisian Blek le Rat, urban art has reached out of the underground and into the fine art studios and museums, and with it the voice of the oppressed is calling from off-stage and receiving world-wide attention.

Andy Warhol mocked our repetitive addictive capitalistic existence with repeating Campbell's Soup cans and Marilyn Monroe faces. At heart he was a trouble-making Carnivalesque artist, as evidenced by the proliferation of quotes supposedly attributed to him, such as this, *"I like to be the right thing in the wrong place, and the wrong thing in the right place. Being the right thing in the wrong place and the wrong thing in the right place is worth it because something interesting always happens."*

The beat poets, the musical revolution of rock and roll, the hippies of the 60s, Pride Parades, trance festivals, flashmobs, the Occupy movement and the Tea Party: whether we agree with the activities, the direction and/or philosophy of any number of these phenomenon, they each carry (or, at least once carried) the power of the Carnivalesque with them. They represent moments of a "Carnival Flip." They arrived, and our world was turned upside down, and a popular uprising with the mocking of authority ensued.

Philosophers and social critics had paved the way for these moments of upheaval. Radical thought has started movements, influenced culture, and launched revolutions. Hegel, Marx, Nietzsche, and Freud are some of the most influential voices from the past still invoking revolution today, but Michel Foucault, Jacques Derrida, and more recently Slavoj Žižek carnivalize us with a radical clowning philosophy.

The Carnival Flip is most observable in protest movements. Few people seem to remember the beginnings in the short history of the recent American Tea Party. Renegade Republican Ron Paul garnered national attention, and a faithful following with an all too common sense approach and libertarian leanings in 2007. In February of 2009, people were asked to mail their used tea bags into their representatives as a protest against high taxes and massive bailouts. Just days later, on February 19, Rick Santelli of CNBC morning news reported from the trading floor in Chicago before the opening of trading. He criticized a government plan subsidizing bad mortgages. The traders on the floor cheered, Santelli joked that they were holding a tea party in reference to the famed Boston Tea Party of Colonial America. The video went viral. Within 10 hours of the report from the floor in Chicago, small tea parties were being arranged all around the nation to take place on Independence Day as a protest. Within days the term "Tea Party" was being used by Fox News as though it was a potentially game changing third party addition to the American two-party system. This began as a grassroots revolutionary momentum couched in humorous carnival behavior looking like a tea party from Alice in Wonderland.

From the left, the Occupy Movement camped itself in front of the Federal Reserve building in Boston, in Zucotti Park near Wall Street in New York, and 919 other places around the world where voices against a centralized world control of the economy, which betrays the interest of the common person (the "99%") could be heard. Small tent villages of protesters refusing to move from public spaces popped up in 82 countries. This was another example of a grassroots, participative protest against an economic system oppressing the average world citizen. It was a Carnival Flip with world impact, but like the Tea Party before it, which was tamed and overrun by Republican voices and mocked by Democratic voices, the Bread and Circus ringmasters on both sides of the aisle were powerful enough to suppress Occupy's beautiful Carnival momentum.

Like the philosopher, the artist, and the revolutionary, the preacher has also been a master of the Carnivalesque in world history – both ancient and modern. The wild Syrian ascetic Saint Simeon Stylites lived on a pillar for 39 years in the 6th century. His insane mysticism made him renowned, and even popes sent emissaries to beseech the favor and wisdom of Simeon. Saint Francis of Assisi has been called the clown of God. Yet, many of his most notable marks – his vows of poverty, and itinerant preaching among the common folk were already happening in France under Peter Waldo and the besieged Waldensians at least 50 years earlier. The season in which Saint Francis arrived was alive with religious Carnival revolution.

In more recent Christian history, what now feels like a too-oft-repeated cliché was a once subtle Carnivalesque turnaround phrase given by Evangelical Christians to their detractors who were quick to reject the trappings of Organized Religion. *"It's not about religion. It's about relationship,"*[115] was the quick retort. This response was at one time a surprise comeback to people who had never heard it before. It dialed back the fears about lists of dos and don'ts. It removed the dread of the smothering wet blanket of a dull liturgy, and presented a spiritual experience of interactive participation with an imminent God, Who wants to walk and talk with us and cares for us deeply. It was a response in every way Bakhtinian Carnivalesque, though I am not sure that Bakhtin – from a Russian Orthodox upbringing, and living under the suppression of Stalin would have recognized this simple but brilliant Carnival Flip.

In the late 1950s the "Death of God" theology used the most radical of religious terminology to capture popular attention. Gabriel Vahanian suggested that the God we have imagined needed to die, and a new theology of a radically transcendent Godhead needed to be resurrected in our post-Christian era. The theological movement carried all the surprise of a Carnival Flip. It stole the show from the dreary pulpit and placed the impetus for transformation in the individual thinker. This theological movement seeming to echo Nietzsche preceded John Lennon's interview statement of being more popular than Jesus, and Time magazine's famous "Is God Dead?" cover by at least 10 years.

The examples of the Carnival Flip above found in artists, philosophers, revolutionaries, and preachers are often foolish moments

---

[115] It is quite possible that this now common theme among evangelicals has only served as a way to shoot the movement in foot, as churches in the US struggle talk about not being religious and still attempt to invite people to church.

of surprise, and this is the nature of the revolutionary power of the Carnivalesque. It is a surprise forcing open the doors of interpersonal relationships and honest dialogue. Alexandar Mihailovich speaks of this moment in almost painfully erotic terms, *"In Bakhtin's view, as in Gumilev's, true life begins with rupturing the protective membrane of individual existence….."*[116] So radical was Bakhtin's insistence upon the dialogical sharing nature of Christianity, that it defined his thoughts on the Kingdom of God,

> *"Bakhtin several times repeated the phrase that, as it were, objective idealism maintains that the kingdom of God is outside us, and Tolstoy, for example, insists that it is 'within us', but I think that the kingdom of God is between us, between me and you, between me and God, between me and nature: that's where the kingdom of God is."* (Kozhinov 1992, 114 15)[117]

It is the prepositions, which make all the difference here. Bakhtin envisions the hand of God at work in the relationships, in the "between." It is in the dialogue we establish with one another, and in the openness we have toward one another. Although there is much to be said about the prepositional variations not being an either/or proposition, but rather existing in simultaneity, it does not negate the power of Bakhtin's observation. The Kingdom outside of me, and the Kingdom inside of me both lend themselves to a potential non-participative puppetry with a god who simply does something to me, but in the interaction "between us" lies the dialogical. This is where we hear and are heard, where working together, playing together, and hoping together all happens. The dialogical is the dance that separates spectators in the Bread and Circuses Big Top from the wild transformative Carnivalesque marketplace of Gospel revolution. This between-ness places God in the impossible space between secular society and religion. The un-navigable gap is already bridged by a voice, by a relationship, and as impossible as it is for humanity to live in this space – I contend that someone is already living there, and has spread His bleeding wrists across the gap.

In the 1964 World's Fair, a controversial short Christian film made for the Lutheran Council played in the Protestant pavilion. Parable by Rolf Forsberg was on a continuous loop during the fair.[118] People protested the showing of the film, because Jesus was portrayed as a

---

[116] Alexander Mihailovich, Corporeal Words, page 42
[117] Ruth Coates. Christianity in Bakhtin: God and the Exiled Author (Cambridge Studies in Russian Literature) (Kindle Locations 153-155). Kindle Edition.
[118] You can witch a low quality version of this rare film on YouTube here: https://youtu.be/cCkqyyBClmU

silent, white mime-like clown following a traveling circus, and this was considered sacrilege. In the twenty-two minute film, the clown interjects himself into four scenarios, and in each scene he takes the place of beleaguered circus workers winning both followers and enemies along the way. In the last scene of this substitutionary activity, the clown enters the Big Top, and with his newfound followers he begins brushing the shoes of children in the stands who are staring blankly at a performance up in the center of the circus tent. Circus performers high up in Big Top are dangling like living marionettes in a mock fight, with the Master Puppeteer pulling at their ropes. The entranced children snap to their senses, and begin laughing with the clown as he brushes their feet. The clown frees the living marionettes, and takes their place in the ropes. He is lifted to the top of the tent, and as the children leave the Big Top laughing, the Puppet Master cruelly pulls at the ropes and the clown's enemies beat him to death. It is in this scene that we see the full movement of the Carnival Flip – the transition from the manipulative circus to the participative and revolutionary carnival inherent to the Gospel. The children transition from a silent hypnotized audience to a laughing crowd. The oppressed are freed from their bondage, and the liberator steps into the place of their oppression.

Without this participative element in life, which Bakhtin called the dialogical, the Gospel itself becomes a Bread and Circuses motif, where we are not sure if we are the spectators or the puppets in the cruel momentum of our world. Only in the Carnival Flip – in the transition from Bread and Circuses to the celebratory carnival are we liberated into a wild new world of adventure and participation with God.

Bakhtin referred to this power as "carnivalistic mésalliances" and observed,

> *"A free and familiar attitude spreads over everything: over all values, thoughts, phenomena, and things. All things that were once self-enclosed, disunified, distanced from one another by a noncarnivalistic hierarchical worldview are drawn into carnivalistic contacts and combinations. Carnival brings together, unifies, weds, and combines the sacred with the profane, the lofty with the low, the great with the insignificant, the wise with the stupid."*[119]

The Apostle Paul understood the nature of this foolish momentum. He foresaw that through history it would not be power, money, or intelligence that would become the abiding influences of Christianity. The Roman model of Bread and Circuses was rejected by Paul in favor

---

[119] Bakhtin, Mikhail (1984-06-21). Problems of Dostoevsky's Poetics (Theory and History of Literature) (p. 123). University Press of Minnesota - A. Kindle Edition.

of something more common, more intrusive, and much more subversive.

> *"For it is written: "I will destroy the wisdom of the wise, And bring to nothing the understanding of the prudent." Where is the wise? Where is the scribe? Where is the disputer of this age? Has not God made foolish the wisdom of this world? For since, in the wisdom of God, the world through wisdom did not know God, it pleased God through the foolishness of the message preached to save those who believe. For Jews request a sign, and Greeks seek after wisdom; but we preach Christ crucified, to the Jews a stumbling block and to the Greeks foolishness, but to those who are called, both Jews and Greeks, Christ the power of God and the wisdom of God. Because the foolishness of God is wiser than men, and the weakness of God is stronger than men.*
>
> *For you see your calling, brethren, that not many wise according to the flesh, not many mighty, not many noble, are called. But God has chosen the foolish things of the world to put to shame the wise, and God has chosen the weak things of the world to put to shame the things which are mighty; and the base things of the world and the things which are despised God has chosen, and the things which are not, to bring to nothing the things that are, that no flesh should glory in His presence."*[20]

Carnival and the Gospel

> *"The Gospel, too, is carnival."*
> *– Mikhail Bakhtin*[121]

Lest I lose you in this quirky pseudo-philosophical rambling about circuses and carnivals, I should back up a few miles and describe in simple terms how this revolutionary activity, proposed by an obscure and persecuted one-legged Russian philosopher, which he called "Carnivalesque," applies to the Christian message. And it might do me well to give some descriptions of what it is and what it is not. Of course, I say this with the hope that you are still reading this book, and I have not already lost you. If I have lost you, you won't know that I am thumbing my nose at those of you who have stopped reading, and I am giving you a sloppy Bronx Cheer right now.

Akin, to Shakespeare's "life is a stage", my use of "carnival" is not just something that happens on an abandoned dirt lot in your town when the trucks arrive and unload dizzying rides, and cotton-candy booths. The Bakhtinian carnival applies to all of life. It is the place

---

[120] 1 Corinthians 1:20-31
[121] Mikhail Bakhtin as quoted in a interview with Turbin. Ruth Coates pg.126

surprise meets you in a discussion, and you say, "I've never thought of it like that before." It is the space in which you change your mind almost in opposition to your own will. It happens in a book, when you are offended or delighted, and gasp or laugh for disgust and/or joy. Carnival hides between the laughter and tears of friends. It is, as Bakhtin described it, "ambivalent," and in this sense, it is possible for carnival to be revolutionary for good and for bad purposes, even for competing and un-reconcilable purposes. The 1960s hippie movement with its anti-war, anti-establishment, free-love motif was one type of carnival revolution, yet that carnival itself was carnivalized from within by the Jesus People Movement and crazy hippie preachers like Lonnie Frizbee.[122]

Carnival as a concept may be ambivalent, yet in its individual expressions – when it arrives on the scene of human history – is directed toward revolutionary change. It is sometimes the impetus behind impassioning you or surprising you, and certainly it is the persuasion that invokes you to laugh mockingly at the structures of power. It causes you to consider if things should be the way they are, and prods you, not so gentle (to riff off Dylan Thomas)[123], toward an uncomfortable alliance with insurrection.

The historic universality of the Carnivalesque was noted by Bakhtin in the closing words of Rabelais and His World, which is the seminal work on his thoughts about the subject,

"… *every act of world history was accompanied by a laughing chorus. But not every period of history had Rabelais for a coryphaeus.*"[124]

In simple terms, Carnivalesque has been described as "world upside-down." And this is why Bakhtin can say that, "the Gospel, too, is carnival."

If ever the world was turned upside down, it was in the 1st Century AD, when the obscure carpenter from Nazareth, in the Roman occupied territory of Israel, traveled around his tiny region teaching and performing miracles. After His unfair trial and execution, His followers

---

[122] Lonnie Frisbee's amazing and tragic story was documented by his friends in the film Frisbee: Life and Death of a Hippie Preacher. Two separate fellowships/denominations (Calvary Chapel and The Vineyard) owe their initial growth to his wildly anarchic and charismatic influence. Yet, his name has been effectively removed from their corporate memory. Purchase or rent movie here: http://www.amazon.com/Frisbee-Life-Death-Hippie-Preacher/dp/B00L40IW1Y
[123] A humorous and brilliant reading of the Welsh poet Dylan Thomas's piece, Do Not Go Gentle into that Good Night was done by Rodney Dangerfield in the movie Back to School. http://www.youtube.com/watch?v=mTv1Dmu5CYc
[124] Rabelias and His World, Bakhtin pg. 474

shared His compelling story across the empire and initiated what has become the largest, and most influential religious movement in world history.

Yet in saying this, it should be noted that carnival is not the Christian Gospel. Although this seems contradictory to Bakhtin's quote above, it is a simple logical equation. Carnival is found in the Gospel, but it is not the Gospel. The Gospel is a "world upside-down" revolution. Yet, not all things that turn the world upside-down are the Gospel. Otherwise, A (the Gospel) is B (carnival), but not all B is A.

Carnival is also not simply laughter and mocking. There is a serious and sometimes dark side to this revolutionary power. Recently, Banksy's graffiti appeared on a wall in Clacton-on-Sea, Essex, UK. The city was soon to vote on a local law concerning immigration. Banksy painted a piece on the side of a storage facility depicting a power line with five pigeons sitting together. A short distance down the power line and sitting alone was a small exotic bird looking back over his shoulder at the pigeons. The pigeons held protest signs with sayings like, "Migrants not welcome", and "Go back to Africa." The city painted over the art, calling it racist. When Banksy posted a photo of the piece on his website, the city realized their mistake. They had erased an invaluable work of art, which was a dark and serious social commentary on the tensions over immigration in the UK.

Banksy's pigeon piece also highlights the fact that Carnival is not always easily understood. It carries a degree of mystery, which is often the nature of subversion. It can be sarcastic, and mocking. It may juxtapose the way things are with the way things should be. It comes as a surprise you weren't expecting, and often will simply go over your head using illustrations, which offend or challenge while expounding on truth, as in the example of the clown Jesus in Rolf Forsberg's film Parable.

It is these moments of intellectual and emotional exchange I call the "Carnival Flip." When a subversive concept emerges in dialogic exchange, and turns social construct, political expectation, or philosophical and theological ideas on their head, the "Carnival Flip" has occurred. And moments of "Carnival Flip" fill the pages of the Bible, and the history of the Christian Church. This world can be a cruel Roman circus, but I believe that God is directing us by surprise to the interactive joyful carnival.

Carnivalesque in Scripture – a Hermeneutic of Wonder

The Carnivalesque surprises of God are marbled through the pages of the Bible. Our 21st century vision is trained by a skeptical and obscene hermeneutic.[125] We anticipate all cruelty and tragedy – a mean God in the Bible, but the laughing jester, hiding in the sacred pages, must be rediscovered by people with eyes for the surprises of God. The task of a complete Carnivalesque commentary on the Bible would be a wonderful service to the generations trapped in fear of the tragic and a foreboding anticipation of the apocalyptic, but only a few most notable examples are possible here.

Just in the first story of interaction between God and humanity we should already be standing on our heads hoping to see the world aright.

Humanity is made from the dirt of the ground. We are "but dust." Popularly, we say today that we are made of "star stuff." There is no effective difference between star stuff and the dust of the earth. So, the crowning act of God's creation is made of dirt, and this does not strike us strangely, perhaps even as ancient brilliance? I have already carnivalized the story of the tree of the knowledge of good and evil, and the prohibition against eating one particular fruit, with human society having its genesis with this one peculiar law. The skeptical obscene hermeneutic calls this an arbitrary and cruel law. The carnival hermeneutic calls this crazy – only one law for the entirety of human culture, and it is connected to fruit on a tree. What a wild act of grace and trust!

The story of the Fall continues with the first couple camouflaging themselves in fig leaves and hiding amidst the bushes of the garden, hoping God won't find them; an absurdity which laughingly highlights our own behavior when we've been caught with our hand in the cookie jar. And the story ends with God sending a once holy and naked couple into a struggling world where they are clothed, but perform a good deal of their unholy activities in a shame-based and shame-full nakedness. This is a story of a world turned upside-down by a tiny human action, and the utopian world that was lost has been the dream of philosophers, artists and adventurers since history was recorded. Ponce de Leon hunted for the fountain of youth. Rousseau enamored himself with the concept of the noble savage. The impressionist painter Gauguin has been accused of following Rousseau's ideals. He left a family in Denmark to cavort in Tahiti. The ancient inversion of the current human condition appears embedded into our soul. It subversively and against our own will, seeks the roots of a holy

---

[125] Please note, that in making a reference to a skeptical and obscene hermeneutic, I am not insinuating that skepticism is obscene. I, in fact, remain a skeptic in many ways. I am only saying that there is an obscene skeptical interpretation of religion, which is popular today. It automatically assumes that faith and religion carry inherent oppression and cruelty. To see evil in others at first sight is a prejudice, which should not be considered anything but obscene.

innocent beginning, but the story of that utopian loss is framed carnivalesquely in terms of apples and snakes, of fig leaves and flaming swords.

The history of Israel is filled with stories of inversion and surprise. A Hebrew slave boy becomes a powerful leader in the land of Egypt, because he interprets dreams, and this absurd story repeats itself in the Babylonian empire. A skinny Jewish kid with a slingshot kills one of the world's most feared warriors in a face-off and emboldens the army to victorious battle. Musicians lead the nation into battle, and donkeys talk to mad prophets. Prophets are swallowed by big fish, sleep with hungry lions, and are thrown into bonfires and live to tell about it. Ezekiel mimes his way into Israel's prophetic history. The devil becomes consumed with the destruction of a single man, but poor ol' Job hangs on with his integrity intact. Israel builds idols on the mountains, and the omnipotent God weeps like a jilted lover.

The tragic and the cruel are found in the pages of scripture, just as they are found in our world today. Eyes that see nothing but cruelty are prejudicially trained against seeing stories of wonder and delight with their accompanying life-inverting lessons.

The Carnival Flip is at its most obvious in the messianic story. Jesus' life becomes the greatest story ever to blow our minds. God incarnate is born into an obscure occupied nation, and an inconsequential town, in an unimportant family. God becomes the disenfranchised 99%. Miracles are performed, but in contrast to the horn-toting, self-promoting marketing of our age, Jesus tells people to remain quiet. The declaration of his kingship over the Earth occurs on a donkey ride processional into the capital, and the pauper-God story continues to unravel before our eyes. In the end of the story we kill God and He does not retaliate. Rather, He initiates His fisherman friends, outsiders to the classes of high ranking, into the highest levels of Church leadership.

In Jesus, sinners are sought, and religious leaders are rejected, and all our thoughts on God are inverted. God comes down to initiate the dialogue with us and hang out in the local tavern to have a brew, and the authorities get upset about it.

This is the engaging, sometimes humorous, sometimes tragic, always surprising story of Christianity, but it seems that our culture has lost that story in a haze of skeptical bias and visions of a cruel God exacting torture, when in fact, the story tells of the power brokers of this world slaying the God Who visits them offering healing and deliverance.

Could it be that our eyes see the cruel Bread and Circuses God, because that is all we are trained to see? Could it be that He came with a dialogical "Carnival Flip" to bring the party back into our lives?

It may be that our interpretation of the Bible is a kind of psychological transference or projection test telling us more about ourselves than it does about God.

The Carnival Flip and the Individual

> *"The true being of the spirit begins only when repentance begins… I am infinitely bad, but someone needs me to be good."* – Mikhail Bakhtin[126]

Metanoia – a change of mind. This Koine word, fundamental to the Greek New Testament, is typically translated "repentance." The word "repentance" primarily invokes thoughts of sorrow and remorse for wrongs committed. A "change of mind" somehow seems less morose, and yet, more transformational.

When the carnival comes and satirizes our lives, it is a call to change. Mikhail Bakhtin astutely observed that others' opinion of us is more accurate than the opinion we hold of ourselves, and though this cannot be universally claimed, the nature of metanoia assumes this is true. Someone, sometime, writing somewhere described, critiqued and at times parodied your life, and in doing so seemed to know all about you. Such is the sense of properly interpreted scripture. James speaks of the Word of God as a mirror, and when we read the words but do not apply them to our lives, we walk away ignorant of who we truly are. Like transformational festivals, where the experience is only a true experience when the transformation occurs in the heart and mind of the individual, an interpretation of scripture without application is effectively not a helpful experience of the scriptures at all. Words are intended to have life beyond the written page. A good word has the power to transform a life in a positive manner, and it begins with pinpoint accuracy in an interaction with our hearts. Boris Gunjevic uses surgical terminology to describe this accuracy.

> *"An unexpected clinical incision can provoke a entirely new vision of ourselves which we couldn't have seen until that shift, having been obsessed by our own phobias and fixations."*[127]

This surgical incision on the human heart is the beginning of the inversion of our little world. Fixing corporate structures and systems using unchanged individuals is effectively no change at all. The best of systems is corruptible by creatively selfish people. In the spirit of this

---

[126] Bakhtin, as quoted in lecture notes from Pumpianski, Bakhtin and Religion, pg. 209
[127] Žižek and Gunjevic, God in Pain, pg. 259

principle, the Apostle Paul spoke about sin taking advantage of the law to betray me – even slay me.[128] Even that most holy of systems, the law of God, is powerless against unchanged and stubborn subtleties of our self-absorbed inner conflicts. But metanoia is the surgical cut of carnival surprise transplanting new hearts, and correcting vision.

The Carnival and Freedom

> *"In the spirit of the Chalcedonian formula, Bakhtin is critical of any utter fusion or merging of difference."*[129]

The Chalcedonian formula Mihailovich comments about above is a reference to the Council of Chalcedon in 451 AD, and the Chalcedonian Creed that came from it. This creed was one of the foundational moments in the development of doctrine in the Christian Church. The focus of the Chalcedonian Creed was the dual nature of Jesus Christ. He is described as being both God and man, not in some kind of hybridization, but fully and completely both. The Chalcedonian formula does not attempt to demystify the nature of the Son of God, but allows it to remain unmixed, and enigmatic.

> *"... the distinction of natures being by no means taken away by the union, but rather the property of each nature being preserved, and concurring in one Person and one Subsistence..."*[130]

This unmerged difference of man and God being found together in the one person of Christ is a model of polyphonic literature, and of a multi-voiced world for Bakhtin. Each voice carries its own world of value, and stands independent in its own right within the Bakhtinian polyphony. Never does two become one in a way that destroys the independent life of either voice. This is the nature of carnivalesque revolution: it does not make two one and the same, but rather liberates the one trapped in the expectations or oppression of another. The circus turns a large number of individuals into a crowd, acting in unison. The Bakhtinian carnival comes to liberate the herd back into individual actors, whose parts are equally valuable – no longer a mesmerized mass, but a free and rebellious throng of independently thinking members.

In the Gospel, many are not one because they are the same, but many are one in their difference. Bakhtin's severe critique of a unity,

---

[128] Romans 7:8-10
[129] Mihailovich, pg. 139
[130] Chalcedonian Creed

which diminishes the individual, is aligned with the Pauline concept of the "body of Christ." Many become one, but not one loses its radical uniqueness.[131]

Sinclair Lewis' 1927 satirical novel Elmer Gantry was listed as the number one fiction bestseller of the year. The book was banned in Boston, among other places, and was a favorite enemy in Christian pulpits for a season. The book, and the 1960 movie based upon it tell the story of an alcoholic charlatan preacher, who becomes a manager and eventually the lover of the popular female evangelist, Sharon Falconer.[132] In the end, as a newly erected tabernacle burns to the ground and kills Sharon Falconer, Elmer Gantry escapes the fire leaving Sharon behind and only thinking of himself. Undaunted, he goes on to marry up, and take over a large church.

Elmer Gantry may be a prophetic announcement of the Christian Church in its often return to a Bread and Circuses model of church life, and the self-immolation inherent to the model.

Unfortunately, the weakness of the somewhat anarchic, interactive carnival revolution is the inverse of the weakness of the circus. Just as the Roman Bread and Circuses is susceptible to the revolutionary, the carnival revolution of the Gospel is susceptible to manipulative and charismatic super stars, and lazy hedonists who only want the party without the responsibility of hosting others. Both religion and the secular are susceptible to this. Even that most radical expression of Carnivalesque today, the Burning Man Festival, is struggling with the pressure of a Roman Bread and Circuses invasion. The three-ring circus of capitalism is taking over with a corporate commodification of the event. Many fans of the event are losing their respect for Burning Man. Plug-and-play luxury camps with everything pre-arranged, and selfish rich people driving around in rented art cars with high priced hookers on their arms does not evoke a sense of radical self-expression, radical self-reliance, and gifting, nor any other kind of carnival revolution.[133]

Both religion and secular society are susceptible to being manipulated by frail human passions and a lust for power and money, and yet, there is hope for a better church and a better world. Sergei Averintsev describes Bakhtin's relentless hope for this better world.

"and yet, Bakhtin was right, profoundly right, when he placed his hope in the

---

[131] 1 Cor. 12:12-27
[132] Trailer for the movie Elmer Gantry: https://youtu.be/0f4ZQW-XBWs
[133] The movie Spark highlights this tension, and shows Burning Man struggling with the changing dynamics of the festival.

fact that as long as the people were the people, the last word has not been spoken..."[134]

Andy Warhol's prescience seems most astute in his supposed prediction of a world in which every person would experience a short spurt of fame, *"In the future, everybody will be world famous for fifteen minutes."* "As long as the people" maintain their individual voices the carnival will continue to invade the Bread and Circuses and turn it upside-down. The Savior peeks through the tear in the circus tent bringing liberation and transformation in the face the people. Of course, we expect the Savior to peek through the tear with the face of the artists, the philosophers, the revolutionaries and the preachers, but God has chosen the "foolish things of this world" to turn the world upside-down. So, any old fool will do. It just might be me, and it just might be you.

---

[134] Sergei Averintsev, Bakhtin and Religion, pg. 89

Engage: Do you feel trapped between the Circus and the Carnival?

Religion, politics, and economics all appear to be a circus of action. Everyone wants our attention, our money, and for us to jump on their bandwagon. In this chapter, the carnival is used as a motif of interactivity and freedom, which breaks away from the three-ring circus advertising for our attention and allegiance. Can you imagine politics and religion in an interactive space with everyone holding equal value? I acknowledge that this is in many ways idealistic, but can you picture it? If so, what tiny steps could each of us take to move us toward this goal?

Interact with the Burning Religion community on the website at www.burningreligion.com.

Tales from the Land of Jaw: The Adventures of Gwyn Dee
The Feast at Little Finger

A few short hours after leaving Salvatown, Gwyn Dee happed upon a lonely, struggling, and long-faced old woman with an overly large stone yoke upon her neck.

"May I help you with your burden?" Gwyn Dee flinched with memories of years of stone shoe wearing, and desperately wanted to help unchain the poor woman.

"Please, do not come near to my yoke. You shall only make my burden greater, if you seek to help me." Hopelessness was measured in the dropping tone of her voice, and the long-faced old woman trudged on.

Gwyn Dee walked beside her for a short distance knowing that being there was sometimes as good as lending a helping hand. The long-faced old woman looked down at Gwyn Dee's unshod feet, and stopped. She looked Gwyn Dee up and down, once or twice.

"It is not wise to walk in these parts unburdened from the Stones of Discipline, my dear."

Gwyn Dee understood the import of her words, and pulled from the shoulder bag the magically light stone shoes from Salvatown. Gwyn Dee smiled and slipped them on, and the long-faced old woman strained a small smile back.

"Your stone shoes are not large enough for the Elders of Little Finger, but they will do for now." And the long-faced old woman trudged onward.

Soon, long-faced people young and old were to be seen sitting along the road side with massive stone shoes, enormous stone yokes, and ponderous stone bracelets chained to their bodies. Few gathered the energy to look up and nod a weary hello, and Gwyn Dee felt the sadness of the growing crowd. It weighed upon Gwyn Dee like the stone yokes the people carried upon their necks.

"These are the people who have no homes, and not enough strength to find another town in which to work and live. They are the poor of Little Finger." The long-faced old woman glanced at Gwyn Dee and a little sparkle flickered deep inside the wizened, weathered eyes.

"Welcome to Little Finger", the sign said. It was large, and freshly painted, and contrasted with the shacks hugging the eastern edge of the wide, wide road. The shacks piled haphazardly against the road, as if hoping to spill out and tumble away. Across the road a large temple gleamed white and beautiful, and cast it's long shadow upon the rickety town.

The long-faced old woman stopped in the shade of the temple. She looked at the long faces of the weary people, and then standing taller than Gwyn Dee thought it was possible for the long-faced old woman to stand, she pulled a large stick from the pack on her back, and drew a line down the middle of the road. Gwyn Dee watched the strange liturgy with curiosity.

"Dear people of Little Finger. I come with friends, and we come with hope. We come with strength for the journey, and we come with a feast today!" The long-faced old woman shouted with the strong voice of a liberator.

The long-faced people looked up listlessly, with hollow eyes, and in the face of their hopeless stares ten strong young men burst onto the street. They wore heavy stone gloves on their hands, and their strong arms rippled with the muscles of seasoned soldiers. Their stone gloves had excessively long and disproportionately thick little fingers. They rushed into the street with tables, and running back into the shacks on the road returned with large steaming pots of stews, and plates of warm breads, and fruits and cheeses of all sorts.

The long-faced people looked up with empty stares. Some looked away, and others yet scoffed.

"They will not rise to come to the feast. We must bring it to them, and hope that they will eat. Will you help me serve them, Gwyn Dee of the Clown Caste?" The twinkle in the long-faced old woman's eyes exploded like the stars on a clear new moon night.

Gwyn Dee was surprised at being known once again in a strange place, but laughed and loaded plates of food, and with the strong young men with stone gloves, and a growing crew of both men and women, ran back and forth serving the plates to the long-faced people of Little Finger.

Some ate voraciously. Some looked at the plates with trepidation and glanced toward the towering white temple across the street. Others refused to eat, and set the plates aside, and others still mocked and shouted for the generous strangers to go away.

Suddenly, a siren sounded from the large white temple, and every long-faced person stopped what they were doing, and looked submissively at the ground. The doors of the temple flew open and a small army of sword wielding warriors poured into the wide, wide road and stopped unconsciously at the line the long-faced old woman had drawn in the road. Twelve well-dressed elders stepped out of the temple and stood at the top of the stairs. They raised their hands into the air, and splayed their fingers to the sky. Each of the twelve elders had four fingers on each hand – all missing their little fingers.

"We, the elders of Little Finger are your servants, ordained by Jaw to be your leaders. These intruders have poisoned you with weakness. Place the food aside and do not partake in their devilish, lustful dainties." *The Elders of Little Finger hummed in unison as the chief elder spoke.*

The long-faced old woman laughed. "We mock your soldiers. We mock your disciplines, and your demand to the huddled masses to live the hard life, while you sit cozily in your dead white temple. We come with help, and we will lift our little fingers and our strong arms to help your starving people!"

The Elders of Little Finger shook their four fingered hands, and howled. The soldiers rushed across the line in the road. The long-faced old woman wielded her stick with deadly accuracy, and quickly flattened three warriors. The strong young men dropped away the long-little-fingered stone gloves, and began to swing the gloves by chains. The stone gloves suddenly exploded into fire, and the strong young men danced and spun and clobbered the warriors like they were swatting flies. Before the battle started it was done, and thirty warriors were moaning in the road. The few remaining scattered and hid like squirrels.

Gwyn Dee ran swiftly with a plate of steaming food to the top of the steps, where the Elders of Little Finger stood, and looked into the eyes of the chief elder.

"How dare a member of the Clown Caste defy the Elders of Little Finger. You shall pay dearly Gwyn Dee." The chief elder spoke calmly and glared with the eyes of a demon planning his revenge.

"You bind heavy burdens upon people, and will not lift a finger to help them. May you reap what you have sown.", Gwyn Dee responded.

And with these words the people of Little Finger ran to the top of the temple steps. The Elders of Little Finger fled into the temple, barred the doors, and the long-faced people pounded with rage on the temple doors.

The long-faced old woman called the people back to the feast. They ate, and they laughed. The strong young men put their stone gloves back on, and began to use them to break the stone yokes, the stone shoes, and the stone bracelets off of the people of Little Finger.

Gwyn Dee looked with wonder at the long-faced old woman. "Surely, you know the way to the borders of the Land of Jaw. I have been in search of them for many days."

The long-faced old woman smiled. "You on are the right path Gwyn Dee, but you may find that the borders are not as clear as you might have supposed." The long-faced old woman smiled, and Gwyn Dee was sure she had seen her Weathered Old Face somewhere before.

THE BIG STINK BOMB

I am convinced that what we popularly call the Butterfly Effect, a subset of Chaos Theory, is real. The hypothesis has been proven true to me. I have been on the receiving end of its pomposity. The basic premise behind the Butterfly Effect is that nature holds a certain inherent extreme sensitivity to initial conditions. That first gentle flapping of the butterfly's wings may set off a growing chain reaction, which builds into something enormous – perhaps devastating. The illustrations used to describe these reactions are typically powerful negative impact events.

I admit, it sounds strange to say that the flutter of a butterfly's wings in Papua New Guinea could possibly cause a wild chain reaction leading to a hurricane developing off the coast of Sierra Leone, which will wipe out trailer parks in Florida, but it must be true. I have discovered that simple little decisions from high muckity-muck corporate leaders sometimes cause great violence far away in a little city. It appears that in corporate offices, extreme sensitivity to initial conditions is the rule of the day. Simple little actions by people with a great degree of power often carry massive implications for small and powerless people, who despite great effort to defend themselves are overrun by the catastrophic consequences of tiny actions.

The nod of a head, the wink of an eye, the shirking of the shoulders, the small words of disregard, or the signature at the bottom of the page: these are the little things, which have the possibility of triggering massively larger results for people in distant places. These little actions correspond to the dismissal of claims, to the choice to leave someone defenseless in the face of false accusation, to social rejection, to economic suppression, and a host of complex and devastating powers.

When a CEO farts in his office, he may cause a great and monumental stink in some distant place, and small people drown in the sewage of his oozing death blast.

I am convinced that God does not hold the CEO responsible for the little fart, but for the big stink.

The Fourth Square Meal: A Modern Pythagorean Tale

There was a bowl of spicy bean dip, and stone ground tortilla chips on the massive cherry-wood desk.

The Pontifecal Operations Officer (POO) sat sharing the bean dip with James, his Second in command, and a younger CEO in training – renamed by the office staff as the "Brown-Noser."

If you were a Pythagorean, this would have been a clear sign of trouble. Pythagoras was one of history's greatest mathematicians. What some of us did not know is that he was also a religious leader of a unique belief system. One of Pythagoras' fundamental tenets involved avoiding the darkly occult musical fruit. Beans were evil in the dogma of the Pythagoreans, and every child learns early what the mystical mathematician feared about the bean. What child has not used the flatulent producing legume as a weapon against siblings and classmates? In the corporate office, bean dip signals something else: some secret act about to be performed under the practice of the dark arts. The noble Pythagoras understood the potentially evil and powerful force of the bean, and mercifully swore off using the potent legumes early in his spiritual journey. A couple millennia later, religious corporate officers re-discovered the magic behind Pythagoras' fear, and the bean dip on the boss' desk would be renamed the "fourth square meal" in honor of its necessary centrality to the smooth running of a religious corporation.

Church, after all, is business, and business is war.

"By Scott! James. This is just too prickly a subject to handle. Gee, the burr is already under my saddle on this one." The POO took another large chip heaped with spicy bean dip.

James reluctantly shared the ecclesiastical intelligence with his POO, "What should we do? People are taking sides already. Calls and letters have been coming into the office. There is solid support for them, but there are also a few very concerned people. Should we look into this a bit more, or just send our Hatchet Man to handle it?"

"No, no, no. Let's not be hasty. I'm too busy to handle this issue personally," and taking another chip with a spicy mound on top added, "and it will probably go away on its own."

The Pontifecal Operations Officer looked to his underlings and raised his eyebrows, almost, but not quite imperceptibly. He nodded to the young Brown-Noser, who quickly and nervously swallowed a couple stone ground tortilla chips heaped as high with the brown spicy mush as a buffalo dung pile.

The young Brown-Noser had been considered a prodigy since his first word, which was "obey." His parents often noted that the similarity between "prodigy" and "prodigal" was strong with their son. Under the gently smiling gaze of the POO, the prodigy squinted, wiggled into his seat a little more comfortably, and then he farted a stupendous fart.

He farted as long as an ancient rambling tenured professor, or a state of the union address from a second term President with dropping approval ratings, and louder than the crack of a calving glacier, or the 1972 Deep Purple concert, which rendered three fans in the audience unconscious. It was one of those juicy, squirty, slimy, grotesque sounding farts – the kind that causes Junior High School kids to leap out of their chairs screaming and fleeing like cockroaches when the light is turned on – the kind that makes nurses run into a room wondering if the last gasp of life has been expressed when a greasy soul is leaving a struggling body.

The POO smiled in that fatherly caring kind of way, like a dictator observing the malevolent influence of his charismatic powers taking root in the next generation of groping followers. No one said a word, but the stupendous sound was heard throughout the headquarters, and its echo traveled down the street to the nearby city park. A few people at the Temple of the Angels across the street looked up to sixth floor office. Their raised eyebrows conveyed a knowing. The strolling afternoon walkers in the park attributed it to an earthquake. Earthquakes are common, after all, around the headquarters. In most large urban areas, those who are familiar with corporate corruption attribute these earthquakes to the mystical Pythagorean bean arts. But, in fact, the gargantuan flatulence passed only as a sound.

There was no smell to accompany this gas attack, and no quiver of the earth to match its magnificent decibel level. Windows did not shake, and small ceramic objects already teetering on the edge of shelves did not fall. Besides the chillingly gruesome eruption – an aural rendition of the WWI trenches, chemical warfare and all – there was no damage, there were no results from this elephantine sound, which is why everyone in the neighborhood appeared to ignore it. Perhaps only the initiated, or the conspiracy theorists realized the passing of this mysterious corporate right of passage.

James the Second paused. Ecclesiastical decorum dictated he go next. A rumbling lower-stratum turmoil bubbled deep within his belly in the same way maggots crawl around inside the remaining decaying organs of a half-rotted zombie. Pythagoras understood not only the evil power of the legume, but the slow festering price the abuser of the art would suffer. But, James obediently followed suit and farted too. He secretly, and guiltily wondered if "following suit" held a card game etymology, or if it came from the pressure of obeying the dark expectations of the Boss. His fart was less grotesque than the Brown-Nosed prodigy. He performed like a long-time expert of the gaseous art, but James lacked the subtlety of a true master. He counted to ten with his butt cheeks, recited the Ten Commandments and the

Beatitudes, and followed with portions of Roberts Rules of Order, and he did so with a combination of gentle watery tones, and cruel growling thunder, but these were the mere tricks of a showman. It had the volume and power of a scolding and a corrective paddle of a Victorian grade school principle.

The three men smirked knowingly, but without any other acknowledgement.

Sometimes even death gives birth, but death does not crown as a living child. It always squeezes out the canal backwards. Breaching and crowned on the backside, death is birthed hideously, and its cruel twisted form does not appear in the same location as the birthing event. Death somehow escapes as though blasting in reverse through the great vacuum of the universe's Black Hole, and explodes randomly on the unsuspecting in unanticipated times and locations.

In a pause of dark pregnant silence, the POO blinked slowly. The slow blink of a Master POO is the sign of a wind-up, like a major league pitcher with a 100mph fastball, who settles and centers on the mound just before he kicks his leg. He rocked slightly, and settled delicately onto his right butt cheek, lifted his left heel as though preparing for the kick, and a barely audible airy hiss floated across the room with beautiful undertones of a B diminished chord. The notes sang softly for three or four minutes. Like moist lips to the brass horn, he commanded a sphincter skill matched only by the cruelest of ancient inquisitors, and those in the highest tier of world politics. The soft undulating rhythms swayed to rich droning horns, and the careful pluck of harp strings and mountain dulcimers, and settled into a comfortable C chord with the timing of a radio pop song that plays your heartstrings and leaves you wanting more.

Even the reluctant Second was awed by the dark beauty and tonal perfection, and fell into a trance. As it masterfully faded to black, the three men nodded in agreement. The lights, which dimmed on their own for the grand performance, came back to full power, and the officers moved on to other business.

No foul smell. No harm.

"These times remind me of Pentecost," the POO reminisced nostalgically, "with the mighty rushing wind."

Meanwhile, 3,000 miles away, a small church group was huddled in a second floor apartment of a member's house. The small group was slightly larger than the room and crowded onto the couches, sat on tightly arranged folding chairs, or squeezed onto the floor crossed-legged for their tribal meeting. While they talked innocently and happily, a distant rumble rose, at first gently, and then grew in both nearness and volume. Then like a jetliner on the runway, the sound rose to a deafening volume, and the walls of the house rumbled. Windows shook, and small ceramic objects already teetering on the edges of the shelves fell and broke on the tables, and on the heads of the women seated under the knick-knack shelves. The shaking continued for what seemed as long as a State of the Union address, and the small church group began to become seriously concerned; but the bark was worse than the bite, and the temblor passed with only the loss of a ceramic angel or two, and little bump on the head.

The small group heaved a corporate sigh, laughed and returned to talk of simple dreams and humble hopes. But their innocent joy was quickly snuffed out.

The earth began to rumble and snap up and down like privates brought to attention under the gaze of an officer. The walls rocked and the shelves were emptied of their carefully set, precious contents as plates, pictures and the Holy Book were tossed around the room like numbered balls in the lotto selector. The group screamed, they ducked, they tried to get up, but the shaking was too violent. They were banged around like kids in a bouncy house. The windows exploded inward and shards blasted across the room in every direction like an auto accident with the glass company truck. After a few minutes the rumbling subsided. Some of the women and children were crying. Someone ran to the bathroom for a first aid kit, while the two nurses quickly took stock of the situation, and began to check for lacerations, scrapes and bruises.

Before they could fully reorganize themselves, the floor undulated gently beneath them like a sphincter muscle when it tightens, relaxes, and pushes to squirt its unholy gases. Now, even a couple grizzled veterans of ecclesiastical wars were on the verge of panic. A putrefying odor of scandalous, gooey death oozed through the fibers of the carpet. The monstrous, deadly, eye-stinging, festering stench rose to fill the room. They might have fled, but they had nowhere to go. Someone almost died, several people were wounded irreparably, and the little group pulled their shirts over their nostrils, and huddled around the most precarious of the gasping victims.

It was a good thing the nurses were there, because hospitals strictly forbid flatulence-bombing victims. There is an unknown quantity of danger in such anti-Pythagorian gas attacks, and so the little group was quarantined like potentially rabid dogs for a season. Even the local seminary refused to send its counselors due to the fear of the evil bean arts. When asked what the chief psychologist suggested for these situations, someone replied, "Well Sam Hill! He just shoots 'em." In the long aftermath of the healing process, it would later be difficult to tell whether the physical wounds, or the long season of quarantine had the more deleterious and long lasting effect.

Lower-Stratum vs. Upper-Stratum Illustrations: Rabelais and the Gospel contrasted

The above Pythagorean tale is my tame attempt at creating a modern variation on Grotesque medieval carnival literature in the vein of Rabelais, with a nod toward what Mikhail Bakhtin called "lower-stratum" humor.

Mikhail Bakhtin's literary evaluation of Rabelias' 16th Century medieval tales, Gargantua and Pantagruel was written during the height of Stalin's power. Rabelais and His World was a doctoral thesis defended before the State Accrediting Bureau in the late 1940s. The division of opinions on Bakhtin's work was split and tense.

Bakhtin had already spent years in exile for his supposed Christian subversion. Between his connections with rebel Christian scholars, and his literary critique of Dostoevsky's work, Bakhtin was sent off to labor and rehabilitation camps in 1929, and would spend over 20 years in a combination of exile and ill health.

In Rabelais and His World, Bakhtin presented the anarchic comedy of Francois Rabelais as a carnival revolution of grotesque humor – "a laughing truth", which "degraded power." [135] It would be 1965 before his thesis would finally be published.

Bakhtin referred to grotesque humor as "lower-stratum" references – activities of the lower parts of the human body. These were allusions to the passions and secretions of the body as an expression of life and death, and to crude sexual references insinuating both birth and new life. Death and life were not separated in this grotesque humor. Bakhtin described the lower-stratum humor from the 15th and 16th century carnival culture as "ambivalent" voices laughing at the structures of power.

Like Bakhtin, Rabelais lived in dangerous times. He was born the same year as Martin Luther. Heretics were being burnt at the stake. The Huegenots and Waldensians were in the throes of some of history's most tragic persecutions.[136]

Somehow in the midst of this season of beheadings, burnings, imprisonments and scourgings Rabelais wrote a crude, anarchic set of wild tales making fun of kings, princes, priests, popes, and everyone

---

[135] Bakhtin, M. M. [1941, 1965] Rabelais and His World. Trans. Hélène Iswolsky. Bloomington: Indiana University Press, 1993, p. 92f.
[136] The Huegenots are now traceable only through the scattered families who fled to places like Boston, the Welsh Valleys, and the Cape of Good Hope.

else under the sun. Was it the "ambivalent" nature of his wild tales that allowed him to evade the deadly scrutiny of Kings and Kingmakers? Did Rabelais know something Jesus did not, or was there something less subversive, less revolutionary in the activities and words of Rabelais than there was in Bakhtin's critical evaluation of his work? Why did Rabelais survive writing his subversive, carnivalesque tales when Bakhtin was endangered simply for theorizing about Rabelais and Dostoevsky? And why did Jesus lose His life while telling stories that lacked the bawdy, "lower-stratum" degradation of Kings and Priests? The dangerous times of these three characters were not significantly different. Often the French Kings were as brutal in dealing with their enemies, and the Popes were as unflinching in their abuse of the Protestant heretics as Stalin or the Caesars were toward their detractors. Why did Rabelais freely roam while Bakhtin was exiled, and Jesus got nailed to a cross?

These are not questions answered in the short observations of carnivalesque revolution in the life of Christ, but perhaps the crucifixion hints at something inherently more subversive found in the Gospel, and in the upper-stratum story of Jesus. The patterns of life and death were seldom illustrated by lower-stratum degradations and mockings of human defecation and sexual intercourse in the Bible. For Christ, life and death were illustrated in agrarian, hunter-gatherer, and common home-life motifs. Even the wildest otherworldly stories carried these homely motifs forward to a heavenly or hellish time and place. Goats and sheep, seeds and crops, fish and nets, fields and loaves of bread – these were the symbols describing the upward and the downward movement of humanity. It was a movement not between heaven and earth, but a movement between heaven and hell. Bakhtin on the other hand, describes Rabelais' stories as illustrations of the movement between heaven and earth. Rabelais' lower-stratum references drag us back to earth from heaven.

> *"Degradation and debasement of the higher do not have a formal and relative character in grotesque realism. "Upward" and "downward" have here an absolute and strictly topographical meaning. "Downward" is earth, "upward" is heaven."*[137]

Rabelais' tales bring us back to a medieval world of feces and piss in the streets, of fleshly pleasures and penal torments, and it simultaneously mocks and praises all the Bread and Circuses kings and Caesars have used for centuries to numb the common man's passion

---

[137] <u>Rabelais and His World</u>, Mikhail Bakhtin, pg. 21

for deeper freedoms. But Jesus and Paul offer no middle world anesthesia. The passionate drag toward the lower-stratum fulfillment of the earth seems empty, a vacuous space of temporary struggle in the Gospels, and in the Pauline Epistles they reappear, but even then they are couched in the Heaven and Hell motif.

And I submit, that this lower-stratum life was neither as condemned as Fundamentalist Christianity declares it to be, nor as fulfilling as our corporate-capitalist world presents it. Heaven and Hell were not the Go-Daddy girls and little blue pills, or getting "friend-zoned", or struggling with ED for either Paul or Jesus.

Something more radical than Rabelais' subversive medieval carnival was going on, and yet somehow <u>Rabelais and His World</u> still points to the foolishness of God, which turns this world upside down.

Learning to Wipe Up After Cain's Spicy Bean Dip

Despite Rabelais' crazy world of sexual high jinks, crude toilet humor, and common mockery of everything and everyone, his grotesque humor still carries a spiritual attribution. Mikhail Bakhtin recognized this quality, and used it to hint at the subversive power of the Gospel, and he did this during the most dangerous days for religion in Russian history.

Bakhtin saw the ambivalent degrading humor of Rabelais dragging the powers-that-be back down to earth where they belonged. Noblemen were no more noble than the common man, and in fact, were demoted to the lowest of positions. Throughout Rabelais' tall tales, the world is turned upside down. The rich and famous are mocked, the powerful are removed and demoted, the intelligensia are derided as fools, and things as common as knowing the best way to wipe one's butt are given high praise.

In book one, chapters thirteen and fourteen of <u>Gargantua and Pantagruel</u>, Grandgoisier is "ravished with admiration" over his son's wisdom. The thirteenth chapter is dedicated to a rather long description of the best way to wipe one's butt after defecating. When the three-year-old Gargantua concludes the long story of experimentation with wiping his ass with such absurd items as pumpkins, dressing gowns, and clawing March Cats, he comes to discover that wiping with a downy soft goose is the most comfortable and cleanest way to wipe. The Fourteenth chapter describes Grandgoisier's thrill with his three-year-old son's wisdom, and Grandgoisier places Gargantua under the tutelage of the wisest man of his day.

Tubalcain Holofernes becomes the tutor of Gargantua.

The tutor's name is a compilation of two canonical characters: Tubal-Cain who was the ancient and original artificer of brass and iron in the book of Genesis, whose name has been interpreted by some to mean "he who spices the craft of Cain," and Holofernes the attacking Assyrian General, who was beheaded by Judith in the deuterocanonical Book of Judith.

Yet, after much study under Tubalcain Holofernes, Gargantua grew stupider and stupider as the years passed, and this vexed his father Grandgousier greatly.

> *"By that point his father could see that although he was studying as hard as he could, and spending all his time at it, that he didn't seem to be learning much and, what's worse, he was becoming distinctly stupid, a real simpleton, all wishy-washy and driveling.*
>
> *When he complained of this to Don Philippe de Marias, viceroy of Papeligosse, he was told that it would be better for Gargantua to learn nothing at all than to study such books with such teachers, whose learning was nothing but stupidity and whose wisdom was nothing but gloves with no hands in them – empty. They were specialists in ruining good and noble spirits and nipping the flowering of youth in the bud."*[138]

We, like Gargantua, should learn our first wisdom in the art of wiping our own butts – that is to clean up the messes of our own doing. Yet, as we begin to learn the arts of this world, our teachers have "spiced up" the craft of the murderous Cain, and made it palatable to us. Thus we lose our heads in the stench of bloody envy first found in Cain. The grotesque humor of Rabelais speaks an ancient wisdom. In all our designs to dress ourselves up, humanity is still swimming in the sewage of our own making, and our teachers are often teaching us how to increase our dark selfish arts. It is killing us, and killing those we seek to serve, even as we learn to rule.

Judith has entered the tent and removed our head. We have only learned to rule with the grotesque cruelty of Cain, and now, we are separated from the body of our own brethren.

Perhaps Rabelais prefigured the title of a much more recent popular book, All I Really Need to Know I Learned in Kindergarten.[139] The 3-year-old Gargantua was wiser in his feces wiping infancy than he became after years of teaching under the (supposedly) world's best teacher. At least in our youth we learn to clean up our own stinky messes. Could it be that in our adult years we have un-learned how to

---

[138] Francois Rabelais, Gargantua and Pantagruel, Book One Chapter Fifteen.
[139] All I Really Need To Know I Learned in Kindergarten, Robert Fulghum. New York: Villard Books, 1988

clean up the putrid messes we make, and rather have learned to use those messes against others? Are we creating cataclysmic Big Stink Bombs in other's lives, while all the time pointing our fingers at those suffering – whose eyes are burning with the deadly flatulence of Cain's spiced crafts?

Engage: Does mockery have a place in justice?

Rabelais and Bakhtin strike in "The Big Stink Bomb", as we highlight the "lower-stratum" humor of Rabelais and its power to bring the high and mighty down to earth. Although, a very different and less grotesque "upper-stratum" style, we see something similar in Jesus and His parables. The contrast of heaven and hell, or heaven and earth is the narrative behind these stories. My simple attempt at a Rabelaisian tall tale is an example of the power of humor to speak into the high places of corruption. Yet, I present this as a dangerous space from which to speak. Why is this a dangerous space? And, why did it become more dangerous for Jesus, than most other people in history?

Interact with the Burning Religion community on the website at www.burningreligion.com.

VALIDATING REDUCTIO AD HITLERUM

Slouching Toward Nuremburg

If the Catholic Church grants canonization to a patron saint of protection against 20th century false accusation, talismans of Elizabeth Loftus will soon be sold in small markets next to Virgin Mary statues.

Elizabeth Loftus is a researcher of memory,[140] but she is not the person you would contact to learn how to remember someone's name, or how to find the glasses you put on top of your head. She began her career as a cognitive psychologist studying memories by observing eyewitness testimonies in auto accidents. Eventually, her work expanded to some of the most controversial and socially sensitive subjects of our time. She identified the "misinformation effect." This occurs when our memories are influenced by the expectations of others, or we attribute events to wrong sources. She also demonstrated in lab settings how false memories could be planted into a person's memory bank. She became a regular consultant and expert witness in high profile cases, and began to challenge the accuracy of repressed memory therapy. In the 1980's and 1990's when repressed memories were stirring up allegations of sexual abuse, and "satanic ritual abuse" (SRI) in the American courts, perhaps Elizabeth Loftus stood as one of the few voices of reason in a season of witch hunts.

If Elizabeth Loftus' studies are correct, things we remember about our experiences of religion may be tainted by the influences of our church experience, the voices from our culture, and the regular mental rehearsal of our victories or our pains. These things replay themselves in our heads daily with ever so subtle modifications.

So, the past may have been much better than you think it was. Of course, it could also have been much worse than you remember. The twisted memories of our past have the potential for highlighting our experiences and magnifying their intensity. Every time we retell a story with an ever-tightening twist of the "misinformation effect" or the subtle weave of planted memories, it moves closer to a tall tale, a false allegation, or a convenient self-justification.

The stories of our interaction with religion may be mutations of actual events. Do we who tell our stories of abuse have a greater sense of victimization than is legitimate? Do we who rehearse stories of

---

[140] Elizabeth Loftus speaks at TED: https://youtu.be/PB2OegI6wvI

tough leadership decisions place ourselves in heroic positions we do not deserve?

While playing the inside corporate game-of-power we may not be heroes at all. Rather we may be complicit in the abuse of others. Mao's cadres justified abusive behavior as a necessary route to their communist utopian hopes, and this is only one example of history providing us with the details of people, corporations and even nations creating complex self-justifications around even the most heinous crimes. Churches and church leadership have been participants in this self-justifying misinformation effect. Once we begin to dance down this path of the self-justification of even minor abuses, we, like the anti-heroes of history are slouching toward Nuremburg.

Power Corruption

Power corrupts. So, we have been told, but what if this isn't true, and in fact something else is going on with the man behind the curtain?

Oscar Zoroaster Phadrig Isaac Norman Henkel Emmannuel Ambroise Diggs is the man we do not see till the end of The Wizard of Oz. In the movie we never learn his full name. In the original book, The Wonderful Wizard of Oz by L. Frank Baum, we discover that this great ruler of the Emerald City is a normal, kindly circus magician from Omaha, Nebraska. Years before the accidental unveiling by Dorothy and her little dog Toto, the Wizard arrived at the Emerald City in a hot air balloon, and his technological creativity combined with his self-promotion skills set him up as ruler of the land during a leadership vacuum. Yet, like all of us, the Wizard is fumbling and comedic at best. He uses the initials of his full name in promotion, but decides it might not be in his best interest. O.Z.P.I.N.H.E.A.D. was not a name fit for an all powerful, all knowing ruler, and so he shortened it to OZ.

The Wizard of Oz is a mask for Oscar, the common man from Omaha. The omnipotent veil he creates around himself is a mask of strength and wisdom. Meanwhile, the little circus man from Nebraska hides behind his curtain like a kindly, but gruff priest doing his best to play the part of God behind a confessional screen. Oscar Zoroaster Phadrig Isaac Norman Henkel Emmannuel Ambroise Diggs rules the Land of Oz as best he can despite his pretensions. His corruption is, at its worst, the creation of fear through circus trickery in hopes of doing good.

Does the Wizard do what we all do? Resort to our default positions: our skills, our fears, our clumsy silliness, and/or our dark intentions?

The heroes and villains of our day have all the foibles we ought to recognize in ourselves. Steve Jobs changed the world for better, and yet notoriously alienated friends, family, and business partners in the process. O.J. Simpson would have been in the Hall of Fame as arguably the best running back in the history of the NFL, but Elizabeth Loftus had to be an expert witness at a trial that became more famous than his running exploits. Richard Nixon succeeded in opening the doors to China, and stubbornly covered up a ridiculously small illegal wiretapping and intelligence operation to snag information from Democratic Party Headquarters.

Power in human hands is like nuclear power. It can power a city, or level it. It can provide heat and light, or it can leave a place uninhabitable for generations.

Fortunately, most of us are not playing with massive nuclear power resources. Instead we are like children playing with matches. Our capacity may be small, but it is nonetheless deadly. We play with fire, and sometimes we burn down the house.

Just maybe, it is not the power that corrupts and influences us, but we who corrupt and influence power. By neglect, error, or worst of all – purposeful intent, we play with matches and burn down the house – sometimes even the house of God.

James, the brother of Jesus of Nazareth saw this potential corruption of power on the tongues of people,

> *"And the tongue is a fire, a world of iniquity: so is the tongue among our members, that it defile[s] the whole body, and set[s] on fire the course of nature; and it is set on fire of hell."*[141]

Was James an ancient postmodern? Did he prefigure Michel Foucault's theories on power by almost 2,000 years? James the ever simple, common sense preacher not only challenges the use of our tongues, but the focus of our passions,

> *"Ye lust, and have not: ye kill, and desire to have, and cannot obtain: ye fight and war, yet ye have not, because ye ask not. You ask, and receive not, because you ask amiss, that you may spend it upon your lusts."*[142]

Here, power is not an external force working to corrupt our hearts and minds. Rather, we are seen as the external force working on a morally neutral and ever-present power. Our words at one moment heal and bless, and the next create a world of hurt. The same money that feeds the poor, purchases illegal drugs and guns. The power to influence others can mentor, or corrupt. Fame is used to spread

---

[141] James 3:6
[142] James 4:3

messages of hope and peace, or for selfish empty personal gain. Money, influence and fame are morally neutral, but the people who wield them are not. Power is corrupted by those who wield it.

A little power is corruptible in large ways, but may have less deleterious results than a large amount of power corrupted in minute ways.

Oscar Zoroaster Phadrig Isaac Norman Henkel Emmannuel Ambroise Diggs was a simple man with noble goals, who used his power to hide his true vulnerability and weaknesses, while all the time meaning to benefit the people under him. We similarly hide our foibles in order to maintain the status we have achieved, the money we are earning, or the reputation we think we deserve.

Reductio Ad Hitlerum

In 1951, Philosopher Leo Strauss, a German born American Jew first used the term Reductio ad Hitlerum.[143] It is the name given to the logical fallacy that attempts to insinuate that an opposing position is a view, which would have been held by Hitler and the Third Reich, and therefore is inherently wrong or immoral. The motivations of others are assumed to be the same power-hungry, cruel motivations found in Hitler, and behaviors are compared to that of the worst of Nazi Germany. In the United States both Democrats and Republicans have accused the other party of harboring Nazi-like intentions, or attempting to establish Third Reich type laws and regulations. The emotional impact of this argument is so high, that it ends most intelligent argumentation, and brings a sensible debate to a grinding halt.

The left-of-center political pundits have used the "Nazi-card" against their opponents, most notably President George W. Bush.

The Reverend Jesse Jackson used these comparisons in 1995, *"In South Africa we'd call it apartheid. In Germany we'd call it Facism. Here we call it Conservatism. These people are attacking the poor!"*[144]

Even singer Linda Ronstadt has gotten into the act. She was quoted as saying that the Bush administration was, *"a bunch of new Hitlers."*[145]

Not to be outdone, the right-of-center political pundits, and pop stars have used the same tactic.

On Cinco de Mayo 2014, Representative Stacey Campfield from Tennessee wrote a blog post making the Nazi comparison with President Obama and the national healthcare system, *"Democrats bragging*

---

[143] https://en.wikipedia.org/wiki/Reductio_ad_Hitlerum
[144] Fort Lauderdale Sun-Sentinel, January 30, 1995 quoting a Sunday sermon.
[145] "Linda Ronstadt laments a 'New Bunch of Hitlers'" http://www.wnd.com/2004/11/27610/

about the number of mandatory sign ups for Obamacare is like Germans bragging about the number of mandatory [sic] sign ups for "train rides" for Jews in the 40s."[146]

The aggressively conservative Rocker Ted Nugent compared film executive Harvey Weinstein to a Nazi propagandist for his plans to make an anti NRA (National Rifle Association) film with Meryl Streep called "The Senator's Wife." Nugent said that movie goers, *"will see that Joseph Goebbels and Saul Alinsky is alive in the form a fat punk named Harvey Weinstein, and as he tries to destroy the NRA it will backfire on him."*[147]

In 1968 the tension of pulling out the Nazi card boiled over in the ABC televised debate at the Democratic National Convention in Chicago between Gore Vidal and William F. Buckley. After ongoing verbal fireworks with Vidal making comparisons to Communism and Fascism, the debate climaxed in this now famous interchange:

Vidal: *"...as far as I am concerned, the only pro, or crypto-Nazi I can think of is yourself..."*

Buckley: *"Now listen, you queer, stop calling me a crypto-Nazi, or I'll sock you in your goddamn face and you'll stay plastered."*[148]

This exchange highlights the explosive response one receives by identifying your intellectual, political, or theological opponent with the 20th Century's evilest hour. When reasoned responses end, whether through unchecked emotional tensions, or through manipulative attempts to stoke the emotions of others, the conversation ends and the fight begins. Reductio ad Hitlerum has been used to end the debate and start the fight in both politics and religion.

Each October, street preachers from around the United States wielding bullhorns and Gospel tracts visit Salem, Massachusetts during the month long Halloween celebrations. On the weekend before Halloween in 2008, I received a call asking for help to de-escalate a tense religious argument. We discovered a volatile exchange on the Essex Street pedestrian mall, which started with a young woman telling the street preacher he had no right to say abusive things to people on the streets. He responded by calling her a Nazi for wanting to deny his right of free speech. She was Jewish, and the ensuing argument escalated. Her boyfriend became incensed and threatening, while the street preachers stood their ground, feeling justified playing the Nazi-card.

---

[146] found on the blog Camp4u, http://lastcar.blogspot.com/2014/05/thought-of-day_5.html
[147] National Rifle Association's news show Cam and Company, January 16, 2014
[148] YouTube clip of Gore Vidal and William F. Buckley exchange https://youtu.be/nYymnxoQnf8

Reduced to the Worst Possibilities

Reductio ad Hitlerum is typically used as a debate point against the philosophical positions of an opposing party. Gun Rights advocates cite the 2nd Amendment for their position, and simultaneously cite the strict regulation of privately owned firearms in the Nazi regime. LGBT Rights activists cite the 14th Amendment as a point of protecting the right to marry, but also point to the persecution of the gay population during Hitler's rule in Germany, while railing against their opponents.

The invocation of Hitler as an example of someone else's theological, philosophical, or political position finds it's way into the discussion from both left and right, conservative and progressive – in politics and in religion. We use this argument to critique both the outward control of public behavior by law, and the suppression of thought by community pressure. We call the Fascism card when the government uses the law to control behavior we feel we should be free to practice, or when political correctness forces our opinions underground. Opposing intellectual positions become the quintessential immorality when we cite the Holocaust, but the comparison of gun control, or community standards about marriage to Nazi death camps and gas ovens are not sensible comparisons. These arguments, instead, call up some of the most violent and obscene snapshots of human history.

If I stop the rhetoric for a moment, I will see that there is a face on the other side of every argument. It is the face of another citizen, a public servant, or a friend or family member. It is the face of someone, who despite significant disagreement, has some of the same aspirations for doing good and benefitting society that I have. They have the same hopes for happiness, and the same fears of insignificance or loss, and the same dreams for a successful future.

Unfortunately, beneath our dreams a fight or flight response is hiding. A perceived threat, the belief that we are playing a zero sum game, or the inability to perfectly manage our environment may trigger protective actions. Without disciplined monitoring of our own emotions, our fight or flight response has the potential under any threat, real or perceived, to lash out uncontrollably. Yet, the uncontrollable response is less destructive and damaging than the justification of our defensiveness as a positive model for developing business and personal relationships. A social Darwinian "survival of the fittest" approach to life will justify even destructive, aggressive defensive actions. Problematically, our nervous systems do not know the difference between perceived threats and real threats. When we use internally violent defensive emotional reactions as the energy source for our words, our actions, or our decisions we are playing with the Jamesian fire, which *"set[s] on fire the course of nature; and it is set on fire of hell."*

This intersection of our fight or flight response with the Reductio ad Hitlerum fallacy highlights two insights into human interaction: 1) our defensive responses to someone else's point of view may cause us to unjustifiably and irrationally believe false assumptions about them, and make wild accusations against them, but more importantly, 2) by responding in aggressive defensiveness, we may inadvertently be slouching toward Nuremburg by justifying our own abusive behavior towards people we simply perceive as threats. In doing so, we are turning Reductio ad Hitlerum from a fallacy into a potentially accurate assessment of ourselves.

Perhaps the best antidote to the poisonous rhetoric we drink like grape Flavor-Aid is to acknowledge that Reductio ad Hilterum is an accurate assessment of the human condition, but it is not my first assessment of the radical "other." It best illustrates me. If I can find and acknowledge this tendency in myself before I see it in others, if I can keep my pointing finger in my own nose instead of someone else's, I just might have a chance at keeping the peace.

IMAGO DEI AND DEVELOPING SUBCULTURES

Afraid of Witches?

You might expect to hear about a superstitious fear of Witches from the history of the 1692-1693 Salem Witch Trials, but this was not 1692. It was October 2005. Today, Salem sits on the northern urban edge of Greater Boston – an area filled with some of the world's best institutions of higher learning. Yet, education and fearful prejudice are not always enemies. Sometimes they become lovers in illicit affairs.

This was the setting in which I was accused of unorthodox praxis and beliefs for fraternizing with Witches. The leaders of our small church were called to a meeting, which became something of a heresy inquisition. Thirteen pretentiously stern ecclesiastical leaders, who studied in some of these world famous institutions of higher learning, sat around us in the seats of judgment. Thirteen – the number of a perfectly sized Witches' coven – only highlighted the tragicomic irony of the meeting.

The inquisition happened in the first throes of the Fall, and the twitching leaves of the maple trees were beginning to shiver out their dying yellows, oranges, and reds. Our small church in Salem, Massachusetts was accused of befriending dark and dangerous occult groups, and we were called in to account for our unorthodox behavior.

"How can you be friends with Witches?" The question hung on the air like the thick autumn fog that hugs and smothers the shore in old New England coastal towns. We looked at one another, blinked numbly, and thought, 'We live in Salem, Massachusetts. How could we NOT be friends with Witches?' Apparently, loving one's neighbor, which in Salem includes thousands of people who call themselves Witches or Neo-Pagans, did not apply when that neighbor was a Witch.

History is filled with stories of "good" religious people justifying prejudice through a blind insistence on keeping an overly regimented sectarian purity. This was true in the days of Saul of Tarsus, and the question reeked of a similar ancient hateful ignorance.

The meeting lasted three tortuous hours. I was accused of being ungodly because I did not lift my hands high enough at the pastor's conference. I used the name "Jesus" too few times during the meeting, and this was evidence of my lack of orthodox spirituality. I was derided for allowing my son to work in a Witchcraft shop, which in actuality was simply a museum highlighting the history of the Salem Witch Trials. I was deemed dangerous for learning the Welsh language, because it was an occult language of the Druids. It didn't matter that my mother is a Jones, and I have spent a lot of time in Wales. Meanwhile, a Welsh-born pastor cowered in the room, afraid to defend the long-oppressed minority language of his own people.

Despite the above absurdities, there was no discovery of wrongdoing or heresy, but unnecessary corrections would be administered nonetheless. Impetuous and self-impressed leaders know how to save face when erring in harsh judgment. They quickly invent new justifications for the actions of their unrestrained prejudice. The application of unnecessary correction is one of those subtle leadership tricks. It is sleight-of-hand trickery transforming judgmental meetings into supposedly necessary corrections. Despite an innocent verdict during the foolish inquisition, excommunication would eventually come our way. We were supposedly unrepentant and unworkable. At least two other people in the denomination would lose their jobs while defending us. De Torquemada[149] might have been proud.

Our experience was strange enough to make the front page of the Wall Street Journal the following October.[150]

Our story is a story about the clash of a subculture with a dominant culture. It is also a story about the uncomfortable position of mediation between a dominant religious cultus[151] and a misunderstood and feared subculture cultus. It is a minor but real example of domination and oppression. It is a story of ignorance, fear, and suppression pretending to be orthodoxy, strength, and correction.

After 20 years as a church leader in our small Pentecostal denomination, I collided with the unspoken rules of a powerful but small minority about acceptable and unacceptable behavior. We had dared to challenge unwritten codes by befriending Neo-Pagans, who were perceived to be an enemy to the denominational Gospel. Some leaders in the denomination applauded our work, and awarded us a grant. Others superstitiously feared our work. One person took advantage of the tension, and pitted the two sides against one another in hopes of gaining position, power, and more than likely, the grant money.

---

[149] http://en.wikipedia.org/wiki/Tomás_de_Torquemada
[150] http://www.post-gazette.com/life/lifestyle/2006/10/31/Befriending-witches-is-a-problem-in-Salem-Mass/stories/200610310213
[151] I am using this term "cultus" in the simple and broad anthropological sense of "religious practice." My use of the word here carries no connotation of evil, heretical beliefs, or psychological manipulation.

In sociology, philosophy, and anthropology the perceived enemy we fear and hold biases against is often simply called the "other." The other is something/someone different than myself, whose beliefs, activities, and existence presents a challenge to my own world. Framing a conversation about the scary, misunderstood outsiders by defining their world from our own limited and biased perspectives has been called "othering." "Othering" is something American and British Christianity has been doing to modern day Western Neo-Pagans and Witches since the early 1980s.

Tales from the Land of Jaw: The Adventures of Gwyn Dee
The Great Wall of Jaw

*T*he words of the long-faced old woman from Little Finger echoed softly for days. 'You on are the right path Gwyn Dee, but you may find that the borders are not as clear as you might have supposed.'

The wide, wide road turned ever so slightly until by degrees it listed toward the setting sun in the west. Gwyn Dee passed an arguing couple in a small tent pitched in a grove alongside the road, and the first confused and lost couple Gwyn Dee met along the wide, wide road came to mind. Long journeys with hopeful, but uncertain destinations are as tiring on the mind as they are on the emotions. Only the most disciplined minds arrive at the destination intact, and yet, thought Gwyn Dee, 'losing one's mind may not always be a bad thing.'

As the days wore on, emotions and thoughts wore down, and history replayed itself in tormenting cycles. Rehearsing the gracious words from the Book of Jaw brought little comfort. Small noises in the brush and movements in the sky caught by the corner of the eye mimicked voices and faces from Cominkingville, and Gwyn Dee found fear and longing kissing each other. A strange desire for a return back to a simple, dumb obedience to a dull authority began to rise in Gwyn Dee's heart. At least home was predictable, and although predictability may be boring, it is only dangerous in slow and imperceptible ways. This was the first longing for home to have surfaced on the long, long journey down the wide, wide road.

As the road arched steadily more westerly, a gently cooling breeze with a hint of an ocean Gwyn Dee had never smelled before wafted across the wide, wide road, and the heart for adventure, mixed itself with the longing for home in a confusing emotional blend, and suddenly, out of nowhere, an immense stone wall appeared a mere stones' throw to the left of the road. Gwyn Dee stopped, and stared with nervous anticipation as if waiting to open a long-awaited present.

A short distance ahead the wide, wide road split into two paths. A newer, well-cut wide, wide road turned to the great wall, ending at the closed gate. Guards stood at formal and stern attention at the gates, and a sign above read, "Welcome to the Border of the Land of Jaw. All welcome."

With slow careful steps, the diminutive Gwyn Dee approached the towering gates. The guards made no movements, and before Gwyn Dee could knock on the great gates, they silently opened on their own.

Gwyn Dee peered into the dark, looking for a sign from a greeter or a gatekeeper, but the darkness inside was thick against the blinding light of the late afternoon sun. A voice soothingly and hypnotically, spoke from the blackness, and said, "Welcome. We've been waiting for you. Come across the threshold of the borders of the Land of Jaw. The greatest adventure of your life is about to begin." Feeling simultaneously comforted, excited and unsure, Gwyn Dee stepped across the threshold, and into the dark as the gates silently closed behind.

Slowly shape took form in a great hall, and a dais appeared across the room, with a man seated on a throne. "Come closer. Here to the altar rail, and let me have a look at you." The man seated on the throne laughed the hearty laugh of a grandfather speaking to a child.

A low altar rail was positioned at the foot of the high dais, and Gwyn Dee approached as instructed.

"Perhaps, you would like to kneel and give thanks to Jaw, for bringing you to this place. Those who pass this border are never the same." And Gwyn Dee thought it appropriate to kneel in prayerful thanks, and did so, with a heartfelt prayer, which dispelled the days of confusion.

"You are just in time. A party in your honor is about to begin." And a door to right snapped open to a room filled with light, and with cheering, applauding, happy faced people.

"Please join us in the celebration of your arrival," crooned the voice from the dais.

And as if by a gentle external force, Gwyn Dee walked into the room of smiling faces.

"Welcome to the family! We are so glad you have made it this far!"

"All the goodly spirits in the heavens of Jaw are rejoicing with you today!"

"This is beginning of great things for you!"

These, and a host of other welcomes, and compliments, and greetings, and admonishments, and promises, and encouragements; were accompanied by smiles, and gestures, and pats, and handshakes, and hugs, and kisses. And Gwyn Dee felt the thrill of adventure and comfort of home rush together in one corporate embrace, as the strangers became friends in a moment – albeit a slightly mechanical moment.

Gwyn Dee was gradually herded by the happy activity into the center of the room, and there, met a small group of others, who had only just entered the gates at the border to the Land of Jaw themselves. The grins on their faces exuded relief and acceptance, and Gwyn Dee wondered how many people received such gracious attention upon leaving the Land of Jaw.

Before Gwyn Dee could settle into a conversation, doors on a balcony at one the end of the room opened and the Man from the Dais appeared. He held out his arms as if hugging an invisible friend, and all the people shouted, "Father!"

And the Man from the Dais said, "Greetings newcomers, you are part of the family of Jaw. We welcome you here, and want to extend our offer of support and encouragement for your journey into a grand new world." And the Man from the Dais continued with advice, and encouragement, and stories, and words of hope, and kindly warnings, and simple rules for journeying the path of life. And when it was done, he said, "Now, we send you out as sheep among wolves, but with the promise of standing by your side through any difficulties."

And at the opposite end of the room, doors opened, and the last light from the afternoon sun poured in. Gwyn Dee, and the other newcomers were herded toward the doors through the happy crowd. A Greeter handed a sealed and rolled up scroll to each of the newcomers, and said, "Each of us has received a new name as part of the our induction into this new life. When you step outside, open the scroll, and you will discover your new name."

The newcomers were pushed outside, and were greeted by thousands of yelling, and arguing, and fighting, and stealing, and swearing, and spitting people crowded shoulder-to-shoulder into a tiny high-walled city no more than a couple acres in size. Gwyn Dee had been herded out last, and stood behind the other newcomers, holding the worn travel bag tightly, as pickpockets swarmed around the new faces. Suddenly, trumpets blared, and a door opened to a balcony facing the city square. All the people, stopped what they were doing, shouted, "Father!" and became an instant happy family, and a few thieves slinked off quietly with some stolen goods.

The Man from the Dais stepped out on to the balcony. His voice sonorously filled the small city. "We have new family members today! Greet them with the holy kiss. They have journeyed far, like many of us, and have left the dark and evil world, to join us here in the Land of Jaw."

And the people cheered, and the Man from the Dais returned to his throne, and Gwyn Dee clutched the shoulder bag, and realized this was not what it had appeared to be.

Then Gwyn Dee opened the scroll to read the new name, and found these words,

Welcome to the Land of Jaw. You are now part of the family.
Your new name is...
"10,472"

And Gwyn Dee looked out into the city square, and saw 10,471 other people crowded into a small square, who had returned to yelling, and arguing, and fighting, and stealing, and swearing, and spitting.

215

Two Men, Two Stories, Two Critiques of the Dominant Culture

Emmanuel Levinas was a Lithuanian born Jew, later becoming an immigrant philosopher to France. He was one of the first French philosophers to draw attention to the man who would become, perhaps, the 20th century's most influential and notorious philosopher: Martin Heidegger.

Heidegger's work <u>Being and Time</u> is considered a formational and seminal work of phenomenology. Heidegger would go on to join the Nazi Party, write hideously condemning letters to the Party officials against his fellow academics, and remain a faithful Nazi Party member until the day the party was disbanded.[152] After the war, he spent five years in corrective discipline, unable to teach for his associations with the Nazi Party. When he returned to teaching, he never apologized – never recanted his association with the party. He lived pretending that this dark history never existed.

During the same time, Levinas would be captured by the Germans while serving in the French Army, and spend a few years in a prisoner of war camp in Hanover. His family members in Lithuania would be killed, or would simply disappear. Levinas would later say, *"One can forgive many Germans, but there are some Germans it is difficult to forgive. It is difficult to forgive Heidegger."*[153]

Much of Levinas' philosophy reads like a response to the betrayals of Martin Heidegger. He struggled with the concept of how we relate to others, and created a philosophy describing ethical living as the root of being and authenticity. Perhaps Levinas, more than any other philosopher, gives us our terminology about the "other." The Levinasian other was always looking at us, pleading with us, and calling out to us for mercy. According to Levinas, the other, in the face of our neighbor, our estranged loved ones, our enemies, or the fearfully misunderstood cultures around us are never something or someone we can fully understand. We, nonetheless, are demanded to do our best to understand and to love the other, if we are to live fully ethical and truthful lives.

For Levinas, even the Divine (which he also referred to as the "Other") became a reference point for the infinite distance between others and myself. He described the divine Other as a face confronting us, and calling out, "Do not murder me." It was as if Levinas saw God

---

[152] Heidegger - Human, All too Human, BBC Documentary, https://www.youtube.com/watch?v=cNiF7TVE_Y0
[153] Levinas, Emmanuel. <u>Nine Talmudic Readings</u>, trans. Annette Aronowicz. Bloomington: Indiana University Press, 1994. p. 25

staring with hollow desperate eyes through the electrified barbed wire fence of the concentration camp.

Edward Said (Pronounced Sa-eed) was born in 1935, in a country that no longer exists. At a young age he and his parents had to leave their familial homeland, and he was raised in Egypt. As a US citizen through his father, he later studied at Princeton and Harvard, and went on to teach comparative literature at Columbia University.

As a Palestinian, born in Jerusalem, his country disappeared when the Jewish refugees arrived in Palestine after the Holocaust. The Palestinian state became the nation of Israel almost overnight. In the winter of 1947-1948, the Said family fled to Cairo with other Palestinian refugees, and their land would be confiscated by this new nation. His life was a unique exilic situation. He was an accepted academic with nearly rock star status, while simultaneously always being the potentially dangerous "other." This tension informed his views on the term he coined: "othering", and established his place as an early leader in the field of postcolonialism.

His critique on the field of study called Orientalism (studies of culture, languages, art, and literature from the Middle East through Asia and Southeast Asia), focused on centuries of definition and description by Western scholars about the nature of the Middle East and its people. Said contends that these definitions were biased (even if academic) positions formed by outside Westerners, and later became justifications for the often oppressive European colonial expansion into the overly generic category of nations and cultures called the "Orient."

Edward Said's book <u>Orientalism</u> changed perceptions on how the West views the Middle East, and challenged the entire field of Orientalism. Edward Said was the other, and his observations on "othering" came from his experience as a scholar, and as the exiled other living in a land, which often despised his native existence. The premise to his theory on the oppressive power of Oriental studies led to his conclusion that,

> *"... Orientalism is more particularly valuable as a sign of European-Atlantic power over the Orient than it is as a veridic discourse about the Orient (which is what, in its academic or scholarly form, it claims to be)."*[154]

> *"The Orient was viewed as if framed by the classroom, the criminal court, the prison, the illustrated manual. Orientalism, then, is knowledge of the Orient*

---

[154] <u>Orientalism</u>, Said page 6

that places things Oriental in class, court, prison, or manual for scrutiny, study, judgment, discipline, or governing."[155]

These two 20th Century thinkers form a backdrop of critique for how we think about others: Emmanuel Levinas and Edward Said, a Jew and a Palestinian, both exiled and examples of the disenfranchised – the betrayed "other." In their stories, we see an educated dominant power spinning prejudiced tales of the exiles they oppressed, and using those tales as justification for the oppression.

Yet, in spite of the oppression, Said spoke of exile as both a painful tragedy and a privileged position:

"The fate of exile is a pretty serious and unpleasant experience. I mean...someone's sent away, banished, severed from his or her native place... It was traditionally considered to be one of the worst fates. You could never return to your patriate, your place of origin, your country, your native soil...It's like the Fall from paradise - you can never really go back."

"What is it that exile affords you?...the essential privilege of exile is to have, not just one set of eyes, but half a dozen, each of them corresponding to the places you've been."[156]

The Distance of Othering

The fear of the unknown is a motivational force. Some are motivated to create distance between themselves and the unknown. Some are motivated to discover or experience the unknown.

Zealous micro-managers use the minutia of detail in rules to factor out the possible invasion of potential unknowns. The over-controlling leader suppresses difference, and often innovation, because it represents a leap into the unknown. This is a means of distancing oneself, or one's corporation from surprises with potential negative impact.

In small and large ways, we perform this same distancing activity in our daily lives. Where we choose to live or buy a home is based upon finding the place of comfort. We distance ourselves from the feared other neighborhood we do not know or understand. The neighborhood of ethnic other is perceived as a place of dark criminal intent or oppressive injustice. We distance ourselves from its potential violent intrusion, and move into hoods of safety. We form our alliances and

---

[155] Edward Said, Orientalism, pg. 52
[156] Quotes are from Edward Said: Orientalism the Documentary. Go to http://youtu.be/35MNSW2UnlE to view.

group activities around people of similarity and common interest. Those who live and experience a world unlike our own, seldom sit at our table – seldom are invited into our circle. But, in our own enclave we talk about the other from the infinite distance of our holy huddle. We discuss them with political and philosophical critique. We become watchmen at the gates of our own little culture, defending our walls against the onslaught of barbarians. We see the other as a destroyer, and in our comfortable little social circles, we speak about the other in definitive, academic terms. We are like the Orientalists Edward Said critiqued, who talked about the Middle East with an academic distance from behind their mahogany desks, in their prestigious universities.

The world's foremost Sociologist of Religion, Peter Berger points out the distance between his own academic world and the study of fundamentalist religions,

> *"The concern that must have led to this Project was based on an upside-down perception of the world, according to which "fundamentalism" (which, when all is said and done, usually refers to any sort of passionate religious movement) is a rare, hard-to-explain thing. But a look either at history or at the contemporary world reveals that what is rare is not the phenomenon itself but knowledge of it. The difficult-to-understand phenomenon is not Iranian mullahs but American university professors—it might be worth a multi-million-dollar project to try to explain that!"*[157]

The distance from academia to religious fundamentalism is the infinite distance of Zeno's paradox, and it is not only the Fundamentalists but oftentimes the academic who becomes the tool for broadening that distance.[158] The isolated points of reference between one worldview and the feared other remains a distance impossible to navigate.

We look across that impossible space between the other and ourselves, and define that space from our own position, but our position is our bias. We tell ourselves we know the motivations, feelings, and intellectual (or lack of intellectual) content, which we see in the other, but in reality, it is hidden from us. Levinas likened our understanding of the other to peering into the face of another person. There is more behind the face than its physical likeness. The face is like a façade. The façade represents something magical, yet illusory. It is at best pretentious for us to think that we can understand the other when

---

[157] Berger, The Desecularization of the World, Kindle loc 77
[158] see section "Parallaxis as the Infinite and Impassable Distance", in the chapter "Paralyzed in Parallaxis"

we only see the face. It is as though we have judged the book by its cover, or someone's attitude by the look on their face.[159]

> *"By the façade the thing which keeps its secret is exposed enclosed in its monumental essence and in its myth, in which it gleams like a splendor but does not deliver itself. It captivates by its grace as by magic, but does not reveal itself."*[160]

Killing Otherness

> *"To kill is not to dominate but to annihilate; it is to renounce comprehension absolutely. Murder exercises a power over what escapes power."*[161]

Otherness does not behave appropriately in my world. Otherness does not think as I think. It does not hold the same values and cultural norms. It evades my control, and introduces anarchy to my ordered little world.

In one culture, the young child is expected to look down to the ground – avoiding eye contact with an adult who gives correction. To look into the eyes of the elder is to stubbornly and arrogantly challenge. To look down is to show respect. In another culture, the parent may shout, "Look at me when I talk to you!" and the child may be punished for avoiding eye contact. The assumption being that not looking means rebellious inattention. Strangely, though these cultural differences are infinitely distant from one another in praxis and worldview, they may be as geographically close as crossing the border from Tijuana to San Diego, or traveling to a nearby Native American Reservation from your predominantly white American city.

Annihilating cultural norms, which are foreign and uncontrollable within my own culture is an act of killing. It is an attack upon the face of difference with the goal of eliminating – assassinating that difference.

A conquering culture dominates through the enforcement of sameness. The elimination of differences in the conquered culture is the final expression of domination, and language is a primary target of the conqueror. Alexander the Great created a Greek-speaking world in his conquests. Aboriginal Australian languages once numbered well over 300, and with the onslaught of British colonialism only about 50 languages survive today, and those are rapidly dying. Among Native

---

[159] Anna Kendrick on the Late Show discusses her "Resting Bitch Face." https://youtu.be/wIZybnmE4x8
[160] Levinas, Totality and Infinity, pg. 193
[161] ibid pg. 198

American languages, Navajo is the strongest, but there are less than 150,000 speakers. That represents 50% of the people still speaking the disappearing tongues of North America.[162] For centuries, the British tried to exterminate the Welsh language, and the French brutally suppressed Breton, but these Celtic languages have stubbornly survived nonetheless.[163]

Language represents the other we cannot understand. Walking into a room filled with people speaking another language, we are intimidated. Are they talking about me? Are they laughing at me? Are they making plans against me, which I cannot prepare for? Another language represents that impenetrable wall, through which I cannot see or hear. It is a power ambivalent to and ungovernable by my desires and demands. It is something to be feared, and consequently to be conquered. If I can kill the other language, I kill the intimidating and uncontrollable threat of otherness, and reinstate the safety of sameness found in my little monoglot world. That monoglot world does not whisper about me from the dark corner tables of the pub. It is controllable, because I can demand and intimidate in a world that speaks my language and no other.

This historic conqueror's destruction of culture through the annihilation of a language represents the dark intentions we all hold against cultural variations we do not understand – do not trust – do not like. By demanding sameness, we murder otherness and exercise "power over what escapes power."

Whether we are talking about different languages, which perhaps represent the deepest heart of another culture, or the strange and misunderstood behavior of developing subcultures; the dominant powers and traditional majorities have often become masters at suppressing difference.

The Insane Clown Posse (ICP) is a rebellious white horrorcore hip-hop duo from Detroit. Their fans, called Juggalos, dress in horror "wicked clown"[164] makeup like the band. In 2011, the FBI listed the Juggalos as "a loosely organized hybrid gang." There is a lawsuit against the FBI from the ACLU and the ICP. Criminalization of that which we do not understand is a governmental method of isolating, controlling, and killing developing subcultures. What we see happening on national

---

[162] This is number has been considered as high as 1,000 in the Americas by some guestimates, and perhaps 250 in the United States. In either case, this represents a massive ethnocide and with it the assassination of aboriginal culture.
[163] The program "Language Matters" tracks the survival struggle for aboriginal Australian languages, Welsh and Hawaiian. http://www.pbs.org/program/language-matters/ to see the entire video go to http://video.pbs.org/video/2365391566/
[164] There is a history to the motif and theatrical art of the "evil clown." See https://en.wikipedia.org/?title=Evil_clown

and international levels, as in this case with the Insane Clown Posse, is a macrocosm of the biases and prejudices we individually hold against those we do not understand and whom we consequently fear.

We are fooling ourselves if we think that the calamitous world prejudices, which have destroyed cultures, annihilated languages, committed ethnocide, and oppressed races, or simply suppressed developing subcultures do not reside in our own hearts. Our expressions of fear and control may manifest themselves differently and more subtly than the historic tragedies we detest, but they are harbored nonetheless in milder insidious forms within our own hearts. It is in the corporate expressions of our biases that we see individual human desires take on their historic and most heinous activity. Once again, the ancient wisdom of James calls our attention to this microcosm of war residing within our hearts:

> *"From whence come wars and fightings among you? Come they not hence, even of your lusts that war in your members?"*[165]

The Othering Other

> *"...fundamentalism in America shares with other disaffected groups the sensibility of the colonized, in its defiant self-assertion and in a determination to recover one's own identity and culture against a powerful Other."*[166]

Richard Dawkins, Sam Harris and the current cadre of new atheists making the rounds of popular debates and conferences, arguing against the existence of God and the benefits of religion, make a common error in logic despite their persuasive presentations. Audiences ignorant of the actual history and the subtle, but fundamental differences in theology are swayed by showmanship bereft of serious intellectual content. Many of their arguments are informal fallacies called straw man arguments,[167] and/or false binaries.[168] They assign the beliefs and practices of the wildest fundamentalist religious groups to the larger body of religious believers. Thus, they argue, every Muslim carries the propensity toward terrorism, and every Christian the obscene prejudices of the rather noxious "God Hates Fags" Westboro Baptist Church,[169] or the inherent violence of the Crusades. The argument is

---

[165] James 4:1
[166] Armstrong, Karen (2014-10-28). Fields of Blood: Religion and the History of Violence (p. 306). Knopf Doubleday Publishing Group. Kindle Edition.
[167] An informal fallacy based upon a misrepresentation of an opponent's position.
[168] The false binary fallacy is also called a black and white fallacy or a false dilemma. https://en.wikipedia.org/wiki/False_dilemma

presented in such a way as to assume that fundamentalisms are the basic building blocks of the world's faiths. Thus, our culture is presented in polarized terms. There are only two options: stupid religious people, or intelligent skeptics. Such generic and blind argumentation is the Orientalism of current pop culture. It stands at a distance with pretentious academic prowess debating unreal opponents. Like the Orientalist who made general observations about all things Oriental, overly general and false arguments against religion and religious beliefs are created using the actions and beliefs of extreme (and extremely small) groups.

I am a Christian pastor, but I am not the Westboro Baptist Church, and my faith makes no place for me to hold signs at the funerals of soldiers, which say "God Hates America." My Muslim friends have no place in their theology for strapping a bomb to their chests and killing innocent noncombatants. Insinuating that religion inherently harbors violence and prejudice against others is a popular "othering" technique today.

Yet, it is also true, that atheists have been misrepresented throughout history. Karen Armstrong's observation on fundamentalism now rings true for a number of new atheists, who have created a skeptical fundamentalism. They are fighting back against traditional false binaries about atheism created by popular Christian thinkers. The result is, that the oft maligned and misunderstood atheist has his/her own version of fundamentalism in the writings of Dawkins, Hitchens, Dennett and Harris. This fundamentalist atheism has been growing – often to the dismay of other atheists. Dawkins popularity exploded to the point that he was named the most influential world thinker in a 2013 Prospect magazine poll,[170] despite openly displaying his fear and unwillingness to debate one of the world's foremost Christian apologists, William Lane Craig, only two years earlier.[171]

The growing atheist fundamentalism and the number of growing religious fundamentalisms are evidence of an ever-widening cultural divide – a growing impossible space between worldviews.

Outwardly, this appears to be driving religion underground in an increasingly secular society, but contrarily, evidence is indicating increasing religious social engagement in our world, and if this is true, we may see the tension between secular society and religion increase in America and Western Europe.

---

[169] The website for the Westboro Baptist Church is http://www.godhatesfags.com/
[170] http://www.theguardian.com/books/booksblog/2013/apr/25/richard-dawkins-named-top-thinker
[171] http://www.bethinking.org/atheism/dawkins-refuses-god-debate-with-william-lane-craig

Despite decades of academic prediction that secularism would grow in the public sphere, and religion would diminish, scholars like sociologist Peter Berger and political scientist Monica Duffy Toft have reversed their predictions, and have tracked both the growth and a powerful momentum of religion in the political and public spheres. In this light, the misdirected arguments of the new atheists look like a last gasp of the failed 20th century policies to completely secularize politics in the nation state. The worst manifestation of that secularization gave us Chairman Mao and Josef Stalin. Here, atheists who in the past, have been branded as immoral, satanic, communist...are rebranding themselves, and are fighting back in debates, conferences and best-selling books. Yet, when passionate faulty logic comes from some of society's most intelligent people, it carries more of a sense of final desperation than a victorious declaration, echoing Peter Berger's observation that secularization theory is a "last-ditch thesis."[172] While the struggling fundamentalist secularist defines the "religious other" in pseudo-academic terms, we are reminded of the Orientalist's definitions of Islam formed by colonialist power structures. And in fact, many of us – atheist and religious people alike, are currently utilizing the same refuted and biased Orientalist arguments when we speak of Islam.

The new atheist – a cultural other – plays a reverse othering and mimics Fundamentalist Christian groups who protect themselves from the corrupting influences of modern culture by forming apocalyptic, separatist communities, but the atheist cynic uses street preacher tactics in symposiums and classrooms.

Meanwhile standing apart from the world they reject, fundamentalist religionists sometimes stand on actual street corners with signs and bullhorns declaring the impending judgment of God. This vocal aggression from the bullhorn preacher models the dance movements of political protest in its call for change (repentance), and the demonization of the status quo. Signs and bullhorns may bring the protesting message close to our faces, but the distance between the Fundamentalist street preacher and the offended public is infinite. The sign and bullhorn appear only as prejudice and hatred to the passersby, and the near proximity to our faces and ears only lengthens the distance to our hearts and minds.

In the strange and wonderful city of Salem, Massachusetts where I live and pastor a church, the gap between the Fundamentalist street preachers, and the people who live in our city comes to a head every October. The Bullhorns and the signs come out to the streets filled with people, and the locals gather around to drown them out with song,

---

[172] The Desecularization of the World: Resurgent Religion and World Politics (Kindle Locations 256-257). Eerdmans Publishing Co - A. Kindle Edition.

drumming, and shouting back. Even as they stand toe-to-toe, and face-to-face, they could not be any further apart. Paradoxically, the distance is all the more evident in the close physical proximity.

Christian Fundamentalism was not always this distant from our society. It had its genesis in the 1940s in America, and was initially a broad description of those who wanted to return to the simple basics (fundamentals) of the Christian faith. Billy Graham identified with Fundamentalism in these early days, but distanced himself from the movement as its definition narrowed and became more controversial. The remaining Fundamentalist core became more militant as society and much of Evangelical Christianity moved away from its ultra-conservative Christian values. Karen Armstrong defines this social tension:

> *"Although American Protestant fundamentalism was not usually an agent of violence, it was, to a degree, a response to violence: the trauma of modern warfare and the psychological assault of the aggressive disdain of the secularist establishment."*[173]

The one who is treated as the ridiculous or dangerous "other" responds in return, and sees the surrounding society as a real and present danger. In this process, the infinite distance of Abraham's bosom and the rich man's torment is established in the Fundamentalist religious mind. It is strange to see that it is now beginning to be established in some of the new atheist minds as well.

Yet, we should not be surprised to see this occur. Rather, we should guard our hearts against forming this tragic distance from our fellow humans. It too easily takes seed, and forms a new defensive fundamentalism within us. Each defensive fundamentalism becomes a misunderstood subculture to the surrounding dominant culture, and treats the dominant power as the dangerous other, while simultaneously being treated by the dominant culture as a dangerous other. Here the other begins othering others, while misunderstanding and distrust are magnified and exaggerated in this hopelessly isolating cycle of othering.

We become the demons we battle. In the face of our perceived enemies, we find our own faces twisted by bias. Could it be that even as we distance ourselves from those we see as our enemies, that we also distance ourselves from ourselves? And from God?

Common Suppressive Roots of Relativism and Fundamentalism

---

[173] Armstrong, Karen (2014-10-28). Fields of Blood: Religion and the History of Violence (p. 306). Knopf Doubleday Publishing Group. Kindle Edition.

> *"But it should be noted that both relativism and dogmatism equally exclude all argumentation, all authentic dialogue, by making it either unnecessary (relativism) or impossible (dogmatism)."*[174]

As I was writing this chapter, the Supreme Court of the United States, declared gay marriage to be a constitutional right. The 5-4 split decision loosely represents the split in the US public opinion. As I follow social media responses to the decision itself, and to the opinions of the four dissenting judges, the shout of public opinion is a deaf polemics. Public responses are often shouts across the infinite divide without honest consideration of other opinions.

Much of the dissenting public considers the support of gay marriage to be based upon immorality, or stupidity. The supporting public uses the same bases in their arguments: dissenters must be either immoral suppressors of freedom, or stupid.

The nuanced opinions of the four dissenting judges cover topics such as states' rights versus central government mandates, the reach of the constitution on the subject of marriage, the definition of marriage itself, and whether the Supreme Court ought to be a place of public policy activism. Dissenting opinions even voiced support for equal rights for the LGBT population, but disagreed on the means for accomplishing that equality, not seeing it as an either/or proposition that universal marriage rights was the only path forward. Yet, many public supporters of the decision have the unreasoning audacity to call dissenting Supreme Court Justices "stupid" or "immoral." Similarly, the same rhetoric of immorality and stupidity came from many public dissenters against the decision on gay marriage rights.

When we come to the opinion that men and women who sit in the highest court in the land, and have a long track record of academic and judicial excellence must be either stupid or immoral, because they disagree with us, this can only be the result of a blind and deaf distance between ourselves and our neighbors.

A call for silencing dissenters has been trumpeted by the more radical activists. This is the place where Bakhtin's observation rings true: relativism and dogmatism carry similar suppressive roots. Dogmatism seeks to silence argumentation by crushing it with monologic shouting. Relativism seeks to suppress it under the pretentious guise of moral and intellectual superiority. Perhaps, today's sexual issues carry this tension between the dogmatic and the relativistic further than any other issue in early 21st century American culture. Both relativism and dogmatism establish an unnavigable space between

---

[174] Bakhtin, Mikhail (1984-06-21). <u>Problems of Dostoevsky's Poetics (Theory and History of Literature)</u> (p. 69). University Press of Minnesota - A. Kindle Edition.

academics, politicians, and next-door neighbors, thus making real discussion and understanding impossible.

For some people, listening seems tantamount to relativism. Dialogue with the other seems dangerous. Allowing dialogue appears to be the same as accepting the entire worldview as valid, and giving it precious airtime, thereby promoting the dangerous position. Even a relativist position becomes a harmful fundamentalism when it refuses to listen and silences opposition. A mature person understands that dialogue does not mean agreement, but on the other hand, the refusal to enter a dialogue does promote fundamentalisms.

Sexuality may be the hottest topic, but it certainly is not the only topic where sides are refusing to listen to one another, and new fundamentalisms are being born.

Listening and Believing: an Antidote to Othering

> *"I think it's very horrid on your part, for it's very brutal to look on and judge a man's soul, as you judge Ippolit. You have no tenderness, nothing but truth, and so you judge unjustly."*[175]

Dogmatism will not believe the best in the other. Relativism will not listen to the voice of the other. Yet, it is not possible to practice true Christian spirituality without listening to others, or believing the best in others. Neither is it possible to be a decent neighbor, or a citizen who is beneficial to our whole society without listening to and believing in others.

Pop psychology appears at times to call for us to believe in ourselves, sometimes even to the aggressive defense of our own desires against the needs or desires of others. Contrarily, Emmanuel Levinas described true authenticity as something born out of our ethical response to others, and these ethics carry the Golden Rule to an extreme position. Our response to the other is our chief act in life. Though we can never fully know the other, our patient listening is an attempt to know others deeply, and it embodies authentic living and community peacemaking. Silencing, on the other hand, is a suppressive annihilating murder of the culture and beliefs of another. Unfortunately, as the pendulum of popular opinion in a nation swings, one form of suppression often merely replaces another in a Foucauldian power shift.

Understood this way, being a listener is a necessary component of being a good citizen, and an authentically caring person. Lessons in

---

[175] The Idiot, Fyodor Dostoevsky pg. 399

deep listening have been with us for millennia, but they are not simple techniques. They are character traits involving caring about others, thinking of another's needs before my own, honoring other people, and developing patience. In pretty little meter we now use for wedding ceremonies, the Apostle Paul laid out the life-changing character traits of authentic ethical living. These same traits are true for real listeners.

"Love is patient, love is kind. It does not envy, it does not boast, it is not proud. It does not dishonor others, it is not self-seeking, it is not easily angered, it keeps no record of wrongs. Love does not delight in evil but rejoices with the truth. It always protects, always trusts, always hopes, always perseveres. Love never fails."[176]

Without the internal self-controls of Paul's love regulation, we cannot become the kind of listeners who are culture-changing citizens. Without these traits, we tend toward self-absorption. What has appeared to us as a benign poetic phrase applicable to weddings is in fact a radically countercultural passage of postcolonial import.

In a monologue, we make assumptions about others, and believe we have the answers they need. In a dialogue, we open our hearts to hear others, and we learn as much as we teach. In the monologue, the feedback we receive does not come from the other person, but from ourselves. Like the guitar in front of the amp exciting the squeal of feedback from the tones of the amplifier reverberating on the strings, we become excited by our own words, and mistake our excitement for transformation in the other. In the dialogue, it is not just our own words, but the words of another, which play upon our heartstrings.

Looking for God in All the Wrong Places: a Model of Grace

If listening to another challenges our sensitivities, and appears to be a dangerous social practice, believing the best in those with whom we disagree will appear tantamount to declaring war against our own beliefs. To assume that there is something good, and right to be found in the individual whose philosophical positions are contradictory to my own position, challenges basic assumptions in my own worldview, and in those of my friends and family. The immature response will see me as an enemy when I identify good things in the dangerous other. A holy history is marked by people who have stood in the demilitarized zone between embattled positions working as peacemakers. Many of these people have suffered as a consequence. Gandhi and Martin Luther

---

[176] 1 Corinthians 13:4-8

King Jr. are the contemporary popular figures of this peacemaking. This, in fact, is the story of Jesus. But Jesus represents an even more radical expression of this kind of peacemaking.

In theology and lifestyle, Jesus was closer to the Pharisees than He was to the people he protected and defended. He believed in a resurrection, and angels and demons. He lived a strict lifestyle: avoiding excesses, praying for hours on end, having fluent understanding of the Hebrew Scriptures, and living as a celibate. He lived, to a great degree, as the Pharisees lived. Yet, the tax-collectors and sinners were His friends, and He protected them from the dominant Jewish religious culture. Unlike, Gandhi who was Indian and stood up for his own people, and Martin Luther King Jr. who was black and stood up for his people, Jesus could not be numbered among the people He supported and loved. He was the holy, (and wholly) religious other in practice. Yet, to the religious elites, He represented an acceptance of the sinful, irreligious other. Reaching across the divide, from the position of a politically powerless holiness, He took the hands of the sinful other and drew them near. He identified possibilities and a seed of the divine with them. Yet, we cannot mistake His acceptance of the sinner as an embrace of sin itself.

It was once popular in Evangelical circles to say that we should, "Love the sinner, but hate the sin." In recent years, this theological sound bite has been mocked by progressive Christians and intellectual non-Christians alike. Could it be that the mocking of this pop-theology is in fact another example of isolating polemics? Could it be that concept of accepting all people regardless of agreement with their opinions, philosophical disagreements and lifestyles is embodied in this pithy aphorism? Could it be that a few bad examples of abusive people using the axiom to justify their bad behavior are used to argue against a generally beneficent meaning behind the phrase?

Somehow, Jesus models full acceptance of people and a rejection of the destructive power of sin simultaneously. He does so without diminishing either the power of His love, nor His deep concern for the injurious effects of sin and evil.

I have a good friend who has been struggling with life-threatening alcohol and drug addiction for years. A group of his closest friends have ganged up together over the years to be there for him: listening for his breathing through the night to make sure he was still alive, taking him to the emergency room during dangerous overdoses, gathering around and telling him that he needed to stop the self-destruction, and doing our best not to enable his addictions. Is this perhaps an embodied caring meaning behind, "Love the sinner – hate the sin?"

In Levinas' thoughts, we see acceptance of the radical other as a means of knowing God,

> "*His very epiphany consists in soliciting us by his destitution in the face of the Stranger, the widow, and the orphan.*"[177]

Yet, millennia before the arrival of Levinasian ethics, Jesus shared this same wisdom with us in a parable about the Kingdom of God.

> "*When the Son of Man comes in his glory, and all the angels with him, he will sit on his glorious throne. All the nations will be gathered before him, and he will separate the people one from another as a shepherd separates the sheep from the goats. He will put the sheep on his right and the goats on his left.*
>
> *Then the King will say to those on his right, 'Come, you who are blessed by my Father; take your inheritance, the kingdom prepared for you since the creation of the world. For I was hungry and you gave me something to eat, I was thirsty and you gave me something to drink, I was a stranger and you invited me in, I needed clothes and you clothed me, I was sick and you looked after me, I was in prison and you came to visit me.'*
>
> *Then the righteous will answer him, 'Lord, when did we see you hungry and feed you, or thirsty and give you something to drink? When did we see you a stranger and invite you in, or needing clothes and clothe you? When did we see you sick or in prison and go to visit you?'*
>
> *The King will reply, 'Truly I tell you, whatever you did for one of the least of these brothers and sisters of mine, you did for me.'*
>
> *Then he will say to those on his left, 'Depart from me, you who are cursed, into the eternal fire prepared for the devil and his angels. For I was hungry and you gave me nothing to eat, I was thirsty and you gave me nothing to drink, I was a stranger and you did not invite me in, I needed clothes and you did not clothe me, I was sick and in prison and you did not look after me.'*
>
> *They also will answer, 'Lord, when did we see you hungry or thirsty or a stranger or needing clothes or sick or in prison, and did not help you?'*
>
> *He will reply, 'Truly I tell you, whatever you did not do for one of the least of these, you did not do for me.*'"[178]

Unlike Jesus, Who begins from a position of perfection and moves toward the brokenness of this world, we are at best wounded healers, impoverished philanthropists, and stupid teachers. We must assume that we start from partially correct/partially incorrect beliefs and standards. Every other worldview, every other lifestyle, and every other

---

[177] Totality and Infinity pg. 78
[178] Matthew 25:40-45 (NIV)

culture and subculture will have critiques of my own little world, and many of those critiques will be valid.

As a basic beginning point, I choose to believe that imago dei (the image of God) is inherent to the human condition. Yet due to the brokenness of this world, we are all precariously teetering between nobility and criminality. If it is true, that the imago dei resides within every person, it must also be true that it can be found in every gathering of people. Every culture, and every subculture carries marks of the divine. In order to live the life of a peacemaker – in order to discover God in the radical other, I must believe that God's image will bleed through in the subculture markers of all the people groups representing the radical other to me. I must find the hints of God in the Jews, in the Palestinians, and in the Juggalos. For myself, it is easier to find those hints of the divine in ethnic groups. I am challenged more severely to find the fingerprints of God in the crazy developing subcultures and new religious movements around us: in the Goths, in Hip-Hop culture, at Burning Man, in Neo-Paganism, in Scientology, with skinheads, with the Islamic State, and with white and black supremacists.

Could it be that our inability to believe the best in the radical other, and to see the imago dei in them, mirrors our inability to find God? Does our distance from them equate to our distance from God? If I read Jesus with a simple and straightforward understanding, I am forced to say yes. And yet, this acceptance does not demand that I accept all things. It is a discerning and intelligent acceptance. I need not lose strong moral ethics or strong faith in my theological position while embracing an ethic of radical acceptance. I can believe the best in others, without agreeing with them, or participating in things I do not accept.

Perhaps we have been looking in the right places to find God, and we have missed Him, because He has been hiding in the wrong places all along.

> *"The Other who dominates me in his transcendence is thus the stranger, the widow, and the orphan, to whom I am obligated."*[179]

---

[179] Totality and Infinity pg. 215

Engage: Practicing identification with others

Chapter 17 asks if the logical fallacy called reductio ad hitlerum has a practical social application when I reflect upon my own weaknesses and selfish tendencies. Chapter 18 is about looking for the imago dei in developing subcultures – it asks us to find the best in others, even while acknowledging the worst in ourselves. This has application to me as an individual, but also it applies to my worldview and my own culture. Is this the equivalent of Jewish jokes by Jewish people? Is this a helpful way to navigate relationships in our polarized world?

As a practice of this discipline: Can you name something, which is problematic about your own worldview, or the group with which you primarily identify? Can you name something beautiful and positive about a religious, non-religious group or political party with whom you disagree?

Interact with the Burning Religion community on the website at www.burningreligion.com.

THE THIRD RING
THE CARNIVAL CANON

Tales from the Land of Jaw: The Adventures of Gwyn Dee
The Nameless Ones

*P*eople who believe they represent an expression of the totality of anything are most often narrow and limited expressions of anything. There must be a natural law, which describes this strange inversion. The people who lived in the high stone-walled city had come to believe that the Land of Jaw was an exceedingly small place. Artists and thinkers do not live well in small places, and it did not take more than an hour for Gwyn Dee to find the way out.

Despite the fact that the city had only one gate, and it was guarded, Gwyn Dee was standing outside the walls before it was dark. Tucking the name scroll into the shoulder bag as a memorial to absurdity, Gwyn Dee stood outside the walled city, sighed, and looked toward the setting sun.

The wide, wide road was now a distance away, so Gwyn Dee turned back toward the road with a combination of relief and dejection. Danger had been averted, but hope had also been lost in the short experience with the Man from the Dais. The aversion of danger and the loss of hope are secret lovers, and we are always surprised when they meet each other and their illegitimate children run around inside our hearts.

The nearby bushes rustled vigorously, and a birdcall, clearly of human origin, sounded from the thicket. Gwyn Dee walked up to the brush, and a voice whispered, "Hurry, hide in the bushes here, before they see you, and send the guards to drag you back to the Land of Jaw." Gwyn Dee humored the voice in the thicket, and quickly ducked into the bushes.

"Come with me, and I will show you where the others are. We are many now. We've built our own little village." The guide nervously took Gwyn Dee on a short walk through the thick woods of maple and birch. They came to a clearing, filled with stick huts. About a hundred people sat around a fire pit, which was only just being lit, in the center of the village.

"I have found another fortunate escapee from the Land of Jaw!" The guide called out loud, and people of the little village cheered, and ran to greet Gwyn Dee.

"We are so happy to see that you have escaped too."

"I do not remember you from The Land of Jaw, but I want to congratulate you on your freedom."

"Welcome, may your heart find a home here with us."

These, and many other salutations were given by the village people, with hearty hugs attached. Unlike the great party in the stone walled city, something less rote and more genuine was evident in these greetings, and Gwyn Dee was quickly at ease.

The guide turned and held out his hand in greeting, "I am 1,012. What is your name?"

"I am Gwyn Dee."

The guide stared blankly for a moment, and quizzically responded, "That is a strange name. I have never heard a name like that before."

"I only came into the walled city this afternoon, and escaped as quickly as I could. In our village we have many beautiful names. My father gave me this name when I was born, because he had great hopes for me. That is how it is done in Cominkingville."

"That is a queer tradition, I should like to learn more, but for now, allow me to introduce you to the others in our little rebel village. We are all escapees from the Land of Jaw. Most of us were born there, or came to it when we were very little."

The guide and Gwyn Dee moved from person to person and family to family saying hello and learning names. With each person there was a moment of silence, and a strange look when Gywn Dee's name was given, but then it was quickly reciprocated, "I am 4,601," or, "I am 956," and so forth.

Coming to a weakly middle-aged lady warming herself quietly on a log near the now roaring fire, the guide said, "This is a newly liberated soul. Meet Gwyn Dee." The weakly middle-aged lady looked helplessly pensive for a moment as though senility had an early onset, and simple thoughts were too difficult, but then she slowly said, "I had a pretty name like that when I was very young, but my parents brought us to the Land of Jaw, and I do not remember it now." She smiled with a sadness more ancient than her age, and said, "I am 53."

While the greetings circled round, a burly man sat at the edge of the circle watching the introductions, and worked crafting hunting bows. He shouted above the noise of the jabbering crowd, "I am quite tired of being nothing more than a number in a crowd. What kind of father would give his child a number for a name? How do I get a name like yours?"

All the people became silent. They stood quite still, and looked to the older man tending the fire.

The man tending the fire stood.

"I am Number 1. The Land of Jaw was the design and handiwork of myself and 2, whom they now call "Father." I am sure you met 2 this afternoon." Looking rather stern, he measured his words carefully, "It seems you have caused quite a stir with your strange name," and as Gwyn Dee fidgeted nervously, Number 1 added, "but it also seems that you bring something valuable to us this evening."

The man crafting bows dropped his work, and jumped up. "Well, I for one want a real name. How do I find one, O Gwyn Dee of Cominkingville? What would you name me?"

Gwyn looked a little hesitant, but seeing the hungry anticipation in the burly man's face said, "I would name you by your work. I would call you Bowyer."

And the burly man jumped, and shouted, and danced around the fire chanting, "I am Bowyer. Bowyer is my name, and I will make a bow for you today!" And the people laughed, and Bowyer danced, and Number 1 laughed harder than them all until he nearly fell into the fire.

Now, all the people were clamoring for names. The Guide, 1,012, was soon named Avian, and he stood on a tall rock making birdcalls the rest of the night. The numbers were exchanged for names, and soon the people were named for their hair, their smile, their occupation, or the way they laughed. Once they saw how easy it was to find name, they began to name one another without Gwyn Dee's help.

53 seemed to break out of her slumbering stupor and said, "I remember I was called Grace. I think I should like to be Grace again." She smiled such a deep and genuine smile that Gwyn Dee cried, and Number 1 cried as well.

"Gwyn Dee, let us talk while the naming goes on. I am sure this will continue all night on its own." and Number 1 and Gwyn Dee sat by the fire, and talked through the naming party.

"I was told to look for you many days ago, and I was not sure if I should be trustful or worried. Our people are a battered people, and they need a gentle, liberating hand. It has not been long since we escaped the Land of Jaw."

"Where I come from, we call this place where we sit now, and all the land around us for thousands of miles The Land of Jaw. I have been traveling for months in search of the border, and today was the first time I thought I might have found the borderlands and the gates out of the Land of Jaw." Gwyn Dee's sense of disenchantment bled through the words.

"How strange a turn of events for us both. What you call the Land of Jaw, we called the outside world, and yet, you passed into our old home thinking it was the borderlands and the way out."

Both Gwyn Dee and Number 1 stared into the fire, while the happy party was distanced from their heavy thoughts.

"I see now, that you are just what we needed. Will you stay with us awhile?"

"Yes. I would like that, but I cannot stay long. The borderlands, wherever they might be, still call my name."

Number 1 smiled. "I was once called Bob. That was long ago, before I helped build the stone walled city. I think I should like to be called Bob again."

I AM WHAT'S WRONG WITH THE CHURCH

The Neo-Pagan and Witchcraft community is substantial and prominent in my city. They own occult shops, health and herb boutiques, tourist trinket stops, and bookstores. They work in coffee shops, real estate, public schools, and any variety of occupations. In the US, Canada, Australia and the UK Neo-Pagans comprise about 0.15% of the general population. In Salem, MA you would be 50 to 100 times more likely to meet a Witch. The exact numbers of the local Neo-Pagan population are unknown, but are thought to be between 5% and 10%.

This community represents much of the postmodern thought today. Many of them are old enough to be parents of those who grew up completely in a postmodern world, but being the early adopters of new thinking, they represent the way post-modernity thinks of the church.

I am concerned with how the church relates to my Neo-Pagan friends, and from dramatic personal experience, I have found it does not look good.

My friends question the validity of Christianity. They ask about the cruelty of our God, the strict sexual standards of our faith, and the relevancy of the Church.

They practice a religion misunderstood and demonized by Christian pastors. They understand what it means to be persecuted for the faith, but they have experienced this persecution from evangelical Christians who have believed the tall tales, and urban myths about today's Witches. (And that would be a whole other long, long book.)

Church in the 21st century does not identify with their needs, and the television version of Christianity appears to be no more than parlor tricks played upon gullible crowds by ministers who are as much magicians as they are preachers. The wave of a hand, and the people fall trance-like to the ground. Declarations of healing are made without evidence to be corroborated later. Large amounts of money are collected in long drawn out offerings, which play on the emotions of people, and promise a huge blessing by God in return.

I am a Pentecostal, and that means I believe in the miraculous working of God, but I understand the concerns of my friends in the Neo-Pagan community. I too yearn for something simpler, easier, more natural, and honest. I am not sure I see it coming too soon.

Large events will probably continue to be the public face of the church in the coming years. A few dramatic (but quite frankly, overly corny) people will continue to be mocked by the press, and by most of the growing unchurched population. Manipulation, and greed will continue to be seen as the marks of the "Christian trade," whether it is a warranted critique or an urban legend.

My real despair, and sense of hopelessness is found much closer to home though. I find it in myself. I am what's wrong with the Church.

I find that I can quickly jump to conclusions about people. The way they look, the way they talk, the style of lives they live; these are the things, which cause me to quickly disassociate from people, or mark them as a lost cause.

I worry that the church has become too superstitious to see my Neo-Pagan friends as regular people who, like us, were created in the image of God. The church is afraid of their "magic," and refuses to connect with them in any manner except in a rebuke, or worse, an aggressive attempted exorcism rite. Yet, I ask myself, is this same attitude found in me? Is the same superstitious fear found my own heart every time I see the television evangelist wave his hand, or push someone down. Have I automatically assumed that they are playing the crowd, and thereby performing parlor tricks for personal gain? Even if it is true of some, my quick assumptions about television evangelists are no different than the scared Evangelical who assumes every Neo-Pagan is a Satan worshiper sacrificing babies.

So I find that I must purge myself of fearful criticisms about people I have not met, and of the stories about Christianity, which are now the tabloid literature of our society. Perhaps I carry the seed of our trouble in my own heart. Even if I have seen what is wrong with the Church...

...sometimes I am what is wrong with the Church.

I also am concerned that the church has become too proud. Why do we always have the answer to everything, and question very little about even the most complicated issues of life? I have heard the Pentecostal blame game.

"Your sickness is the result of sin, or a lack of faith."

"Your calamities are due to spiritual warfare, which you have not recognized. You must battle Satan to overcome."

I have heard the pat answers, which leave no room for hope.

"You must accept everything which comes your way, because it is the will of God."

Our answers are naive against the complexities of life.

Not only does the Church appear to have the answers to life on all issues, we discuss our faith in such a way as to extinguish dialogue before it begins. We do not question others about what they believe without doing it in such a way as to lead them down the salvation path. Like a smooth lawyer, we bait our friends with set up questions designed to trap them into looking foolish, when in actuality, it is we who look foolish.

We seldom question to learn from people. Assuming that open listening is the same as being persuaded, we listen only to win our arguments about faith. My friends can feel when this is happening, and feel trapped as though being lured by the slick sales pitch.

In Pentecostal circles we have even developed a doctrine to support our habit of telling people without listening to them. "Touch not the Lord's anointed," we say, and using the story of David and Saul, we negate the teaching of James, which tells us that a teacher has greater accountability. We have created a heresy, allowing church leaders to be free of critique. This self-serving attitude runs throughout the leadership of the church. Then it is passed on down to the followers of Jesus, whose neighbors and co-workers wonder why we are so cocky.

Church does not offer a time for people with honest questions to ask them openly. We do not give place to real doubts in any fashion, except perhaps to answer them with our simple platitudes, which make it appear as though we do think we fully understand the complexities of the struggles around us.

Yet again, I must recognize my own little demons of pride (I'm speaking figuratively here, and I am not requesting an exorcism), which rear their ugly heads when I am accosted by the offenses of the Church. Do I carry the sick seed of heresy, which stands up to say that I am right? Is any questioning of my authority therefore a "Jezebel spirit," (sorry for the Pentecostal lingo) or rebellion? Perhaps I carry the seed of our trouble in my own heart. Just as much as I have seen unbearable pride, I find it in me.

Sometimes I am what's wrong with the church.

October of 2006, the Wall Street Journal told the story of our church being removed from our denomination, because we were too friendly with Witches. We have experienced what it is like to be on the receiving end of the inquisition of superstition and pride. It has been a long hard road to avoid giving back what we have received.

At our best, sometimes we are still what is wrong with the Church today. Just because we talk about being 'open,' and 'relational' doesn't mean we are. Is it possible that we express those terms in a way, which fosters a fear of being something other, or a pride about being something better?

Sometimes we are what's wrong with the Church today.

The Inherent Health of a Self-Critiquing Community

"I am a serial deconstructionist. I sound self-deprecating at times. I suppose this is a natural by-product of who I am, and what I've been through. Maybe this is Why I am a survivor – or at least I think I am. Please note: If I seem to question something which seems simple, the best solution is to ask me another question."

The above quote is the heading to a cathartic blog named "The Why Man",[180] which I started during a difficult season in life. I have always considered the capacity to be self-critiquing one of the healthier character traits in an individual. The culture of self-justification permeates not only corporate powers protecting their assets against internal decay and power grabs, or external attack and invasion; but the culture of self-justification is a foundation stone for a certain degree of pop-theology and pop-psychology. Even when the "ologies" do not support an unhealthy self-justification, we sometimes hear teachings and advice through a bias of self-protection, in the same way a CEO perceives a threat against the company and circles the corporate wagons. One of the early stages of maturity is the recognition that we are wrong, and the willingness to admit so. Whether in an AA meeting, a marriage, or a job, this character trait is critical to healthy relationships. The lack of self-critiquing honesty is the bane of homes, and nations, and though self-critique is counterintuitive to a personal sense of self-protection, it is in fact, a mark of health and maturity.

This is especially true of religion. A healthy religion is a self-critiquing religion. Although Christianity has often tried to hide its errors in the same manner as a badly hemorrhaging corporation, the development of new denominations through the long course of Christian history, and the Reformationist and Reconstructionist movements evidence the fact that self-critique is built into both the human psyche and the scriptures of the Christian Faith.

I was born the same day as the reformer Martin Luther. A new Pope was on the cover of Life magazine that Tuesday in 1958.[181] The juxtaposition and irony on the cover of Life magazine could not have been greater, and it unintentionally highlighted the ongoing self-critique and self-correction in the history of Christianity.

Self-Critique as a Healthy Deconstructionist Hermeneutic

"The key moments for understanding Mark's text are not the questions asked of Jesus, nor are they Jesus' answers or his symbolic actions (healing,

---

[180] http://philwyman.blogspot.com/
[181] https://2neatmagazines.com/Life-Magazine-Covers/1958/Life-Magazine-1958-11-10.jpg

exorcisms, the miracles of him feeding the hungry), nor even his parables, but rather the questions he asks his disciples, his opponents, and, in fact, his readers..."[182]

Croatian radical theologian Boris Gunjevic outlines a deconstructionist interpretation of the Gospel of Mark in God in Pain: Inversions of Apocalypse co-written with Slavoj Žižek. In Mark, Gunjevic sees Mikhail Bakhtin's revolutionary carnival,[183] and a formidable deconstructionist tone running throughout.[184] Both the Carnivalesque and the deconstruction pull us into a self-questioning paradigm. Mark's challenge to the 'powers that be' appears frenetic, as the Gospel begins with Jesus jumping from one event to the next. Jesus "immediately" transitions, almost frantically between preaching, and healing, and exorcising demons; and as Mark's Gospel moves forward, the Jewish expectations of messianic promise are simultaneously invoked and disregarded. The liberating good news of "the Kingdom" is the first proclamation in the post-baptismal initiation of Christ's ministry,[185] and yet, paying taxes to the oppressive Roman Empire remains a necessary element of righteous living.[186] From the liberating freedom of the poor, to the call of civic duty everything is turned upside down by Jesus. One moment the structural Empire of Rome or of Israel's religious elite is challenged and called into question, and in the next moment the empire of the individual's heart is assaulted by a graceful but passionate call to repentance. No one and nothing seem untouched by this world-upside-down challenge, and any honest reader of the Gospel should be provoked to both personal repentance and revolutionary action. I, and my world are weighed and found wanting. Both I and the other are broken, but the solution to the coexisting internal and external brokenness is found first in my heart – with a mysteriously growing seed of a word from the revolutionary carnival-like Christ, Who in messianic kingly ceremony rides into His own city on a beast of burden – a creature whose mere mention initiates laughter.

This simultaneous self-critical and other-critical reading of the Gospel of Mark would conjure up Luke's "Physician, heal thyself!" if it weren't for the messianic promise of help, healing, and divine intervention in both our external and internal troubles. Yet, the fact that the internal life of every person is challenged and called to the

---

[182] God in Pain: Inversions of Apocalypse, by Slavoj Žižek and Boris Gunjevic, pg. 245
[183] ibid pg. 259
[184] ibid pg. 258
[185] Mark 1:15
[186] Mark 12:16

healing pool reflects the necessary deconstruction I am called to practice. It is this word from Christ, which "carnivalizes" me, and turns me upside down inside my own world. My surrender to the process of being upended by Christ, is the beginning of my induction into a revolutionary force. I overcome the enemy in me, before I can overcome the enemy in the world. As Gunjevic points out, I am being questioned by Christ. My answers betray my position, and it is only in a process of healthy self-critique that I will be brought into alignment with this upside-down other Kingdom Jesus speaks of.

ONE BIG SORRY CHURCH

It was not a new idea. We read about it in Donald Miller's book Blue Like Jazz. James was the one with the idea of trying it over the month of Salem's Halloween events. I thought it would work well, but we had no idea how well.

James bought a few monks robes. We had the tents and tables. James and Brooke brought some candles and incense, and a handful of friends to man the booth. We made signs, "Free Confessional Booth."

At first people walked by and laughed. Occasionally someone would nervously say, "I don't have the time. It would take all day."

Then a few people began to trickle into the tent, and sit for a confession. They would walk out with big eyes, and occasionally some tears. Things began to gain some momentum when some of my friends who run a Psychic Faire decided to give it a try.

Jeff stood by the door to the tent, handling the people asking questions.

"What do you do in there?"

"Confessions." Jeff said frankly with a twist of wry. Jeff does wry well.

"But what happens in there?"

"I can't tell you. You will have to experience it for yourself." Jeff said, and after a pause, "But it's not what you expect."

"What do you mean?"

"I can't tell you. Are you up for giving it a try?" Jeff asked with that wry smirk sneaking out from the corner of his mouth again.

They entered the tent as a group. Three Witches sat together in support of one another. Witches entering a Christian confessional booth need backup. Who knows what gallows, or stake piled high with dry faggots hides behind the tent?

James spoke first, "Thank you for joining us in the confession booth. I'm sure you nervously entered expecting to share your deepest, darkest secrets, but we are here to offer another kind of confession. We want to confess to you on behalf of the church."

This was the beginning of a deeply moving time for my friends, the Witches. I found them half and hour later standing in front of the confessional booth with tears still streaming down their faces.

"This is the most moving spiritual experience I've ever had," Leanne said dragging long on her cigarette.

"I have been waiting for so many years to hear something like this. This is the high point of my Samhain this year." Shawn's makeup was running as he continued to cry.

James and the other monks confessed ancient and modern sins of the church to my Witch friends. He apologized for the Burning Times, the Inquisitions, and the Witch Trials in Salem. He apologized for the Crusades. He apologized for the prejudice and fear in the church, which has caused people to treat the Witches with anger, and fear – often in quite personal attacks. James confessed for being part of a church, which imposed its morality upon the Witches, even though Neo-Pagans live by another religious ethic.

Later that day, other Witches began to come through the tent. An entire Psychic Fair of Readers and Seers experienced the confessions. Witches from shops around town heard the rumors circulating about the confessional booth, and came to visit. The tears were many, and hearts of people generally antagonistic to Christianity were endeared to us.

Toward the end of the day a Tarot Reader brought one of her clients into the tent because, "she needed to hear this."

We are one big sorry church, and that has been our strength.

Engage: Is making an apology an act of power?

In these chapters, the model of humility, honesty, and honor are shown in the context of actual stories from Salem, Massachusetts with interaction between two cultures typically at odds: The Christians and the Witches. Both individual and group actions of apology are shown in these anecdotes, with the power they carry to change opinions people have about us. How does such activity open up dialogue with people radically unlike ourselves? How can you apply this principle of apology to your interactions with those who are your radical Other?

Interact with the Burning Religion community on the website at www.burningreligion.com.

Tales from the Land of Jaw: The Adventures of Gwyn Dee
The Cod Slappers of Peter Harbor

*T*he wide, wide road rose to the top of a high, high hill, and at the peak, the wide, wide road split into four paths. Gwyn Dee's moment of confusion hid the ocean, which splayed out like a great plain at the bottom of the high, high hill.

Seeing the ocean for the first time in a short life is enough of a surprise to suppress any confusion. A large and prosperous fishing village lay at the bottom of the hill, and hugged the harbor like jewels on a wedding ring, and Gwyn Dee ignored the roads, and ran down the hill across the turf, the heath and the heather, and through the village to the shores, and racing headlong into the water shouted with the joy of a precocious two-year old loosing the stone shoes from their happy feet.

Fisherman coming and going in their small and large boats stopped their work, and watched the strange sight of Gwyn Dee diving headlong, fully clothed, into the mildly lapping waters of Peter Harbor, and Gwyn Dee rose from the water to the laughing fisherman, chortling fishmongers, and giggling fishwives in the boats and on the shore.

Gwyn Dee blushed, and smiled sheepishly. The people cheered, and Gwyn Dee felt an invitation of deep friendship in this brief moment of vulnerability.

Coming ashore, the crowd of children, and women and old men gathered around and jabbered like long lost family. They offered their coats to the chilly swimmer, and offered food and warm drink, and hugs and words of blessing. Gwyn Dee's heart melted with happiness and a yearning, which in the ancient holy tongue of Cominkingville was called "hiraeth."

As the happy party was chortling and swapping tales of city life, a tall gentleman of means, with a top hat and a cane, and a 3-foot long cod hanging from his belt parted the happy crowd, and strode confidently up to Gwyn Dee. One of the children whispered, "Mommy, it's a Fisher-King. Is something wrong?"

The familiar haughty air of the High Clown Caste of Cominkingville was upon the Fisher-King, and this made Gwyn Dee exceedingly uncomfortable. Towering over the wet visitor, he looked down and smiled a big uncomfortable kind of knowing smile, and said, "Welcome Gwyn Dee. We've been expecting you for some days now. Your reputation precedes you from the High Clown Caste. Your family sends their greetings. They are concerned that all is well with you."

He leaned in with a hard penetrating stare, and while Gwyn Dee smiled on the outside, there was a 12-year-old barefoot runner curling up on the inside. The surrounding villagers cowered with the 12-year-old as well.

"While you are with us," the tall important gentleman with the big cod on his belt paused for effect, and the sun seemed to darken for that brief moment, "our homes are your home, and you will be treated like one from the Clown Caste deserves."

And with this declaration, the small crowd of people cheered, and shouted, and the children danced, and the teens popped their poppers, and the women and the old men with smaller cod attached to their belts patted Gwyn Dee on the back. And the people hugged, and kissed Gwyn Dee's face until it was wetter than the sea water dripping down the traveler's grinning face. A dozens homes and a dozen beds were offered with a dozen dinners, and a dozen grandmothers proposed arranged marriages, and Gwyn Dee smiled, and felt quite at home. In the end, the nearby neighborhood Fisherman's Hall was chosen as the location for a feast in Gwyn Dee's honor.

On the high porch above the Fisherman's Hall the Fisher-Kings with their tall hats, their squinting knowing smiles, and their long cod hanging from their belts looked down with the same lofty look Gwyn Dee had come to know from the High Clown Caste. One Fisher-King stood out among the rest. He was the tallest. He was the fattest. He had the tallest stovepipe hat, and a 6-foot-long cod hung from his right shoulder down to just above his shoes. The smell of dead fish and fish oil seeped over the edge of the building, and left the slight hint of putrid decay to the ending of the day.

As the sun slipped over the hills, and daylight came to an end, the last of the fishing boats returned from the day of work. Fish were unloaded, and the village came to life with the hustle and bustle of preparations for the neighborhood party at the Fisherman's Hall. Smoke from the chimneys of the village huts rose straight up in the windless sky, and formed a romantic haze just below the peaks of the hills. The smell of cooking fish, and garlic, and mustard, and paprika, and celery salt, and bay leaf, and black pepper, and crushed red pepper flakes, and mace, and cloves, and allspice, and nutmeg, and cardamom, and ginger filled the air, and in short time dishes of potatoes, and corn on the cob, and beans, and rice, and crabs, and cod and lobster began to fill Fisherman's Hall, as the children ran around, and the teenagers popped their poppers, and young and old men played their banjos, and their fiddles, and their mandolas, and their bodhrans, and their flutes, and their harps, and the young women danced and twirled, and laughed, and flirted with the young musicians.

All the while, three families sat on the seawall by the beach with a distant disenfranchised look in their eyes, which was too familiar to Gwyn Dee.

"Are you not joining the party tonight?" Gwyn Dee asked, not knowing what else to say.

A sad looking mother of two young children looked up from the ground, "We are always welcome they say, but there are a few too many bruises between us and the cod-slapping Fisher-Kings to forget."

The party was all about food, and music, and people asking Gwyn Dee what it meant to be part of the Clown Caste in Cominkingville, and how someone of such a young age had achieved notoriety. Gwyn Dee did not have much to say, but did tell of the dream to re-find the paths of Jane Foole the Jester of Jaw. The people of Peter Harbor were amazed, because they had similar tales of one Jan the Fisher-Queen.

At the party, an occasional young boy misbehaved, and the father would take the small cod off his belt and slap the boy's bare butt with the fish. In the middle of the evening five young boys started a fire in the back of the hall, and their fathers slapped the butts of the screaming boys with cod as the Fisher-Kings looked on approvingly.

Gwyn Dee found the way outside, and sat with a few remaining families on the seawall. The silence was a knowing silence, and Gwyn Dee began to feel like the 12-year-old barefoot runner again.

The evening wore down and the musicians faded, and the dancers tired, and the eaters ate to their full, and the Fisher-Kings relaxed their careful observations of the event. Suddenly, a strong young man ran through the front doors of the Fisherman's Hall with the largest cod anyone in Peter Harbor had ever seen. One of the mothers on the seawall screamed, and ran into the Hall. Gwyn Dee followed. The strapping young man swung the 7-foot cod like it was tree branch. He chased the fathers with their small cod out of the room, and some of them left the Fisherman's Hall air-born. The Fisher-Kings chased the young man, swinging their 3-foot cod with the skill of great batsmen, but the angry young man shouted, "I'll crack your cod pieces and lay your foul bodies on the floor!" And the Fisher-Kings chased, as the swift young man evaded their swings, and he cracked their skulls with his cod, and laid the men out like stacked wood. But, the Chief Fisher-King stood proudly in the middle of the room waiting to snap his massive cod, and toss the young man across the room. The young man's mother screamed. Gwyn Dee found a corner of the room and watched the mayhem. Children were hiding under the tables and crying, and mothers were doing their best to gather them and run out of the Hall. And fish oil, and fish guts, and the stench of decaying cod filled the room. Soon all but the Chief Fisher-King had been dispatched and lay groaning on the floor.

The young man looked at the Chief Fisher-King, pointed, and ran headlong at him with the enormous cod cocked over his shoulder like a bat. The Chief Fisher-King smiled confidently, and wound up for the deadly swing with his 6-foot cod. The young man flew at the massive man with the massive cod, and the two enormous codfish cut the air. And time froze in Peter Harbor.

And when the cod had met their mark, the young man lay dazed and propped against the doors of the Hall, and the head of the Chief

Fisher-King ricocheted around the room, as did the head of his massive fish. His headless body slowly teetered and fell to ground, with the huge headless cod still in his tightly gripping fingers.

The bouncing heads of the Chief Fisher-King and his cod finally came to rest at the feet of the dazed young man, who seeing them, came to his senses, shouted, and fled the Hall.

That night Gwyn Dee stayed with the family of the young man who attacked the Hall. In the dark hours of the early morning, they snuck out of town. The sore young man and his family decided to travel to a distant village where relatives would offer them refuge. Gwyn Dee and the family said a tearful goodbye, and Gwyn Dee understood the plight of Peter Harbor in a single evening of battle, and was strangely grateful for having been raised with stone shoes instead of cod slapping.

UNCOMFORTABLE SEXUAL POSITIONS

I was asked to present a workshop on the intersection of sexuality and theology at a fledgling but quickly growing festival. The Wild Goose Festival draws progressive Christians, conservative Christians and non-Christians. They would all be bumping around together in the woody hills of North Carolina – a state, which at the time was openly wrestling with the subject of gay marriage.

The festival director and I had a two-hour long discussion about sex and Christianity, and at the end of that discussion he asked, "Would you consider leading a workshop on this subject?"

And I asked, "Are you trying to kill me?"

I was joking – sort of joking. I'd been in these woods before.

Into the Deep, Dark Woods

Harold Parker State Forest is a nature reserve north of Salem in Andover, MA. It used to be the yearly gathering location for the Eastern Massachusetts Pagan Pride Day. Some years ago I was invited to present a workshop at that event. This was an honor, and a challenge. I was a Christian Pastor speaking at Pagan Pride. Some of my friends jokingly suggested I was the sacrifice for the ritual.

As my topic I choose to talk about four of the most controversial subjects between Christians and Neo-Pagans. It was a workshop about how Pagans could survive living with their Christian friends and family. My goal was to reframe Christian theology in the minds of my Neo-Pagan friends. I wanted them to see another, more gracious side to the God of Christianity than the misogynistic, oppressive, self-absorbed version they imagined. I had promoted the workshop with this description:

The Circle and The Cross Talk: Re-visioning Pagan/Christian Relationships

Looking back to the Caesars, and to the Burning Times misconceptions and urban myths have had deadly results for both Pagans and Christians. In our own times, though mild in comparison, Pagans have been on the receiving end of religious persecution. Some have chosen to remain in the broom closet, and others have faced the struggle head on – sometimes to bitter disappointment with family, friends, and work associates. This workshop is designed as a deeper look into the worldview differences between Christian and Neo-Pagan thought with a focus upon

255

deconstructing and re-visioning some of the beliefs, which cause the greatest pain. Come learn to navigate this battlefield of philosophical tension. Topics of frustration to be covered include judgment, conversion, spiritual dissonance, and sexuality.

So, there in woods of Harold Parker State Forest, my four Christian friends and I held a workshop for 30 or more Witches and Pagans. We were outnumbered 6 to 1, and we were going to hold short dialogues on Hell and Judgment, Conversion, Spiritual Warfare, and Sex.

Some of you read the above description with its reference to deconstruction, and imagined what you might think is a liberalized Christian pseudo-theology leaning into Paganism. Others have read that sentence and imagined something new and wonderful. As much as I hope for the latter, I will have to allay both your fears, and your excitement. The purpose of the workshop was to help Pagans understand that the conservative theology of their Christian family and friends was more gracious and beautiful than the bad press it gets. And unfortunately, it is the Christians themselves who often give Christianity its bad press. Yet, it was my contention then and still is now, that there is a more gracious way to see a conservative interpretation of the Bible and the words of God than we have been able to express.

The political and social tensions of our days demand we speak up on the subject of sex. The first question many people have about church is the stance it takes on LGBT rights, and both the left and the right expect pastors to identify with the polarizing political talking points. Jesus appears to have avoided those radical talking points. The Pharisees attempted to catch Him in politically radical positions. Somehow, despite taking neither the position of the religious radicals or the Roman oppressors Jesus became the most radical voice in His time, and I would contend, in human history.

And so, to my Pagan friends I had to find a way to make the story of Christian sexuality beautiful apart from the political talking points of this generation.

Pagans understand liturgy, and love it. Pagans understand discipline, and often see themselves as better practitioners of spiritual disciplines than most Christians – and they often have a point. I reframed the sexual commandments of God as a liturgical lifestyle: prophetic annunciations liturgically modeling God's faithfulness, and the eschatology of our redemption story. It is a redemption story, which pictures Jesus as the Bridegroom, and the church as the Bride. Witches and Pagans could see in this story the self-sacrificing sexual ethic outlined by Moses and Paul as a lifestyle choice – a lifestyle chosen to model the character of God and to prophetically retell His redemption story. It is a story of waiting, of faithfulness, and of monogamy. But Pagans do not follow the Bible. They do not feel the overbearing guilt Christians feel when we read the pages of this book we revere as the Word of God. Consequently, I sat Christians and Pagans down together to talk about this tough subject. After a bit of reeducation, and telling the secrets of my Christian faith, my Pagan friends saw for the first time that it was possible to dialogue about sexuality with Christians, and not fight.

Did my Pagan friends and acquaintances buy my theological position, and see my conservatism as beautiful rather than oppressive? I will let this email from George Popham speak for many others who were there:

Pastor Phil,

I just wanted to thank you again for the kind and thoughtful discussion you moderated at pagan pride yesterday. I was so impressed that you managed to neither soft pedal or market away the true differences of belief involved or make those differences excessively confrontational. Usually interfaith dialog between any of the, let's say, 'Abrahamic' faiths and other religions is either so diplomatic that it is dishonest about the true nature of their basic differences, or so focused on the differences that they appear as you aptly put it 'mean and judgmental' Somehow you managed to find a middle course between these extremes and I have seldom seen this done with such grace.

But you also avoided two other mistakes (I believe) Christians commonly make in witnessing their faith. 1. You did not speak as if we non-christians had never heard this message before and 2. You did not speak to us non-christians as if we were in need of rescue. I know you likely believe we *are* in need of rescue, but that you were respectful enough to not explicitly condescend shows a good heartedness and sensitivity I am not used to encountering among evangelicals. This is important because this attitude conveys that you are aware that many non-christians are just as comfortable and assured of their beliefs as you are, and just as contented in their lives and full of spiritual hope as well. That is, we are as committed to our stuff as you are to yours. Too many Christians fail to recognize this and this tends to shut down discussion right from the start.

The sort of discussion we had yesterday is also encouraging in so far as the discourse between Christians and non-christians has become increasingly and dangerously polarized, toxic and political. That you have drawn such fire for even speaking with neo-pagans is yet another perplexing proof of it. It just seems so un-Christ-like to condemn you for ministering to neo-pagans, after all, that is exactly what Christ would have done. If there is to be any peace at all and if the political fiber of our Country and Constitution is to hold together we need to continually remind each other that whatever we may believe we are NOT enemies.

Christian Day was speaking with my wife after the discussion yesterday and told her how kind, generous and basically samaritan-like you and your people have been in the Salem community. And in this respect I think we have at least one common belief: argument and discussion is worthwhile and even fun, but it is far more important to persuade by one's example of loving kindness.

The whole thing made Debbie and I feel great. We've been talking about it quite a lot. We will likely never share your congregation's religious beliefs, but we hope you will consider us allies all the same.

Peace,
George Popham and Debbie Fields Popham

The Deeper Darker Woods?

Teaching on the subject of Christian sexuality was filled with enough tension. I had jokingly asked the director of the Christian festival if he was trying to kill me, but the fact was that I thought teaching on the intersection of sexuality and theology was a tougher task between progressive and conservative Christians than it was between Pagans and conservative Christians.

Large and necessary parenthetical section inserted here: (Conservatives may at this point assume I am saying that progressive Christians are "worse than pagans", besmirching Pagans even as they say that. Progressive Christians could take what I am saying as evidence that conservatives are still in the Dark Ages. Both these assumptions are based on the sophomoric thinking of our polarized society, and my basic contention of this entire book is to break away from that absurd perspective.)

This festival in the hills of North Carolina was a predominantly progressive Christian audience. In the festival's first year, a workshop was taught on sexuality. A young conservative Christian man asked an honest, but polarizing question. He wanted to know how homosexuality could be justified scripturally in light of the creation story. God created man and woman, and this appears ordained by God as a model for intimate relationships. Furthermore, the animal world similarly seems divided up predominantly into a male and female construct. So, how do we justify homosexuality as a God approved relationship?

The response did not come as an answer. Rather it was mocking and jeering. The young man was shouted down, and booed. The director of the festival was saddened by the experience, and felt that the festival was a place questions like this should be graciously and intelligently answered. I suggested that graciously answering the question was not radical enough a position. The festival should be a place where polarizing questions can be intelligently answered, and even if the answer is received as unsatisfactory, deep relationships are built and dialogue continues in spite of ongoing disagreement.

In the end I agreed to lead a discussion about theology and sexuality at the Christian festival, because my comfort zone has never been a deciding factor for my pastoral activities.

It was a tough enough process to contrast Biblical sexuality with anarchic Pagan personal freedom, but I had re-envisioned the commandments on sexuality as a prophetic liturgical lifestyle, which emphasized their beauty.

I knew the success I had experienced creating peaceful dialogue between Christians and Pagans would not be the same experience with a mixed group of liberal and conservative Christians. Differing Christian groups are looking closely at the same book from different perspectives. The proximity makes the parallax more severe. As Christians we are attached to the Bible. I imagined that the cultural dissonance between Christians and Christians was going to be far more severe than the dissonance between Christians and Pagans. Each Christian had their interpretation of the Scriptures. Each political position would have its talking points, and those talking points carried violent ramifications from the perspective of the other side. Christians from different schools of theology are contending to be the definers of our Book to this generation.

I live the conservative Christian sexual ethic as best I can. I am heterosexual. I believe that marriage and sex were made for each other, and that is the place sex belongs. I have lived this ethic for these 30 years of my Christian experience, and I have not adapted with the howling winds of social change, or deep struggles of personal betrayal.

I had four months to prepare for the event, and it seemed too short. So, I immediately called the only two experts I personally knew who were dealing with the subject of sexuality and faith, and began digging for information, and pleading for help. Calling my friends for advice had its own level of uncomfortable tension. They were both women. Beautiful women. They were married – to men I admired greatly. And I was going to talk sex with them.

Insert LP needle scratch sound here.

Is this the kind of dialogue you expect from your local pastor? Me neither, and the problem was I was the pastor, and I was diving into sex issues. Most pastors diving into sexual issues emerge with scandals and front-page news.

Deb Hirsch was the pastor of a small church called Tribe LA. Tribe is the only church I've visited, which feels like our little ragtag band at The Gathering in Salem. They are a free-wheeling, artistic bunch of Jesus freaks and connected seeking friends from Los Angeles, CA. Their church meets in an art laboratory. The church had its beginnings after a few friends returned from the Burning Man festival and asked themselves, "Why isn't church more like Burning Man?" and out of the passion for an artistic, interactive community Tribe LA was born.

Deb and her husband Alan Hirsch moved from Australia to Los Angeles, and Deb took the helm of Tribe, as Al wrote and traveled speaking on missional Christianity. Deb had years of experience working within the LGBT community in Australia, and I knew she would have advice for me. Real experts on any subject are typically practitioners of what they study, and Deb had experience of speaking on the wild subject of sexuality in our revolutionary culture.

Megan DeFranza lives near Salem. Megan had recently completed her doctoral work on what the Gospel has to say to the "intersexed." She had a book contract to publish her doctoral work.[187] I had read portions of her work, and was impressed with her depth of knowledge. She had been raised in a Fundamentalist Christian home, and she was wondering how she ended up as an expert on sexuality and faith. She had been involved on panels with some of the world's most noted "Queer Theologians" (a term they use for themselves). Her husband Andrew is a high energy Italian-American working in non-profit groups helping establish housing for the poor.

I had only a few questions for these brilliant women, but there was one burning question I had absolutely no answer for, and I was hoping they had an answer from their experience. I wanted to know how to get liberal pro-LGBT rights Christians, and conservative Christians to sit down at the table together and discuss the topic of sexuality without fighting.

If anyone had the answer to this question it had to be these two women.

It turned out that they had the exact same answer – used the same exact words, and it was a simple answer. It came in two words: "Good luck!"

Deb explained that in her travels and speaking engagements, when she dealt with the topic of sex, once it moved into political and social

---

[187] Megan's book has now been published by Eerdmans under the title Sex Difference in Christian Theology. http://www.amazon.com/Sex-Difference-Christian-Theology-Intersex/dp/0802869823

justice issues concerning LGBT rights – especially gay marriage, the meetings became unruly, and tempers flared.[188] In Deb's experience, progressive Christians were often angrier than conservative Christians, and often the conservatives were afraid to speak up. Deb had not found a way to approach the subject peacefully in larger groups with opposing opinions sitting at the same table. Deb directed me toward Janell Williams Paris' book, The End of Sexual Identity.

Megan and I met at a coffee house in Salem numerous times to think through the topic. She helped me outline a simple chart of sexual practices from a stringently conservative to a wildly liberal spectrum. On one side was the radically conservative patriarchal polygamy in the Middle East. On the other side was bestiality, and pedophilia. It was by no means comprehensive, but the middle of the chart included uncomfortable and even strange things many Christians don't want to consider, and in some cases have never heard about: masturbation, celibacy, traditional Christian nudism, polyamory, prostitution, Queer Theology and more.

Megan pointed me in the direction of Queer Theologians I should read in order to understand their perspectives, and theology. In the meantime, I read up on the subject from one of the most influential voices of the 20th century: Michel Foucault's History of Sexuality. Slowly a process for helping create a peaceful dialogue emerged from the strangest combination of sources.

Foucault as a Voice of Conservatism?

Michel Foucault was a French Philosopher/Social Theorist, and one of the most influential philosophical voices of the 20th century. Unlike many philosophers, much of his writing is accessible. Foucault was a primary force in the description and movement into post-modernity. His theories on power have become part of our table talk and the politics of human rights organizations. Foucault participated in the gay sado-masochistic scene in San Francisco in the early 80's and contracted HIV. He died from the complications of AIDS in Paris in 1984. At first glance, he would appear to be an unlikely source to find answers for my conundrum, but the controversial philosopher was controversial in every way and did not disappoint me.

Foucault did not see power as something owned by oppressors, but as inherent to every human interaction. He saw power not only in the actions of the strong against the weak, but also in the weak with their

---

[188] Deb Hirsch has since published a book on the subject through Intervarsity Press. http://www.amazon.com/Redeeming-Sex-Conversations-Spirituality-Partnership/dp/083083639X

reactions to the strong. In respect to sexuality, Foucault suggested that those driving the sexual revolution utilized the same kind of power as their oppressors in the fight for liberation.[189] Like medieval institutions separated the lepers from society, could it be that the political changes in the winds of our culture have created outsiders out of those who are reticent to bend to the wind? Foucault was a carnivalesque philosopher who often stood in the place of being neither left nor right, but surprised us with observations from outside the battle lines of contention. Foucault's theory on power put the first piece in place to establish grounds for a peaceful dialogue between warring positions.

Megan suggested I read <u>Radical Love: an Introduction to Queer Theology</u>. Patrick Cheng introduces the various voices of Queer Theologians, who are changing the face of religious thinking with a post-structuralist liberation theology based upon queer theory. Cheng describes "coming out" as gay as a liturgy, similar to baptism. The action of "coming out" is a public announcement about one's inner life, and so it is celebrated in some circles like baptism is celebrated in an evangelical church service. Strangely, this provided another piece towards establishing the grounds for peaceful dialogue, because it represented the Foucauldian power shift in a moment of exchanging one outsider for another.

Janell Williams Paris is a conservative Christian anthropologist. In her book, <u>The End of Sexual Identity</u>, she contends that using sexual preference as a definition for who we are as human beings is an inaccurate and unhelpful category of reference. Interestingly, Queer Theologian Patrick Cheng agrees with Paris on this account. And so, a third piece of the puzzle came together allowing me to prepare a path for dialogue to occur between people with radically different Biblical theologies.

How to Get a Crowd

How to get a crowd: Give your workshop a naughty name.
Festival time arrived, and I was excited, but nervous about the workshop. On the basis of trying to get left and right to sit down together at the table of discussion I called the workshop "Uncomfortable Sexual Positions." A few minutes before it began under an outdoor tent made to seat about a hundred, people started coming. By the time the workshop began I had people sitting in groups of 10-12, and they were squeezing out the sides of the open tent.

---

[189] Michel Foucault, <u>The History of Sexuality, Vol. 1</u>, pg. 10

I apologized for the false advertising – there would be no live demonstrations, and I began with a description of my own conservative Christian lifestyle, before I broke into the teaching time.

I used the chart of sexual practices I developed with Megan, and allowed people to privately identify where they were on the list. I asked them to consider the range of practices, which should be allowable by law, and last I asked them to consider what they thought God's range of acceptable activities might be. People acknowledged that their personal actions, their expectations of the law, and their view of God's opinion were different positions on the scale.

Using the chart of sexual practices I had to explain a number of the unique and strange sexual lifestyles listed. During this explanation I described the post-structuralist Queer Theology with its re-interpretation of scripture in the light of sexual lifestyles. Patrick Cheng's reference to "coming out" as liturgy was one of my examples of re-interpreting scripture to align with sexual liberation.

And here is where Michel Foucault came to the rescue.

The act of celebrating "coming out" turns the power structures, and the social acceptance factors upside down. The person feeling outcast and disenfranchised finds a new community in the moment of the coming out celebration. Their open declaration establishes their seat at the family table in progressive Christian circles. In the moment of liberation and familial acceptance someone else is being shamed. The conservative who does not accept the lifestyle as a God accepted norm for human sexual relationships is suddenly the rejected one. In this movement one leper is exchanged for another.

Foucault would say that the same power initially used to suppress is also used by the suppressed to invert the power. Revolutionaries use the same power modes to find their freedom that their enemies used to suppress those freedoms. Consequently, those who once held the power are often the new lepers. As Deb Hirsch had noted, many conservatives are in hiding today. They have been made to feel ashamed for their beliefs.

I asked the workshop of about 120 people how many identified as liberal. Most of the people in and around the tent raised their hands, and I said, "How must it feel to be the rare conservative in a room full of people who are celebrating a lifestyle you are not sure you can condone? What must it be like to sneak into a place hiding your identity, because you are sure everyone will be against you? Is it possible that the moment we celebrate the choice of one person, that we have turned the tables upside down and denigrated the position of another?"

"But isn't it possible to celebrate everyone, even the honest seeker who believes differently than ourselves, and comes with a desire to learn and love?"

And then I asked, "How many conservative Republicans are here right now."

People looked sheepishly around the tent. Some people stopped breathing. A few seconds later, people were craning their necks, looking around the space to see if there where any Republicans present. After a painfully long few seconds, one woman toward the front raised her hand slowly.

I asked her to stand.

The tent broke out in applause.

The tables were turned again, but this time they were turned right side up, not upside down, and everyone could sit at the table to dialogue, because the dominant power force in the space celebrated the feared other minority. Could it be possible that Jesus turned the tables in the temple over, and is waiting for us to right them and use them as they should be used? Not as places for the power structures to maintain their position, or as places to establish new power structures, but rather as places of open and caring interaction – a house of prayer, not a den of thieves robbing power and acceptance from one group to give to another.

Even in the most difficult religious and political positions we are called to lovingly dialogue as much as it is possible – even when we are talking about uncomfortable sexual positions. This story is a theological and philosophical example of speaking from outside the lines of contention, and finding a carnivalesque mode of communication, which is birthed from the impossible spaces in between.

I mentioned earlier that many conservatives feel they have to hide their identity today. How do I know this? They came to me secretly after the workshop, and thanked me, and they were grateful for the lady who raised her hand. They were not liberated enough to do it themselves.

Where Cognitive Dissonance and Sexual Practices Meet

One of the reference points from Leon Festinger's <u>When Prophecies Fail</u> relates directly to our sexual life:

> *"The person holding the belief must have committed himself to it; that is, for the sake of his belief, he must have taken some important action that is difficult to undo. In general, the more important such actions are, and the more*

difficult they are to undo, the greater is the individual's commitment to the belief."

The amount of counseling I have had to do over relationship breakups, and singles over-committing themselves to another person could be logged as flying hours, and I would have a pilot's license many times over.

Among most Christians, sex seals the deal, and establishes the importance of a relationship. It binds emotional attachments and makes fighting for the relationship critical. If the relationship is desperately unhealthy, the self-justification can become a series of amazing intellectual acrobatics.

This is not true for conservative Christians only. I have been on the phone late into the night with Neo-Pagans, atheists, and an assorted potpourri of faith traditions similarly struggling with these same self-justifying tensions. Even when everything has fallen apart, betrayal has happened, and it should been apparent long before the end came that this was not a wise relationship to enter, they still hold on desperately believing this is the right person. The politics of sexuality are entangled in such a power play, because sex holds immense power over us. Those politics are at play before they take the public stage. Sex itself is like a politician manipulating our emotions through subtle and beautiful sounding words. Sex is a key player in the contemporary Bread and Circuses power structures. Perhaps we are not living in reality to think that we are free to live any sexual lifestyle we want. Rather, it could be that the power of sex is what is free. It is freely running rampant in our minds, emotions, and hormones without restraint, and we are subservient to its power, and this could be true whether we fight against its mastery over us, or give in to it.

Engage: Looking into one of today's hottest topics.

This chapter tells the story of trying to navigate peaceful discussion between people holding radically polarized positions on one of the hottest topics of our day. How do you feel about the issues surrounding sexuality, and how will you seek to approach discussions in the future in respect to this hot topic?

Interact with the Burning Religion community on the website at www.burningreligion.com.

Tales from the Land of Jaw: The Adventures of Gwyn Dee
The Inquisition

Gwyn Dee came to a fork in the road. It looked uncannily familiar. Gwyn Dee read the dilapidated sign pointing down the hill to the village. It took a moment to realize where this was. Gwyn Dee had traveled many months on the wide, wide road in search of the borders of the Land of Jaw, only to discover that the wide, wide road led in a big circle back to the beginning point of the long journey.

Welcome to Cominkingville.

Gwyn Dee flopped down in the middle of the road in despair, and sat for hours, or maybe it was days. Perhaps it was weeks. The sun did not rise or set – it stood still, so it was impossible to tell how long a time had passed, sitting there in the middle of the road. An occasional merchant, or passing child walked in a wide arc around the despairing traveler, and stared uncomfortably.

Then after some long, long time in the wide, wide road chanting could be heard coming up the hill from Cominkingville.

"Shambala, shambala..." and the repetitious shambalas came closer and closer, and Gwyn Dee knew what was coming, but did not have the strength left to flee.

Thirteen robed inquisitors processed up the hill. They formed a circle and surrounded Gwyn Dee. The Chief Inquisitor in a Bishop's robe carried a large hatchet. The Hatcheteer took his hatchet and one by one pulled back the hoods of the 12 monks, and chopped off their heads. He handed the heads of the monks back to them, and they stood calmly in their circle spurting blood from their open necks and holding their own heads in their hands. Eerily they chanted with their disembodies heads. "Shambala, shambala..."

Suddenly the chanting stopped. The Chief Inquisitor/Hatcheteer called out formally and coldly, "We are here to account for your evil ways Gwyn Dee."

All twelve beheaded monks began shouting. Their disembodied heads screamed high-pitched accusations. The blood spewed like small fountains from their over-excited pulsing arteries.

From under the arm of a rather burly monk, his head cried, "Heresy, heresy..."

A petite blonde with a lion's mane of hair held her head in both hands, and leaned forward screaming, "You're a friend of sinners, bewitched, and filled with demons. I've seen you cavorting with the devil in my dreams!"

The twelve headless monks screamed accusations, danced in place in little hissy fits, and created a deep circle of blood around Gwyn Dee. Their heads screamed and their bodies bled themselves out, until they collapsed on the ground.

The Chief Inquisitor smiled with deep satisfaction. "You are not welcome back until you have fully repented Heretic Gwyn Dee."

The Hatcheteer then took each head, and one by one he pulled the top of the skullcap over as though it was hinged, and set the open head upon the ground. Hiking his Bishop's robe up above his waist, he squatted, and groaned, and filled each head with a steaming reeking pile. He closed the skullcaps, and placed the heads back on the bodies.

"Shambala, shambala..." The Hatcheteer marched back to Cominkingville as his chant faded slowly away. One by one, the bodies revived, and followed the Hatcheteer back to the village chanting, leaving Gwyn Dee alone in a circle of blood.

"I think you've got my body. Shambala..."
"I thought it felt pretty nice. Shambala..."
"Hey! Don't be touching it like that! Shambala, shambala..."

THE MAN IN MIDDLE

Sonnet #42 on the Greenman[190]

He hides among the stories past, but now
he has no name. With stonied face he laughs
or scowls, or smiles, or frowns, or cries. Who knows
what mood is carved by ancient cunning crafts?

The wintered face of death after the fall,
the brambled, twisted, tortured crown of thorns
will gently resurrect at springtime's call
with vestal bud and festive flowered horns,
but then from jamb post lustily explodes,
from foliate frieze the summer greens wrap round
and high above the narthex harvest loads
his juicy fruits upon the stirring crowd

he has no name and yet he wears the crown
of life and death and birth upon his brow

---

[190] The Greenman is a wood or stone carving found almost exclusively in medieval churches, abbeys, and cathedrals across the UK, France and Germany. People have linked this symbol to ancient Paganism, but the history of the Greenman is not known. In this sonnet, I compare the Greenman to the life of Christ.

Sonnet #43 on the carnival of God

A song was played. Heaven and earth were formed.
A garden made, where naked bodies warmed,
until the worm slithered from past'ral glade
and with the germ of doubt innocence slayed

and from the leaves of figs we played our game -
the game, which thieves still play to shift the blame.
Covered our shame, leaves over hubris weaved
Naked dance tamed, we dressed in brittle sheaves

But from the dust of Adam, rose a tune -
a tune we cussed, which piped the earth's last moon
the singer crooned in holy, joyous lust
But we in anger slew and stripped unjust

The piper piped. We did not dance his jig.
but hid our joy with barren leafy fig.

Sonnet #44 - 2nd Carnival sonnet, an upside-down sonnet
(to be read in both directions: top to bottom and bottom to top)

T'is He Who turned our planet upside-down
upon the cross of Christ, the Holy Clown

and I would be remiss were I not glad
Though sad the sight of Him whose skin was flayed
So now we ask, t'is He or we be mad?
But we find joy in Him Whom we betrayed

Yet all was lost to us in our estate
We crushed our world, our lovers, and our friends
Like enemies we crushed them to be great
For people became means and became ends

The world was ours to win and win we did
When all was fair in war and love of gain
in winning every battle, every bid
When blessings dropped from clouds like acid rain

The Waning Gibbous Moon

The waning gibbous moon slung low upon the sky
Winks, and bids the dawning day goodbye
It mocks me with its eloquence
It portends darker nights
And with the waning gibbous moon I sigh

The waning gibbous moon slides down to meet the line
Stops, where earth meets sky and dark meets light
Inerrant gibbous moon I sense
Prognosticates my life
and with the waning gibbous moon I cry

The waning gibbous moon slinks out beneath the sky
Flees, to squeeze the nighttime and the tide
O, soothe me omen gibbous moon
Reveal where I might fly
and with the waning gibbous moon I'll hide

The Man in the Middle

You walked with me across this white space
this hard cracked earth like lines upon my weary face
the setting sun cast shadows long and dreary
and the man in the middle dictates the shadows' pace
as we all celebrate the dark

I am the man in this carnival of flame
screaming with the masses to slay myself again
Yet, if I kill him he will come back to claim
his place in the middle of this game
his place in this carnival of flame

You built a home with me for just a season
but we would be evicted, pack up our things and flee him
we tried to slay him with the screaming masses
but the man in the middle will rise again next year from Phoenix ashes
as we all are yearning for the fire

I am the man in this carnival of flame
screaming with the masses to slay myself again
Yet, if I kill him he will come back to claim
his place in the middle of this game
his place in this carnival of flame

WHEN GOD WAS LOST

Finding Jesus at Burning Man

Jesus was walking across the barren landscape carrying a cross. I shouted to my friends, "Look it's Jesus carrying a cross! Let's get a picture of him."

The three of us started walking across the desert toward Jesus, but Jesus turned away. He was walking further into the nothingness, and away from us. So I hastened my pace, and left my friends behind. After a couple minutes I caught up with him.

Referring to a Biblical passage, I told Jesus a fib and said, "Hi, my name is Simon, and the Romans sent me to carry your cross." He, of course, was familiar with the Biblical reference - after all, he was Jesus. Relieved, he handed me his cross and said, "Oh, thank you. It's not too heavy is it?"

I walked and talked with Jesus. I confessed, "My name is not really Simon. It's Phil. My friends and I created an art installation in honor to one of your saints - Simeon Stylites. We'd love to show it to you."

Jesus stopped. He looked me in the eyes, and said, "Are you Phil Wyman?"

Now, I had only told Jesus my first name. This was getting a little weird.

"Uhm. Yes."

Jesus teared up. He said, "I've been looking for you. I was lost and couldn't find you."

'Okay. Now it was getting really weird,' I thought, 'Jesus is lost, and I just found him. How often does that happen?'

But, this was Burning Man, and anything can happen at Burning Man.

Burning Man is formed around the dual values of radical self-reliance and radical self-expression. Yes, it is a notoriously hedonistic event. Burning Man has naked people, but not as many naked people as some of the urban myths suggest. Burning Man does have campsites, which are adult playgrounds for a variety of sexual activities. The activities are openly advertised, but barely veiled behind the thin walls of the cloth domes and large tents. Burning Man has drugs, and an over-excess of free alcohol. By night Burning Man becomes a series of large raves and dance parties, with "sound camps" comprised of walls of woofers and tweeters thumping and squealing until the dawn. It might be expected that even angels would fear to tread the dust of this nomadic adult party, but techno beats and hedonism are not the only things one finds at Burning Man.

Burning Man is about a pursuit of spirituality for many people. It is also about finding a counter-culture, non-monetary way to live. You cannot buy or sell things at Burning Man. "Gifting" is the prime objective, and most Burners bring enough supplies and gifts to give a great deal of it away to others. People give away their art, food, skills and crafts to others at the event. Back at our camp in 2011, espresso was being "gifted," and when the espresso machine broke down Mr. Fix-it, who is about 70 years old, gave us the gift of repairing the machine.

The wild combination of hedonism, art and spiritual pursuit is what dragged me, and my four adventurous friends to Burning Man. We wanted to see if Jesus was there. We were hunting for hints of the witness of God's Spirit in the midst of hedonism and nudity. If it is true that "where sin abound[s] grace does much more abound,"[191] it seemed that Burning Man would be on fire with great grace.

'Why,' I wondered 'has Christianity not embedded itself into these festivals? Why are we not among the leaders of new cultural developments and wildly creative thought?' The God I serve is wildly creative, and certainly creative enough to find His way into human hearts in other cultures of the world, but here at these festivals, and in the newly developing cultures of post-modernity the people of Jesus seem so few. Yet, as the five of us would discover, we were not alone.

Kevin (Kevissimo) Rolly helps build the Man: the five-story tall man-shaped structure, which is burned at the end of the festival. He is on the neon team. About 15 years ago, he and two friends started a church in Los Angeles called Tribe LA. They were yearning for a fellowship, which carried some of the creative elements of Burning Man. They could not find one, so they started their own. Kevissimo and some of Tribe LA are regulars at Burning Man.

The camp we attended was a group of 40 Christians from all around the US. There were at least two other Christian theme camps at Burning Man.

So, for the last 5 years of Burning Man, I have sat with friends like the talented studio drummer David Raven, and his brilliant scholarly wife Rebecca Ver Straten-Mcsparran. I chew the fat, and wander the playa with Alan and Deb Hirsch, and hang out with Kevissimo and Crunchy under the brilliant night sky. Jesus people of significant

---

[191] Romans 5:20

influence are already there. These are people who have not stood looking across the unnavigable zone where religion and secular culture clash. They are those who have done their best to stand at both reference points to capture what Edward Said called, "the essential privilege of exile," and this has afforded them the multi-perspectival eyes of prophets. God was already at Burning Man in people who loved Him deeply.

But, God was also in the pattern of gathering found at the event. Burning Man might be today's best example of the developing festival culture in Western society. Like the Children of Israel in the Old Testament who gathered for holy-days like Passover, Pentecost and the Feast of Tabernacles; millions of people are gathering at festivals such as Burning Man, the Rainbow Gatherings, Glastonbury, and Mind Body Spirit. Unlike the Jewish holy-days, many of these festivals are imbued with a hedonistic party culture. Yet, they often foster a search for deeper spirituality. That deeper spirituality is typically not Christian, but it is not specifically or predominantly anything. Rather it is the celebration of the search for meaning. Many of the adherents and seekers have felt disenfranchised from Christianity. They do not see hope in traditional church forms. So, like the Jews running out to the desert to see John the Baptist, they are running to festivals and finding new crazed prophets.

I also found the grace of God in the "gifting" principle of the Burning Man Festival. I found the heart of Martin Luther's "priesthood of all believers" in the emphasis on interactivity, and the encouragement for every person to become a creator. I saw my Creator God in the innovative, and boundary breaking art being erected on the playa. I saw a call to a primitive simplicity in the location of the event: in the barren desert – a wilderness reminiscent of the wanderings of the people of Israel escaping the bondage of Egypt. In these things I began to formulate a plan for an art installation.

Jesus had preceded us to the event. It was as if He had been walking the playa for years, lost and invisible to the eyes of the church, and with tear-filled eyes He was hoping for us to find Him.

Our fear of newly developing cultures, reminds me of the Prophet Jonah, who ran from God only to discover that running was a futile exercise.[192] The developing culture shifts happening around us today have at least some of the DNA of God embedded within their creative momentum. I believe God is with people in these festivals, whether they see and hear it or not. For the religious people who are afraid to stand in the world of the radically different other, watch out, you may

---

[192] Book of Jonah, Old Testament

find yourself spit up on the beach of Nineveh (or the playa of Burning Man) having to adapt your worldview to accept others God loves.

In finding God on the playa, it seemed that all we needed to do was offer people an opportunity to search for Him themselves - to hear His voice, to sense His gentle urgings, and to see His handiwork laid out on the desert canvas before them. So it was that we decided to allow people to "listen for the voice of the Spirit" without mediating the process, and we believed God would show up - or at least, we hoped He would.

In one respect our installation was a sociological experiment. We were looking for people who heard voices, and we wanted to discover what those voices were saying. On the other hand, we anticipated that the voice of Jesus – the same Jesus who spoke to Saul of Tarsus - was already speaking at Burning Man.

Of course, we did not expect every Burner to be a happy little churchgoer, or even interested in Jesus, but then that was the reason we were going to Burning Man. As a team, we shared this hope: That the Spirit of God would come to meet people upon the Pillars, and speak gently and lovingly to them.

Of Pillars and Fire

In my second year at Burning Man, I found some crazy friends to help me. Hope Deifell, Dennis (Two Tents) Huxley, Scott (Horizon) Veatch, Matt (The Pirate) Bender and I came with a plan to build a simple art installation on the desert playa. It was an interactive meditation project based upon the life of the 5th century Christian Desert Father and ascetic mystic Saint Simeon Stylites. Simeon lived on a pillar for 39 years seeking God, and sharing wisdom with the multitudes coming to seek him. Even Popes desired his advice, and Simeon's work started a small movement of "Pillar Saints."

We planned to erect three twelve-foot to fifteen-foot tall pillars on the barren playa. They would be designed for people to climb from the inside, step out onto the top, and close a trap door behind them. Alone upon the pillars, the participants would listen for the voice of the Spirit as they looked into the empty desert. They would be directed to remain upon the pillars until they had succeeded in hearing something.

Three blank walls, and a flame altar would stand in front of the pillars out in the open desert beyond the Burning Man Temple. The flame altar would call the person to release the hindrances keeping them from hearing the voice of the Spirit. This would be the beginning point in the process of hearing from God.

We called our art installation The Pillars of the Saints.

The five of us arrived at Burning Man early to build our project out in the desert beyond the city. We were creating one of over 300 art installations upon the playa. We started building the project four days before the event was to begin.

Four days later we were finished. Tens of thousands of people began to arrive on the playa. At first slowly, and then in larger numbers, Burners began to visit the Pillars of the Saints, and we shared our vision for the art installation. Standing at the flame altar we would point to the Pillars and say, "This is not an art installation. It is merely a blank canvas for the art. Your experience, and the things you write upon the walls will become the art."

At the flame altar, our Burner friends would write upon a piece of magician's flash paper. They scratched down words describing things, which hindered them from hearing the voice of the Spirit. They tossed the paper into the fire, and watched it suddenly flash and disappear. They gasped. They cried. They often stood at the altar a long time, and considered necessary changes to their lives.

Then they would climb the pillars and sit upon them until they sensed a voice speaking. Some sat for a few minutes, some for many hours. Some cried. Some laughed. Some sat silently, and seriously. Some lifted their voices and their hands to the heavens, and many people had spiritual encounters upon the pillars.

The participants would climb down when they were done, and write upon the walls; giving public expression to the voices they heard. Some of the writings were founded in pantheistic New Age perspectives, others appeared to be driven by personal struggles or pop philosophies, but many of them evidenced God's influence.

God's Voice in the Wilderness

A week later, toward the end of the festival, the walls were filled with scores of simple, graceful, and intensely personal expressions. Sayings covered the walls like holy graffiti.

- "Why do people hurt others only to hurt themselves?"
- "You can stop an invasion of armies, but you can not stop an idea whose time has come."
- "It's no good measure of health to be well adjusted to a profoundly sick society."
- "Let go of everything you know and all will be revealed."
- "Joy is a community that loves. Love heals."
- "Discipline is Freedom. Laughter is Medicine."

- "And darkness has no tickets for this event."
- "To find God one must forgive."
- "The truth will find you."

Daniel came down from the Pillars on the first day of the event. He was teary-eyed, and shared how he felt. "This," Daniel waved at the Burning Man city, "is not what my life is about any more. It's time for me to move on with my life, and make some changes." Dennis told Daniel the meaning of his name, "God is my Judge." Hope prayed with Daniel for some time, and both she and Dennis hugged him before he wandered off into the desert.

An attractive young woman wrote with her fingers in water letters upon a black tablet we provided during the hot days. The word "ME" evaporated into nothing. I asked her what significance the disappearing ME held.

"Well, I've got some changes to make." She elaborated that she knew she was the one who was in the way, and hindered the voice of God's Spirit from speaking into her life.

These examples are just two among hundreds of meaningful interactions we experienced during our week at Burning Man. People cried for joy. People thanked us profusely. People returned daily to find peace. People sat upon the pillars each morning to watch the sun rise over the desert.

We prayed with people. We spoke blessings over them. We encouraged them to make a habit of listening to God, and we shared the crazy story of a 5th century ascetic saint who sat on a pillar for 39 years.

The Spirit of God rode in the winds above the pillars and helped people inch their way toward eternity. They surrendered their struggles and their addictions. They reached out with open arms to the heavens. They discovered peace they had been seeking. These are the things we saw, and the things they shared with us.

Not everyone was convinced that our project was something special. Some laughed at the concept. One blogger later would write about us, "The Pillars of Wisdom (as he called us) had it wrong." He thought that divinity did not care about prayers or poetry, and did not speak in words except to say "yes" or "no." I thought his version of divinity sounded a bit like a capricious two year old, but such discouragements are hollow and inconsequential in the light of teary-eyed thankful faces.

Some of the people who visited the art project wanted to climb and jump around instead of meditate. A few wanted to smooch (or something more) instead of seek the voice of God, but most of the time the mood was respectful and peaceful.

At the end of the week, we burned our art project. Flames from the pillars shot out the trap doors at the top, and reached 35 feet up into the night sky. Our three pillars looked like a set of monstrous Trinitarian candles. The words of those who listened for the voice of the Spirit and had written on our walls burned and rose in the smoke to heaven, but some of those words had already reached heaven before they went up in smoke.

It was the middle of the week when the man dressed like Jesus arrived. He is a follower of Jesus. His name is Bert Flaming (a name made for stories like this). He is a bookseller who lives in Canada. He had seen a video about our project before coming to Burning Man, and wanted to find us, but we found him instead. He spent about an hour with us. He meditated upon the pillars and wrote upon our walls.[193]

"I love you. Be kind to one another, especially to people who hate you. I'll help you, and when you can't do this, I'll forgive you."

We discovered that Jesus was already at Burning Man. We found Him there, and like our friend, the Canadian Bookseller Jesus, He was looking for us all along. The words of our Canadian Jesus reminded us that our task is one of kindness and love, and our place was simply to give people an opportunity to find the God Who is riding in the winds above the desert – whether they appreciate our gifts or not.

To our great surprise Burners appreciated it far more than we could have anticipated, and some of them discovered life-changing experiences in the process.

For those of you, who are worried about people falling into temptation and acting like a bunch of hedonists at Burning Man. Well yes, that does happen to some of the Christians who go to these crazy places. They end up getting stoned, or drinking too much. Typically they rebound, and keep their lives together. Sometimes they do not, and I have seen families destroyed in the process. On the other hand, I have seen that same destruction while people are sitting all showered and pretty at church. As the saying goes, "Wherever you go – there you are." People will take their temptations with them.

---

[193] for a video of Bert as Jesus talking to us go to https://youtu.be/v6apPBsE9pE

Engage: How do art and carnivalesque revolution work together?

Chapter 22 represents poetry, and song lyrics from the interactive carnival perspective. Chapter 23 retells the story of building an interactive art piece at Burning Man and this chapter has been updated and added to since it was first published in Christianity Today. Are you involved with the arts? How might you utilize your talents to help others think outside the lines of today's polarizing positions?

Interact with the Burning Religion community on the website at www.burningreligion.com.

THE CLOWN IN THE CANON

The lessons in this book have not been laid out in bullet points. They have not been presented as a self-help book. This is because radical transformation of individuals and cultures does not often come to us in a set of numbered rules. It is not a do-it-yourself project. The Ten Commandments is an affixed set of ethics and moral edicts, which have informed our world for better. These words are still with us today, but clearly they have not alleviated the problems of humanity, because we the people still break the laws, and we the leaders still use the law for our personal advantage. Permanent transformation is more holistic than a bullet pointed list. That is why this book has been a combination of tall tales, historical vignettes, autobiographical information, and philosophical and theological ramblings. The fictional components were designed to carry you emotionally in the same direction as the intellectual non-fiction sections. Kelly, who helped immensely in editing the book, often pointed out my use of "$50 words" in the sections of philosophical content. Some of those words I changed. Some I did not, because, well, because….just because. I'm a nerd.

Since one of the theses of this book is that we need a carnival-like revolution to turn this violent world upside down, this book may have felt a bit like tumbling, or clowning around. Of course, that was its intent. I sought to turn the way we see the world upside down. I even sought to turn the way we see turning things upside down upside down, and yet, in doing so, I hope we have not landed back on our feet. If our societal order is broken and already askew, a proper inversion should not set one's feet on a ground of temporal stability in a broken world. As Jiddu Krishnamurti wisely reminded us, "It is no measure of health to be well adjusted to a profoundly sick society."

Here now, I suppose I am breaking some unspoken rule, prohibiting the creation of a list for a carnival revolution (and yet, I recognize the inherent contradiction of this sentence itself). Despite proposing a topsy-turvy sense of revolutionary momentum, I have, for the sake of simplicity, created a numbered list outlining the basic theses of this book here in the conclusion. So, as though in opposition to the very anarchic nature of a clowning rebellion, these are my foundational thoughts behind this effort:

1. There is an unnavigable space between religion and secular society, and this is inherent to many other polarized contexts in our world.
2. That gap is also inherent to the human condition. It resides within each of us, and consequently it is found in all our social interactions.
3. Every person and every people group is precariously balanced between great nobility and great evil.
4. Because of this unnavigable space, our observations of "the other" are often twisted. We have a tendency to see the other only in extreme polarization – as a monster, or as a hero.
5. Rules are not the final or best method of suppressing evil. The selfish side of humanity is creative, and will find a way to break the rules, and/or use them for personal gain.
6. Changing the patterns of internal and external violence requires turning our world upside down.
7. An ongoing Carnivalesque revolution is a peaceful resistance and a power inversion, and needs to occur in every generation as a means of resisting oppression and evil.
8. The first stage of a Carnivalesque revolution is self-mockery. This turns my own world upside down, and with it the need for defensiveness.
9. The second stage of a Carnivalesque revolution is to look for the best in my enemy. We must anticipate and search for imago dei in what we perceive as the dangerous "other." This is true for other cultures and subcultures as well as individuals. Discovering the imago dei in "the other" turns the external world upside down and softens the tendencies toward violence: by us, and against us.

I consider these points to be some of the fundamentals of a Carnival Canon. Without having to learn how to deliver a punch line, or juggle – without having to learn to tumble, or perform sleight of hand magic – without painting our faces, or twisting balloons, we can still perform revolutionary clowning arts. Beginning with an understanding of the world outlined by the simple points above, we will surprise people, and hopefully help them see the world anew. When we live as though the above points are true, people will not know what to make of us. These are foolish ways to live. They are the foolishness outlined by the Apostle Paul. To believe that the world is broken, that evil resides within people, and yet, to purposely observe that it resides in myself first, is a position of weakness. To believe that great nobility simultaneously resides in people, and to look for it in others first, is to bow a second time to weakness. I recognize the goodness in another, and the evil within me. This is a vulnerable position.

In Orthodox Church history, a venerated position has been reserved for the clown. Simeon of Emessa, Blessed Basil of Moscow being some of the greatest examples, and even the Catholic Saint Francis of Assisi is considered to belong to the history of "Holy Fools." The Russian Orthodox Church has a special name for this category, *"yurodivy."* From Sufism, Hinduism, Shamanism, and Native American Medicine Men we find variations on this ancient Holy Fool, which appears to indicate that the revolutionary possibility of Carnivalesque is a universal value not limited to an individual culture.

The above nine points are by no means a step-by-step guide to living the dangerous life of a Holy Fool. They are merely a beginning point upon which to build a foundation of a dialogical Carnivalesque rebellion. Although, these are principles, which are discoverable through the Christian scriptures, I believe that they are available to all people (regardless of their faith or lack thereof) as powerful tools for establishing peace between warring parties. This Holy Fool vocation is not for natural clowns only. It is not simply for the people wanting to don the white makeup, and wear the big shoes and the polka dotted puffy pants. This is a clown school for everyone who wants to bring peace to the world.

> In all the seriousness, with all its corruption
> In all the pain, and all the consumption
> We need to break some unspoken rules
> We need an army of clowns, an army of fools

Our Corporate Attention Deficit

For years, I thought I had a serious attention deficit disorder. It was not of the ADHD variety, which the Center for Disease Control incredibly attributes to 11% of the children in the US. Rather, it seemed I simply needed more attention than I could get at meetings, shows and concerts. Every single time I went to a concert, sat through a church service, or a pastor's conference; I wanted to be on the stage. I thought to myself, 'Self. Why are you so selfish? Why do you have to be the center of attention?' Of course, the common and simple explanation is that I felt a need, or harbored a greed, to be the center of attention. People, who struggle with that hubristic desire will tell you that this was the motivation of my heart. They see the world through the tainted lenses of self-reflection, and if they must restrain their passion for fame or power, then clearly, that is what is going on inside you and me as well. So, I restrained the impetus to interrupt – to want to be part of the spectacle that was the stage, but the desire never diminished.

Soon I realized that I was wrong, and so were those who told me I was just a troublemaker, and a hog for attention. They were dead wrong. Instead, I discovered I was simply a clown.

What was happening inside me was something very[194] different than ADHD. It was something revolutionary. After a short time being the center of attention on the small stage, and occasionally on a large stage, I discovered that the inversion of this same feeling I had as a spectator, occurred when I was in the limelight. I wanted to be with the audience, even while I held the position of power on the stage.

And so, I wondered for years why I struggled with dissatisfaction as an audience member when I was a spectator, and then struggled being in the limelight while I was on the stage. Calling this a lust for attention, fame, and power was not only too simple an explanation, but did not make sense of the conflicting and contradictory desires.

This tension, it turns out, was connected to my passion for community, and dialogue, and for releasing the freedom of expression to everyone.

I was in a fight in every highly structured meeting I attended. I battled the line between the stage and the audience, and if I could break that line and bring a party to what I felt was a controlling monologic setting, I was happiest. The un-crossable space between the audience and the performer was the gap between listening versus doing, seeing versus being, sitting versus participating, and receiving versus sharing. Listening, seeing, sitting, and receiving are necessary components of a learning personality, but they will never be fully transformative characteristics on their own. They require the follow up of doing, being, participating, and sharing, and these were the transformative elements of interactivity I desired all those years.

Throughout the latter half of this book, my use of the words "circus" and "carnival" have been specific and limited definitions, which draw attention to the impossible distances between beliefs, worldviews, politics, and as a consequence – all human interactions. The troubling stage line, which separates the audience from the "anointed" is one of the pregnant public expressions of these gaps. It represents the space between conflicting worldviews. In both politics and religion, a strict space is created in the public arena, where the powerful take the stage and the weak are anesthetized by the spectacle.

---

[194] Yes, I used the word "very." That terribly overused and abused English word. My use here is purposeful, because I want to emphasize its sense of "truly" as well as "extremely", and there seemed to be no better single word for this combination of meanings. I am sorry for bothering the sensibilities of the grammar Nazis.

The circus performer is typically an expert performing his/her art for an audience. So is the pastor. So is the politician. The experts and an entourage of support systems maintain the stage line, and the crowd is awed to a numb pseudo-liberation. The carnival, as outlined and described by Mikhail Bakhtin, is an interactive event with no spotlights. Everyone is an actor. Everyone has something to say, and they are important in this idealized medieval Bakhtinian carnival. And, this is true whether we agree with one another or not, and whether we are happy with one another or not. Maturity knows that it is more valuable to listen than to be heard, and certainly more valuable than simply and robotically to be agreed with.

In real life, the circus performances are not necessarily this strict and controlled, and today's carnivals are not perfectly interactive. My limited definitions for the words "circus" and "carnival" have been motifs for me to express my passion to see the stage line erased and replaced with interactivity and participation in everyday life: in politics, in religion, and in education. There are creative circuses all around the globe breaking the conventional lines of audience and performer in revolutionary ways.

Despite this movement toward interactivity in the circus arts, we live in a capitalistically driven pop culture, which elevates the famous, the rich, and the popular. We as individuals have been driven to the spectator seats in politics, media, and sometimes even in religion, and the space between ourselves and the stage lights appears to be growing wider and wider, year after year. For the average person, there is a severe attention deficit, and their voices go unheard in important issues of life, power and spirituality. Our voices do not carry the community value they should in our nation, in our church, or sometimes even in our homes.

Fear, Loss of Control and the Clown

Coulrophobia, the fear of clowns, is a new word to the English language, and the phenomenon it represents is growing. Serial killer John Wayne Gacy[195] and Pennywise the Dancing Clown from Stephen King's It, are considered some of the major influences of this phobia. The wicked clown motif exploded into the horror genre of film and literature, along with the simultaneous infamy and popularity of the Insane Clown Posse. These public images have animated the growing phobia, and psychological studies have been done on coulrophobia to describe its parameters.

---

[195] https://en.wikipedia.org/wiki/John_Wayne_Gacy

Does this fear of the clown correlate to an individual's distaste for interruption and surprise, or to the fear of a loss of control? Does the person with a fear of public speaking feel invaded by the clown, who may drag them into the limelight? Does the painted face create a façade of unknown quantity and quality, allowing the clown to be perceived as an uninhibited and uncontainable force? It seems that a clown can get away with almost anything. Does that scare us? Does the anarchic foolishness of the clown break convention, and cross lines we are uncomfortable seeing crossed?

The loss of control corresponds to other losses. Safety and creature comforts are threatened by the loss of control. Yet, for some people the loss of control is a welcome experience to the oppressive existence of a tedious life. In a world filled with well-established cultures of suppression, when things go wrong, they potentially equal a Messianic flipping of the tables. This is the value of the philosopher, the artist, the revolutionary and the preacher. These positions inherently carry public clowning capacities. They are vocations with an innate quality of line crossing and rebellion, and they carry the invocation of public participation and change.

These clowning occupations interrupt the so-called experts and invite the audience into action. In this sense, the clown is radically democratic, offering a place for all the people to experience the stage, which is usually reserved for the performer, and the stage is recreated into a community space. When the stage line is broken and the carnival begins – everyone is a performer. Everyone takes on a position of biblical proportions. We all become holy fools, prancing as kings and queens on the stage of religious experience, and even on the stage of political participation. Christianity demands this kind of participation, because it calls the average man and woman to rise up as "ministers" – a term we also use for positions of political appointment. Democracy in a similar manner demands the same participation. Without it democracy is not democracy at all.

Strong monolithic voices suppressing democracy are mocked by the clown, and we are engaged by a momentary non-violent anarchy, where power has no place. Bakhtin viewed the clown as a multi-voiced being, simultaneously ridiculing all other voices, and opening the doors of dialogue. This was an affront to the poetic, flowery language of the court, and a challenge to the *"cultural, national and political centralization of the verbal-ideological world"*.

> "...*on the stages of local fairs and at buffoon spectacles, the heteroglossia of the clown sounded forth, ridiculing all "languages" and dialects"*[96]

The languages of power and control are not the same thing as the voices of honesty. The language of power often carries ulterior motives, and subtle stratagems beneath its attractive façade and well-crafted words. The language of power is described by Bakhtin as a mask.

> "...the "languages" of poets, scholars, monks, knights and others, where all "languages" were masks and where no language could claim to be an authentic, incontestable face."[197]

The formal "court language" is a restraining power, but this language when mocked by the clown is cast down from its pedestal. Yet, the mocking evokes both fear and hope in all of us, because it leaves a vacant power space.

In our tension filled world, loss of control is typically connected to violence and war. The streets of America rage with violent protest, while Africa and Asia roil with political land grabbing, religious fervor, and blood. We should be afraid of this kind of anarchy as much as we should fear oppressive control. Violent anarchy not only kills, but it sets the stage for cruel and oppressive rulers to step into and fill the power void. Looking like saviors, they turn out to be false prophets living for their own profit rather than the profit of the people, but the story of Jesus is not a power and control story. It is not a story of His political control over nations, His physical mastery over His enemies, or of economic strength. The Jesus story looks more like a model for a foolish rebellion. The Jesus story turns the patterns of this world upside down. Weakness is celebrated as a means of strength. Silence overcomes detractors. Loving and wooing people is the means of influence, as opposed to wowing and subduing people. The Gospel rejects power grabs, and forces us to deal with our control issues.

The ambivalent, peaceful, humorous rebellion of the clown creates the corporate metanoia we need. It changes our corporate mind. It has the potential to steal control from the control freaks and give it back to the people who suffer.

The Clandestine Insurgent Rebel Clown Army[198] emerged in the UK in 2005 protesting war and the invasion of Iraq. Groups soon popped up in Ireland, the Netherlands, Belgium, France, Denmark, Germany, and Israel. Clownsec[199] is another group, which has joined the ranks of clowning peaceful protest. Ed Holmes, whom I met at

---

[196] The Dialogic Imagination Kindle loc 3856
[197] ibid
[198] http://beautifultrouble.org/case/clandestine-insurgent-rebel-clown-army/
[199] http://www.clownsec.com/

Burning Man in 2014, leads the First Church of the Last Laugh[200] in San Francisco, and in their celebrations they mix social justice protest with humor. The most famous of the social justice clown protest artists today has been going strong since the 60's. Wavy Gravy was called, "the illegitimate son of Harpo Marx and Mother Teresa," by the Grateful Dead's Bob Weir. His life's work is documented in the movie, Saint Misbehavin': the Wavy Gravy Movie.[201]

It is not only Christianity, which would benefit from a revival of the Holy Fool: but as evidenced in the voices of clown rebellions above, the world would be a better place with the happy mockery of the *yurodivy*.

Emerging from the Spaces in Between

With our separation of categories like "church and state" (both ill formed concepts), right and left, conservative and progressive, black and white, good and evil, academic and uneducated, and the powerful and the poor; I contend that the seemingly anarchic interruptions of the clown are a carnival invasion birthed from the spaces in-between all polarized positions. The clown does not come from the right or the left, from the establishment or the disenfranchised. The clown presents himself/herself as neither educated nor uneducated. The true clown does not hold my monological perspective, or the similarly limited perspective of my ideological other. The clown stands on nobody's point of reference, but emerges from the space in between us, and is birthed from nobody's point of view, and yet somehow, the clown speaks into everybody's point of view. The clown is at one moment a performer among spectators, the next a spectator among performers, and is birthed from the space other than that of the audience and the so-called experts.

The space between "religion" and "secular society" has been the primary point of discussion in this book. To some degree, I have done you a great disservice. I have not defined the words, "religion" or "secular society." Instead, I have purposely left these words undefined, because as much as they have been poorly defined on the street corners of our culture, they are perhaps even more bereft of definition in academia. Academia has spoken poorly for both words in the studies on violence.[202] Movement forward across this great divide is not

---

[200] http://www.saintstupid.com/event.html
[201] http://www.rippleeffectfilms.com/
[202] On this point, I am in agreement with William Cavanaugh, in <u>The Myth of Religious Violence</u> and his observations on the lack of definition given to these terms by many scholars today.

possible as things are, because there is no middle ground from which to work. "Third way" approaches have often been swallowed up in the black and white circus of our six-second sound bite world.

In this impossible predicament, we need an invasion of foolish adventurers, who believe in the impossible. The answers need to come out of an impossible ideological nowhere, because we have created a world with no intellectual middle ground. The vocation of the Holy Fool is the invasion emerging from the non-space of the unnavigable gaps. It literally comes out of nowhere.

We jokingly remark about the clowns in Washington, or the clowns in religious leadership, but I am convinced this is where we need the clowns. I am not talking about bombastic, attention seeking individuals who suck the oxygen out of a room. I am talking about positive revolution, which comes with passionate fire. These are people who will surprise us; people who will steal the show away from those in the spotlight, and give it back to the suffocating audience of common folk like you and I. Many of us feel as though we have been played like puppets by manipulative ringmasters. I dream of a day when the seemingly out of control clowns take control of the center stage, and steal the control from the powerful and give it back to the poor, acting like white-faced Robin Hoods crashing the public square.

Lest you think that I am expecting politicians and pastors everywhere to don the makeup and the over-sized shoes, that is not what I am talking about – although, that might be an improvement. I am imagining instead the same set of interruptive surprises, which mark a Bakhtinian Carnivalesque revolution, bringing with it metanoia and freedom. It is a rebellion, which is not conservative or progressive, academic or common, nor right, nor left. It is based in respect, even while it is mocking. It is based in love, even while being challenging and pointing cartoonish gloved fingers. It steals the limelight, only to diffuse it, and leaves the stage with everybody dancing and celebrating on it.

This vocation of the Holy Fool is not limited to the circus performers, professional clergy, or political revolutionaries. It was something the early and ancient Christians considered the activity of daily life. They were a people whose purpose included turning broken families, troubled neighborhoods, and even the oppressive empire upside down – without using violence, without obtaining economic strength, and without having notoriety. They were crazy enough to believe that *"the foolishness of God is wiser than men"*[203] and this was their calling card as deliverers for the oppressed, and as troublemakers in the

---

[203] 1 Corinthians 1:25

palaces of power. It was tied to being a child of God, because it was an act of revolutionary peacemaking, and it had been modeled by their Savior at the cross, thus making it foundational to godly living.

Being a Holy Fool does not require a wildly outgoing personality, or great intellectual powers. It sometimes is as simple as refusing to join sides in the debates of our times, while people wonder what makes you tick. It can be as commonplace as being willing to find value in the opposing sides of dissenting positions in today's polarized issues. It does not require great bravery. In fact, it is often perceived as cowardice by the blind, who may not be able to see that there are more than two sides to many issues. Not everything is divided up neatly into right and wrong, or intelligent and stupid, and the person who takes on the revolutionary position of the ancient Holy Fool knows the world is not simply black and white. They bring color into a dreary world of infighting. This vocation is natural for those of us who feel like Treebeard from The Lord of the Rings, when He was asked about taking sides in the wars, "Side? I am on nobody's side, because nobody is on my side, little orc."

The Cost of Clowning

The development of these concepts of carnival revolution found their genesis in the exiled musings of a one-legged Russian philosopher who lived during the reign of Stalin. They were birthed in dangerous places. The interruption of Forsberg's clown in "Parable" is an illustration of this danger – it cost him his life. So too, did the messianic interruption of Jesus, and He most perfectly illustrates living between the worlds of the religious and the political arena.

Both the bully pulpit of politics, and the sacred pulpit of religion need to be invaded by an army of self-sacrificing, dangerous people – people who are willing to live by the principles of a holy foolishness.

I imagine a world where the reformer whose birthday I share can look up from the grave and see a "priesthood of all believers" in action. But, these things are hard to imagine in our bifurcated world. Perhaps it is impossible to imagine, but then, I believe in the impossible.

Perhaps as a simple starting point, we can begin to reframe the words "religion" and "secular" into less biased definitions. Even should these words remain relatively undefined, I hope for a generous interpretation of them in our minds. Today, we speak these words with venomous lips. As noted by people like Karen Armstrong, Peter Berger and William Cavanaugh, the word "religion" often experiences either an intensely negative, or a quizzically snickering bias in academic circles. Yet, among the poor, the oppressed and the downtrodden the same word, and all that it represents often becomes a sanctuary of hope. One might anticipate that it would be natural for the academic to respond to the world of poverty with unbiased eyes and ears of understanding, and consequently see the world of religion through the eyes of the poor, but apparently it takes a fool – or a clown to see things in this manner during this season in Western academia. It is my hope that a biased "secular" world would burn the prejudiced definitions of religion, and would discover some of the great benefits, which have stood alongside the pitfalls of "religion" for all these centuries. Examples of this unbiased secular approach are already exist. Žižek leans in this direction. Alain de Botton's Atheism 2.0[204] is a modest nod in this direction, as is the work of my friend Kile Jones who graces the forward of this book.

Similarly, I call to my religious fellows: let's toss aside the prejudiced definitions of secularism, and the biases against religions not our own, and begin to see value in people simply because they are fellow humans on this wobbly sphere we call home. John W. Morehead's work with the Multi-faith Matters team, of which I am a member, is looking for the best practices of Evangelical churches working to bridge traditional prejudicial divides between religious groups. Mike Stygal, current president of the Pagan Federation in the UK (also writing in the forward) has been swimming hard upstream in turbulent waters with difficult interfaith work for years now. Such actions are typically the efforts of pioneers, who are willing to keep working until a few people begin to 'get it.'

Strangely, we live in a day, when both the religious and the non-religious despise the word "religion." Many who practice religion have avoided using the word as a self-descriptor, because of its loose connotation to violence, greed, and the suppression of freedom. Yet, as we are reminded by Fr. Pontifex's video, religion remains the world's largest contributor to aiding the poor, and one only need look to Martin Luther King Jr. Day in the U.S. to discover the rich role of religion in liberation and peace movements.

The word "secular" does not carry the same shame as "religion," at least, not in most circles. It has been embraced as a panacea to governmental distress by non-religious secularists, and the progressives in religious circles. Others have gone as far as to suggest that a religious/secular divide does not truly exist. Yet, among some conservative religious groups, the word "secular" houses a universe of prejudice against religion, and carries demonic connotations. To view

---

[204] see de Botton's TED Talk on Atheism 2.0
http://www.ted.com/talks/alain_de_botton_atheism_2_0

secularism as either a messianic cure-all against violent religious tendencies, or as a demonic attack is to broaden the impossible space between worldviews, and enact an intellectual war. I contend that, "secular" cannot hold either a messianic position or a demonic definition in our minds if we strive to be people of peace.

Because this work calls for the self-immolation of my prejudicial leanings, and I am asked to rebel against the status quo of the popular thinking within my own little tribal group. I must become a fool among my own people to accomplish this task of redefinition. This reframing work is an ambassadorial path toward reconciliation. Until a sufficiently sized group begins to follow a peacemaking work between radically disagreeing factions, the pioneers risk wearing the fool's cap.

Only in burning our prejudicial definitions toward the "other" will we rediscover a burning passion of care and concern our world desperately needs. The passion of my biases burns the other. The passion of my self-critique, and my redefining of "the other" in positive terms burns my own oppressive tendencies, and will work to benefit those I have previously viewed as enemies.

I am foolish enough to believe that I do not need to agree with the other in order to negotiate peace with the other. I am not forced to surrender my firmly held Christian convictions, or compromise my ethics to navigate the impossible space between worldviews. In fact, this is what keeps the space impossible and the work miraculous: that I retain my unique views without compromise and embrace the radical other simultaneously.

The deep transformative value of foolishness, and carnival surprise would be the treatise for a whole other project. As for now, I will be looking to the bully pulpits of politics and to the sacred pulpits of the churches, and I will be hoping to find clowns in the pulpit.

I am also looking for the fire of a burning religion – not the external self-destruction many of us have seen or experienced, but the internal fiery passion for turning the world upside down. This is the path of a Phoenix-like, burning religion.

Engage: Is the clown (as one who breaks the stage line) a good model for revolutionary peacemaking?

The medieval interactive carnival has been presented as the motif representing the way out of the destructive polarizations in our society – primarily in respect to religion and secular society. Here, the clown is presented as the model revolutionary for a new way of navigating troubling issues. What do you think about this pattern for peacemaking and dialogue?

Interact with the Burning Religion community on the website at www.burningreligion.com.

Tales from the Land of Jaw: The Adventures of Gwyn Dee
A Bloody Full Circle

Gwyn Dee sat in the circle of blood left by the inquisitors of Cominkingville. When the chanting finally faded into the distance, a small troupe of itinerant carnival performers appeared from the nearby bushes. They stood around Gwyn Dee and stared for a few moments, and a thin old clown finally spoke, "Well, seems like yo' got yo'self in one bloody mess dere. Come on now. Let's get you outta de middle o' de road, and find yo' a place to lay yo' head tonight."

Someone took Gwyn Dee by the arm, and Gwyn Dee with the obedient will of a broken horse followed. They strode off into the bushes, and walked a narrow path running parallel to the road down to Cominkingville. When Gwyn Dee realized this, there was a fearful hesitation, and the thin old clown eased Gwyn Dee's raw nerves, "Now, don'chyo worry. We is gonna go someplace yo' nevva been befo'. Might do yo' some good too."

After a silent half hour of walking into the thickening forest, the small troupe came to a cottage, which melted into the trees, as though it was birthed from the ancient yew. It seemed that it had grown from the very ground with the tree. The arched door was wide open, and a happy bustling could be heard inside.

Voices whispered from the trees above, and suddenly, the small troupe of carnival performers were joined by artists and actors of all kinds. They dropped from the trees above, and gathering in close they stood in silence. The bustling house too, silenced, and its tenants joined the circle. The growing crowd parted, and a weathered ancient woman with a cane, tottered slowly up to Gwyn Dee. They gazed at each other face-to-face, and the weathered ancient woman stared with a gentle smile for what seemed like an hour, but passed as though it were only a few seconds.

"Gwyn Dee, we have been watching you for a long time. When you left Cominkingville, we thought we might never see you again, but here we are full-circle – and a bloody full circle it has been."

"Here, in this place," she waved at the cottage and to the trees, where Gwyn Dee saw houses hidden in the branches, "you are always welcome."

And the carnival performers cheered. Clowns ran and tumbled in the shadowed glade laughing. Jugglers juggled, and spinners spun, and people swung from the tree vines hooting, and fire breathers spat fire in the air, and dancers danced, and drummers drummed, and singers sang, and in between it all every person hugged Gwyn Dee, twice perhaps. Gwyn Dee smiled, and yet, reluctantly embraced the moment. The long journey had proven that things are not always what they first appear to be, and even acceptance and celebration are sometimes tools of manipulation.

When the party quieted, and the hugs were finished, Gwyn Dee was ushered to the yew cottage. A fire in the hearth of a large comfortable room sizzled with a cauldron of mushrooms, and greens, and onions, and sage, and rabbit. And the weathered ancient woman with the cane and Gwyn Dee were seated, and were left alone to talk.

Staring into the fire, Gwyn Dee queried, "How is it that I have never seen this cottage, here in the forest I wandered as a child, and know so well?"

"Some things are hidden in the wide open, we are all blind to the very things beneath our big noses." The weathered ancient woman with the cane smiled. "I have watched you for many years. I was there when the sun darkened and you were presented to the village at your birth. I was there the day of the stone shoe race, when you were 12, and the crowd turned against you. I sat alongside the road watching as you left Cominkingville some months ago, and I wondered what you might discover, and whether you would ever return."

"All I was looking for was the borders to the Land of Jaw, but I could not find them, and I cannot shake my yearning to find the adventures I learned about in the tales of Jane Foole, but now the wide, wide road has taken me in this circle, and I am back where I started – the very place I fled."

"Hmmmmm, the bloody full circle. Most of us have been around that road, and have discovered the borders to the land were both nearer and farther than we ever imagined. Jaw is not contained by borders, but we knew that all along, didn't we?" And the weathered ancient woman with the cane moved to rise, and Gwyn Dee offered a hand, and they walked arm in arm to a table with a weathered ancient book upon it.

"The Book of J-A-H" was written on its cover.

Gwyn Dee's face scrunched in confusion, "What is this?"

"You know this book well, Gwyn Dee. You studied it with the Clown Caste of Cominkingville for many years." And in a pause where time crawled like a snail, Gwyn Dee's thoughts tried to focus, failed, and then tried to refocus, and yet they were captured in a blurry tension like eyes you cannot uncross.

And the weathered ancient woman with the cane smiled softly, "Amazing what one letter in a name can do to our view of life, and even of our God – isn't it?"

The stew in the bubbling cauldron was set at the table with fresh bread, and wine, and Gwyn Dee and the weathered ancient woman with the cane sat together and ate and talked of adventures in the Land of Jaw.

"You seem to know me well, but I do not remember you, or even know your name." Gwyn Dee looked up from the stew, took a bite of the warm bread, and lifted the cup to sip the wine.

"I am known by many names, but the people of Cominkingville, when they still remembered me, called me Jane." And with the sip Gwyn Dee gulped down much more than wine.

Tiredness settled upon the weary traveler. The million racing questions tumbled into an exhausted darkness, and would have to wait for another day. A room with a soft downy bed was prepared, and Gwyn Dee was tucked away into a long sleep.

A gentle cool breeze floated in from an open window with soft rays of light breaking through the thick foliage of the ancient yew. Gwyn Dee awoke after a long deep peaceful sleep. Rubbing foggy morning eyes, Gwyn Dee looked around the room. A man stood by the window with his fidgeting hands crossed behind his back, as though he was waiting for something important.

Gwyn Dee sat up and the man turned and nervously smiled.

"Hello, sleepy traveler."

The bleary morning eyes slowly unfogged, as Gwyn Dee blinked, and looked at the man in the window. The world cleared up, and Gwyn Dee gasped.

"Father?"

Engage: What have the tall tales of Gwyn Dee done for you?

Gwyn Dee represents the struggle for authenticity many of us go through. How did you relate to these tall tales, and by the end of the book how did they leave you feeling? Who is Gwyn Dee? Is there anyone you feel Gwyn Dee represents?

Interact with the Burning Religion community on the website at www.burningreligion.com.

Bibliography

Abbott, Edwin. Flatland: A Romance of Many Dimensions. n.p. Kindle Edition.
Alighieri, Dante. The Divine Comedy. n.p.
Armstrong, Karen. Fields of Blood: Religion and History of Violence. New York: Alfred A. Knopf, 2014. Kindle Edition.
Bagshaw, Hilary. Religion in the Thought of Mikhail Bakhtin: Reason and Faith. Farnham, Surrey, England: Ashgate, 2013
Bakhtin, Mikahil. The Dialogic Imagination: Four Essays: University of Texas Press Slavic Series, 1981. Kindle Edition.
Bakhtin, Mikhail. Problems of Dostoevsky's Poetics: Theory and History of Literature. University Press of Minnesota, 1984, Kindle Edition.
Bakhtin, Mikhail. Rabelais and His World. Bloomington: Indiana University Press, 1984. Print.
Baum, L. Frank. Oz series. n.p.
Berger, Peter. A Rumor of Angels: modern discovery and the rediscovery of the supernatural. Garden City, NY: Doubleday, 1969. Print.
Berger, Peter. The Desecularization of the World: Resurgent Religion and World Politics. Washington D.C.: Ethics and Public Policy Center, 1999. Kindle Edition.
Cavanuagh, William. The Myth of Religious Violence: Secular Ideology and the Roots of Modern Conflict. Oxford: Oxford University Press, 2009. Print.
Cervantes, Miguel de. Don Quixote. n.p. Kindle Edition.
Chaucer, Geoffrey. The Canterbury Tales. New York: Simon and Schuster, 1971. Print.
Clawson, Julie. The Hunger Games and the Gospel: Bread, Circuses and the Kingdom of God. Englewood: Patheos Press, 2012. Kindle Edition.
Coates, Ruth. Christianity in Bakhtin: God and the Exiled Author. Cambridge: Cambridge University Press, 1998. Kindle Edition.
Collins, Suzanne. The Hunger Games (The Hunger Games, Catching Fire, Mockingjay). New York: Scholastic Press, 2010. Print.
Cox, Harvey. Feast of Fools: a Theological Essay on Feast and Festivity. Cambridge, MA: Harvard University Press, 1969. Print.
Davis, Mike. Planet of Slums. London: Verso, 2006. Print.
DeFranza, Megan K. Sex Difference in Christian Theology: Male, Female, and Intersex in the Image of God. Grand Rapids: Wm. B. Eerdmans Publishing Co., 2015. Print.
Dikötter, Frank. Mao's Great Famine: The History of China's Most Devastating Catastrophe, 1958–62. New York: Walker and Co., 2010. Kindle Edition.
Dikötter, Frank. The Tragedy of Liberation: The History of the Chinese Revolution, 1945-57. New York: Bloomsbury Press, 2013. Kindle Edition.

Dostoevsky, Fyodor. Notes from the Underground. n.p. Kindle Edition
Dostoevsky, Fyodor. The Brothers Karamazov. translation Constance Garnet 1912. Online pdf.
Dostoevsky, Fyodor. The Idiot. n.p. Kindle Edition.
Felch and Contino editors, Bakhtin and Religion: a Feeling for Faith. Evanston, IL: Northwestern Unversity Press, 2001. Print.
Festinger, Leon, When Prophecy Fails. Minneapolis: University of Minnesota, 1956. Print.
Foucault, Michel. The History of Madness. London/New York: Routledge, 2006. Print.
Foucault, Michel. The History of Sexuality. New York: Random House, 1986. Print.
Frankl, Viktor. Man's Search for Meaning. n.p.
Giddens, Anthony. Modernity and Self-Identity: Self and Society in the Late Modern Age. Stanford: Stanford University Press, 1991. Print.
Goffman, Erving. Stigma: Notes on the Management of Spoiled Identity. New York: Simon and Schuster, 1963. Print.
Grizwold, Eliza. The Tenth Parallel: Dispatches from the Fault Line Between Chrisitainty and Islam. New York: Farrar, Straus, and Giroux, 2010. Kindle Edition.
Harris, Sam. The End of Faith: Religion, Terror and the Future of Reason. New York: W.W. Norton, 2004. Print.
Hebert, Paul. Transforming Worldviews: An Anthropological Understanding of How People Change. Grand Rapids: Baker Academic, 2008. Kindle Edition.
Hebridge, Dick. Subculture: the Meaning of Style. London: Methuen 1979. Print.
Hirsch, Debra. Redeeming Sex: Naked Conversations about Sexuality and Spirituality. Downers Grove, IL: Intervarsity Press, 2015. Print.
Karatani, Kojin. Transcritique: on Kant and Marx. Cambridge, MA: MIT Press, 2003. Kindle Edition.
Levinas, Emmanuel. Totality and Infinity: an essay on exteriority. Pittsburgh: Duquesne University Press, 1969 (translation by Alphonso Lingus). Print.
Mihailovich, Alexandr. Corporeal Words. Evanston, IL: Northwestern Unversity Press, 1997. Print.
Mills, C. Wright. The Sociological Imagination. New York: Oxford University Press, 1959. Print.
Nele Bemong, Pieter Borghart, Michel De Dobbeleer, Kristoffel Demoen, Koen De Temmerman & Bart Keunen (eds.). Bakhtin's Theory of the Literary Chronotope Reflections, Applications, Perspectives. Gent, Belgium, Academia Press, 2010. Print.
Newbigin, Leslie. Foolishness to the Greeks: The Gospel and Western Culture. Grand Rapids, MI: Wm. B. Eerdman's Publiching Company, 1986. Kindle Edition.

Pinker, Steven. The Better Angels of Our Nature, Why Violence has Declined. New York: Penguin, 2011. Kindle Edition.
Putnam, Robert. Bowling Alone: the Collapse and Revival of American Community. New York: Simon and Schuster, 2000. Kindle Edition.
Rabelais, François. Gargantua and Pantagruel. New York/London: W.W. Norton & Co., 1990. Print
Said, Edward. Orientalism. London: Penguin, 1977. Print.
Smith, Lalitha, and Hawk Editors. Evangelical Postcolonial Conversations: Global Awakenings in Theology and Praxis. Downers Grove, IL: Intervarsity Press, 2014. Kindle Edition.
Thomas, Dylan. Collected Poems. New York: New Directions, 1957. Print.
Thomas, Gordon. The Pope's Jews: The Vatican's Secret Plan to Save the Jews from the Nazis. New York: Thomas Dunne Press, 2012. Kindle Edition.
Vahanian, Gabriel. The Death of God: The Culture of Our Post-Christian Era. New York: George Braiziller, 1957. Print.
Williams Paris, Janelle. The End of Sexual Identity: Why Sex is too Importnt to Define Who We Are. Downers Grove, IL: Intervarsity Press, 2011. Kindle Edition.
Wyman, Phil. Witches are Real People Too: Understanding American Neo-Paganism from a Christian Perspective. Charleston: Phil Wyman, 2015. Print.
Y Beibl Cymraeg Newydd. Llundain: Y Gymdeithas Feiblaidd Frytanaidd a Thramor, 1985. Print.
Žižek, Slavoj, and Gunejvić, Boris. God in Pain: Inversions on Apocalypse. New York: Seven Stories Press, 2012. Print.
Žižek, Slavoj, and Milbank, John. The Monstrosity of Christ: Paradox or Dialectic? London/Cambridge, MA: MIT Press, 2009. Kindle Edition.
Žižek, Slavoj. Living in the End Times. London/New York: Verso, 2010. Print.
Žižek, Slavoj. The Parallax View. London/Cambridge, MA: MIT Press, 2006. Print.

Articles, Websites, Videos...

Abdi, Hawa and Mohamed, Deqo. "Mother and daughter doctor-heroes" Online video clip. TED.com, Dec. 2010.
"Aristides de Sousa Mendes – Filme" Online video clip. *YouTube.* YouTube, Jun 13, 2009
Bethke, Jefferson. "My Heart Behind 'Why I Hate Religion, But Love Jesus'". Online video clip. *YouTube.* YouTube, Mar 11, 2012
Bethke, Jefferson. "Why I Hate Religion, But Love Jesus || Spoken Word". Online video clip. *YouTube.* YouTube, Jan 10, 2012.
Biola University. "Interview With Amos Yong - Center For Christian Thought" Online video clip. *YouTube.* YouTube, Jul 9, 2012. Web October 8, 2015.

Campfield, Stacey. "Tennessee senator Stacey Campfield criticized for comparing Obamacare to the Holocaust" Christian Today, May 6, 2014. Web October 8, 2015.

CBS Global. "Mexico takes title of "most obese" from America" July 8, 2013. CBSNews.com, October 8, 2015.

China Daily. "'Generous beggar' helps child with cancer" China Daily, December, 16, 2014. Web October 8, 2015

"Constitution of Massachusetts" Massachusetts Constitution, Part The First, art. XXX (1780). National Humanities Institute. Web October 8, 2015.

Dawkins, Richard. "Is Religion Good or Evil?" Interview by Al Jazeera interviewer Mehdi Hassan with Richard Dawkins. Online video clip. AlJazeera.com, July 20, 2013.

de Botton, Alain. "Atheism 2.0" Online Video Clip. *TED*. TED. July 2011. Web October 9, 2015.

Dobrev, Dobry. "Elder Dobry from Baylovo" SaintDobry.com

"Elmer Gantry". Online video clip. *YouTube*. YouTube, Apr 12, 2014. Web October 8, 2015

"Evil clown". Wikipedia. The Free Encyclopedia. Wikimedia Foundation, Inc. October 6, 2015. https://en.wikipedia.org/wiki/Evil_clown

Forsberg, Rolf. "Parabola". Online video clip. *YouTube*. YouTube, Nov 22, 2012. Web October 8, 2015

Fr. Pontifex. "Why I Love Religion, And Love Jesus || Spoken Word." Online video clip. *YouTube*. YouTube, Jan 18, 2012.

Glass, Ira. "Retracting "Mr. Daisey and the Apple Factory."" This American Life, NPR, March 16, 2012. Web October 8, 2015.

Grubin, David. "Language Matters" Online Video. *PBS*. PBS. Jan. 19, 2015. Web October 9, 2015

Heidegger. Martin. "Heidegger - Human, All too Human – Documentary" Online video clip. *YouTube*. YouTube, Dec 9, 2014. Web October 9, 2015

Hitchens, Christopher. "Christopher Hitchens: Mother Teresa's life should be attacked" Online video clip. *YouTube*. YouTube, Jun 12, 2014

House, Christian. "Sousa Mendes saved more lives than Schindler so why isn't he a household name too?" The Independent, October 17, 2010. Web Oct. 8, 2015.

Human Notions. "Benny Hinn: Let the Bodies Hit the Floor" Online video clip. *YouTube*. YouTube, May 9, 2007. Web October 8, 2015

Jackson, Jesse. "Sermon By Jackson Sways Voters"Fort Lauderdale Sun-Sentinel, January 30, 1995. Web October 8, 2015.

"John Wayne Gacy". Wikipedia. The Free Encyclopedia. Wikimedia Foundation, Inc. October 9, 2015. https://en.wikipedia.org/wiki/John_Wayne_Gacy

Jon Offredo and William H. McMichael, The (Wilmington, Del.) News Journal. Jonestown Massacre remains found in Del. funeral home. USAToday.com. August 7, 2014.

Jones, Malcolm. A Bakhtinian Approach to the Gospels: The Problem of Authority. Scando-slavica Journal Vol. 42, 1996. Pgs. 58-76.

Leadership Journal. "Willow Creek Repents?" Christianity Today, October 18, 2007. Web October 8, 2015

Loftus, Elizabeth. "Elizabeth Loftus: The fiction of memory" Online video clip. *YouTube*. YouTube, Sep 23, 2013, Web October 8, 2015,

Moon, Connyoung Jennifer & Tae-yeul, Park. "Arirang Special: "Comfort Women" One Last Cry." Online video clip. *YouTube*. YouTube, March 4, 2013.

Oxfam. "Statement by 52 NGOs working in Somalia on rapidly deteriorating humanitarian crisis" Oxfam America, October 7, 2008

Pooley, Roger. The Kingdom of God is Between You: Bakhtin and the Christian Reader. The Glass, Number 18, 2006, Page 4

"Reductio ad Hitlerum". Wikipedia. The Free Encyclopedia. Wikimedia Foundation, Inc. August 29, 2015. https://en.wikipedia.org/wiki/Reductio_ad_Hitlerum

Sampson, Will. Bakhtin, Sartre and Hiedegger: Missed Connections. From Academia.edu

Sataline, Suzanne. "Befriending witches is a problem in Salem, Mass." Wall Street Journal. Oct 31, 2006. A1. Print

Satō, Kemmyō Taira and Kirchner, Thomas. "Brian Victoria and the Question of Scholarship." The Eastern Buddhist 41/2, 2010, pgs. 139-166

"Seat 12". Wikipedia. The Free Encyclopedia. Wikimedia Foundation, Inc. September 20, 2015. https://en.wikipedia.org/wiki/Seat_12

Simpson, Christopher Ben. Between God and Metaphysics: An Interview with William Desmond. Radical Orthodoxy: Theology, Philosophy, Politics. Vol. 1, Numbers 1 & 2 (August 2012)

Stobard, Eleanor. Child Abuse Linked to Accusations of "Possession" and "Witchcraft". Research Report RR750, Department for Education and Skills. Crown Copyright 2006.

Strobos, Tina. Holocaust Encyclopedia. United States Holocaust Memorial Museum. Online video clip. Web October 7, 2015.

Tatusko, Andrew. Transgressing Boundaries in the Nine Inch Nails: The Grotesque as a Means to the Sacred. Journal of Religion and Popular Culture, Vol. 11, Fall 2005.

Terkel, Amanda. "With Recession Looming, Bush Tells America To 'Go Shopping More'" Think Progress, Dec 20, 2006. Web October 8, 2015.

Thomas, Dylan and Dangerfield, Rodney. "Rodney Dangerfield Dylan Thomas Do not go gentle into that good night Back to School" Online video clip. *YouTube*. YouTube, Jul 29, 2008. Web October 8, 2015

Thompson, Dennis. "Ecstasy Use on the Rise Among US Teens: Report" HealthDay Reporter. Dec. 3, 2013. Web October 8, 2015.

"Tomás de Torqemada". Wikipedia. The Free Encyclopedia. Wikimedia Foundation, Inc. October 7, 2015. http://en.wikipedia.org/wiki/Tomás_de_Torqemada

University of California, San Diego. Measuring distances to stars. Earthguide. UCSD.

Vidal, Gore and Buckley, William F. "William Buckley Vs Gore Vidal" Online video clip. *YouTube*. YouTube, Aug 15, 2007. Web October 8, 2015.

Whitaker, Roger. "Psychiatric Drugs and Violence: A Review of FDA Data Finds A Link" Psychology Today, Jan. 5, 2011, Web Oct. 8, 2015.

Wilson, Simon. "Letter: That Notorious Fake". The Independent, March 14, 1994. Web October 7, 2015.

"Witch-Hunt". Wikipedia. The Free Encyclopedia. Wikimedia Foundation, Inc. October 5, 2015. http://en.wikipedia.org/wiki/Witch-hunt

World News Daily. "Linda Ronstadt laments a 'New Bunch of Hitlers'" Nov 18, 2004. Web October 8, 2015.

Wyman, Phil. "Left Behind: The Song (May 21st Rapture, May 22nd Party!)". Online video clip. *YouTube*. YouTube, Apr 26, 2011.

Yad Vashem. "The Righteous Among The Nations" 2015 Yad Vashem.

Zac, Paul J. "How Stories Change the Brain" Greater Good. The Greater Good Science Center at the University of California, Berkeley, December 17, 2013. Web October 7, 2015.

Žižek, Slavoj. "Slavoj Zizek on Religion" Online video clip. *YouTube*. YouTube, Apr 25, 2011. Web October 8, 2015.

Žižek, Slavoj. "Slavoj Žižek: God in Pain: Inversions of Apocalypse conversation with Jack Miller". Online video clip. *YouTube*. YouTube, May 18, 2012.

Žižek, Slavoj. The only church that illuminates is a burning church. Religion & Ethics: Content from Across the ABC (Australian Broadcasting Company) 8 Aug, 2011

Phil Wyman is a Christian pastor with a rich history of relationship building with people from other religions and worldviews. Originally pastoring close to home in Carlsbad, CA, he moved to Salem, MA 1999 to start a church called The Gathering. Here he began befriending the Witches and Neo-Pagans of Salem to break down the barriers of mistrust between the Christians and the Witches, which had developed over many years His work with Neo-Pagans and atheists, and his forays into places like Burning Man has been highlighted on the Front page of the Wall Street Journal, in the Christian Science Monitor, Christianity Today, and numerous local papers and radio programs around the world.

Phil is a pastor, writer, editor, musician, songwriter, poet, wannabe philosopher, creator of interactive "blank canvas social art", and a general instigator looking for people to join him in a revolution.

This is the first of a series of theoretical works about relationship building and peacemaking across the impossible gap of polarized worldviews and belief systems. The Burning Religion series will continue with the next work, <u>Clowns in the Pulpit</u> highlighting both the bully pulpits of politics and the sacred pulpits of religion.

If you are interested in contacting Phil for speaking engagements, gigs, becoming a team member in transformative festivals, or you simply want to connect to say hi and debate a bit; you can find his contact information at BurningReligion.com and PhilWyman.org.

Printed in Great Britain
by Amazon

23034964R00189